Living in the Light

Living in the Light

An Exposition of the Letters of John

DERRICK MCCARSON

RESOURCE *Publications* • Eugene, Oregon

LIVING IN THE LIGHT
An Exposition of the Letters of John

Copyright © 2013 Derrick McCarson. All rights reserved. Except for brief quotations in critical publications or reviews, no part of this book may be reproduced in any manner without prior written permission from the publisher. Write: Permissions, Wipf and Stock Publishers, 199 W. 8th Ave., Suite 3, Eugene, OR 97401.

Resource Publications
An Imprint of Wipf and Stock Publishers
199 W. 8th Ave., Suite 3
Eugene, OR 97401
www.wipfandstock.com

ISBN 13: 978-1-62032-903-0
Manufactured in the U.S.A.

All scripture quotations, unless otherwise indicated, are taken from the Holy Bible, New International Version®, NIV®. Copyright ©1973, 1978, 1984 by Biblica, Inc.™ Used by permission of Zondervan. All rights reserved worldwide.

This book is dedicated to my grandmother, Aliene McCarson, who courageously walked in the light for many years and is now worshipping in the presence of Christ

Contents

Foreword / ix
Acknowledgments / xi

1. The Message of 1 John / 1
2. Foundations of the Faith (1 John 1:1–4) / 12
3. Walking in the Light (1 John 1:5–7 / 23
4. Total Confession (1 John 1:8–10) / 30
5. Looking for a Good Attorney? (1 John 2:1–2) / 39
6. Birthmarks of the Believer (1 John 2:3–11) / 48
7. How is Your Worldview? (1 John 2:12–17) / 58
8. Living in the Last Days (1 John 2:18–27) / 67
9. Rapture Ready? (1 John 2:28–3:3) / 78
10. That Nasty Three Letter Word (1 John 3:4–10) / 88
11. What's Love Got to Do with It? (1 John 3:11–18) / 99
12. Becoming a Confident Christian (1 John 3:19–24) / 110
13. Learn to Discern (1 John 4:1–6) / 119
14. The Supreme Ethic (1 John 4:7–21) / 129
15. We Shall Overcome (1 John 5:1–5) / 140
16. How to Be Absolutely Sure (1 John 5:6–12) / 149
17. Living above the Level of Mediocrity (1 John 5:13–21) / 158

Contents

18 The Message of 2 John (2 John 1–3) / 168

19 Balancing the Truth with Love (2 John 4–13) / 171

20 The Message of 3 John (3 John 1–4) / 177

21 Three Men and a Church (3 John 5–14) / 180

Bibliography / 189

Foreword

THE WRITINGS OF THE apostle John are a treasure for those seeking to discover and know God for the first time, as well as those who have been followers of Jesus for many years. In fact, having a robust understanding of the Gospel of John is to make great strides in understanding the Person of Jesus Himself. Here in the letters from John, we find answers to the great theological, cosmological, and even practical questions of that Gospel to life and living. In these short letters near the end of the New Testament, God has revealed His very nature and plan for humanity throughout time as well as real ground-level insights for life here and now. These are reason enough alone to pick up this commentary, but added to those is the specific way in which Derrick McCarson approaches the letters of John. This is a great resource for the pastor and layperson alike.

As a friend and colleague over the years, Derrick has proven to be a man of keen insight and practical wisdom, deep scholarship and approachability; of biblical understanding and cultural discernment. He is a student of history and the human condition. All of this being birthed out of a heart for seeing people come to know and love God. The explanations and applications in *Living in the Light* are quite profound, yet somehow familiar; as if you have known Derrick all of your life and are chatting over coffee. Rarely is the warmth of Appalachian humor married with such exegetical rigor. The apostle John was the son of a Galilean fisherman, yet the rich theological truths explored by John in his letters to the church soar to the heights of human understanding of God. In this way, Derrick is much like the Apostle John himself—a well-grounded, red-blooded man with simple roots that has had his heart and mind set ablaze with the knowledge of who Jesus really is.

These are the types of insights you will find as you explore the letters of John with Derrick. You will find yourself at one moment nodding your head with laughter in recognition of one of life's truisms, and at the next moment pausing with your mouth open at what you have just unearthed

Foreword

about the glory of God. This is all carried along by personal stories we all can relate to. In this commentary you will find the rare blend of big-picture contextualization and careful exegesis of the nuance of Scripture. The historical details that are brought to life through Derrick's background in history education from the universities of UNC-Chapel Hill and Western Carolina University are married with systematic theological understanding and weighty intellectual defense of the historical Jesus from Southern Evangelical Seminary. The reader will appreciate the depth of knowledge from a scholar of Derrick's caliber as well as the familiarity of a country pastor. If you have read Derrick's first book, *Origins,* which dealt with the foundational chapters of the book of Genesis, you will be glad you added this second commentary to your collection.

It is with great excitement that I recommend *Living in the Light* to Bible students of all levels of exploration. May God greatly use these words to guide your study of His Word!

Terry Hollifield
Lead Pastor, Paradigm Church
Asheville, North Carolina

Acknowledgments

I WOULD LIKE TO express deep gratitude to my wonderful mother-in-law, Trudy Rogers; my beautiful wife, Caitlin McCarson; and a faithful church member, Kelly Carpenter; for helping me proofread and edit this book. Without your meticulous eye for detail this project would have never made it off my computer.

1

The Message of 1 John

A FEW YEARS AGO I was shopping for a new acoustic guitar. Personally, I believe that if you are going to buy an acoustic guitar then you could not do any better than a Martin. Few instruments have the mellow sound of a Martin. I searched all around town for the perfect Martin; and I found one at a discounted price.

When I finally got the guitar home, I opened up the case and the smell of the new guitar was amazing. Before I pulled it out to play, I noticed that in between the strings was a certificate. It had written in gold embossed letters "Martin" and below it said, "Congratulations! You are the proud owner of an official Martin instrument." The card gave some facts about the instrument: its dimensions, what kind of wood it was made of, when and where it was assembled, the model number, and an assurance of quality.

This certificate struck me because it signified that the instrument I had purchased was authentic. In other words, I had not bought some cheap knock-off of a Martin guitar, but what I had in my hands was the real thing. This precision instrument was made in America and came straight from the factory in Nazareth, Pennsylvania.

It would have been a tragedy to spend hundreds of dollars on a guitar that looks like a Martin, feels like a Martin, smells like a Martin, but when you strum the stings it doesn't sound like a Martin. Authenticity is important. In this world things that are of the highest value are often counterfeited, copied, and poorly imitated.

The same is also true in the arena of spirituality. That's why the study of 1 John is so essential for believers. John was adamant about believers knowing that the faith they practiced was "the real McCoy."

Before we begin our journey, it is essential that the reader have a basic overview of the entire epistle so that you will get the big-picture before we systematically go through each verse. First John is a short book of only five chapters, or 105 verses, or 2,523 words. The average reader can make it through the book in a ten minute sitting. If you could read it in the original Greek language you would notice that 1 John has the simplest vocabulary of any book in the New Testament. Inevitably, this is the book that first-year seminary students learning Koine Greek cut their teeth on. But don't be fooled. This brief letter, although written hundreds of years ago in unpretentious language, contains some of the most profound truths about the Christian life. Christian scholar D. Edmond Hiebert had this to say about 1 John:

> The forceful simplicity of its sentences, the note of finality behind its utterances, the marvelous blending of gentle love and deep-cutting sternness of its contents, and the majesty of its ungarnished thoughts have made 1 John a favorite with Christians everywhere. The plainness of its language makes it intelligible to the simplest saint, while the profundity of its truths challenges the most accomplished scholar. Its grand theological revelations and its unwavering ethical demands have left their enduring impact upon the thought and life of the Christian Church. First John is indeed a singular, irreplaceable gem among the books of the New Testament.[1]

AUTHORSHIP: WHO WROTE 1 JOHN?

If you are looking for the name of the author in the text you will not find it. In fact, 1 John, like Hebrews, is anonymous. In spite of this we can be sure that this epistle came from the hand of the beloved apostle John. There are two ways we know this—internal and external evidence.

Let's first look at the internal evidence which links it to the Gospel of John. The similarity in writing style and vocabulary convincingly shows that the Gospel of John and this epistle came from the same pen. For example, let's compare the prologues from the Gospel of John and the first epistle of John to see their similarity.

---

1. Hiebert, *The Epistles of John*, 1.

John 1:1, 14	1 John 1:1-2
"In the beginning was the Word, and the Word was with God, and the Word was God . . . And the Word became flesh and dwelt among us, and we have seen His glory, glory as of the only Son from the Father, full of grace and truth."	"That which was from the beginning, which we have heard, which we have seen with our eyes, which we looked upon and have touched with our hands, concerning the Word of life . . ."

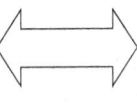

As you can see both introductions are very similar in wording. The theology is also identical; both emphasize the deity and humanity of Christ in His incarnation and both concentrate on the personal experience the writer had with Jesus. The author clearly identifies himself as an eyewitness to the life and ministry of Jesus, noting that "what we have seen and heard we proclaim to you also" (1 John 1:3).

As far as external evidence goes, the early church fathers attributed the authorship of this epistle to John. The first writer to quote directly from 1 John and name the apostle John as its author was Irenaeus, who lived in the closing decades of the second century. His testimony is especially significant since he was a disciple of Polycarp, who in turn was a disciple of John himself.[2] Moreover, the fourth century church historian, Eusebius, wrote, "But of the writings of John, not only his Gospel, but also the former of his epistles (1–3 John & Revelation), has been accepted without dispute both now and in ancient times."[3]

Tradition holds that by the time John took up his quill to pen this epistle he was an old man. John was probably in his eighties or nineties as he wrote at the end of the first century. In fact, one ancient story relates that John was so feeble that the deacons of the Ephesian church where John ministered had to help him up to the pulpit in order for him to preach. Some scholars even believe that the epistle is actually a sermon that John delivered and was copied down by a scribe. Imagine as you read this ancient correspondence that Grandpa John is speaking to the infant church of his day, telling them what it means to be a Christ-follower. John Phillips comments:

---

2. MacArthur, *The MacArthur New Testament Commentary: 1–3 John*, 3.
3. Eusebius, *Ecclesiastical History*, 3.24.

Living in the Light

John was a very old man, feeling the weight of his years and aware that his days on Earth were about done. A godly life lay behind him and a very long memory thrilled him. His native land was far away in the land of Israel, although he now lived in Ephesus, a pagan Asiatic city on the edge of the European world. Probably he had come there to escape the Roman war, which had engulfed his homeland and brought about the downfall of Jerusalem, the destruction of the temple and a virtual end to national Jewish life. If she was still alive, at that time, which is not altogether impossible, we can suppose he brought Mary, the Lord's mother, with him . . . He had lived through a turbulent century . . . Nero launched the Roman Empire on a three-hundred year persecution of the church . . . Then came Domition . . . he launched the second official Roman persecution of the church—spies and informers lurked everywhere and there stood "an executioner at every door." Such was the world in which John lived and survived. Such was the world in which the church, assailed by implacable forces from without, was now being threatened by error within. John thus felt compelled to write.[4]

There is much we can learn about the life of the apostle John by going back into the Gospels. When we first meet him and Andrew, they were fishermen and disciples of John the Baptist (John 1:35–37). However, once they met Jesus everything changed. John the Baptist saw Jesus from a distance and declared, "Behold, the Lamb of God who takes away the sin of the world!" (John 1:29). John even remembered the very hour that he met Jesus, for it was the "tenth hour" when Christ gave his first invitation to follow him (John 1:39). Later, Jesus came to the fishing boat of James (John's brother) and John as they were mending their nets and invited them to begin the adventure of a lifetime (Matt. 4:21–22). Not understanding what they were getting themselves into, they agreed and never looked back.

John became one of three disciples, along with Peter and James, allowed into the inner circle of Jesus' ministry. In Matt. 17:1–9 John accompanied Jesus up the mountain where he saw His glorious transfiguration and the unveiling of Jesus' deity. John and his brother James were called the "Sons of Thunder" which was a term denoting their fiery passion and endless zeal. On one occasion they suggested that Jesus should rain down fire from heaven upon the Samaritans who snubbed their noses at the Lord (Luke 9:54). In his book, 12 *Ordinary* Men, John MacArthur noted:

---

4. Phillips, *Exploring the Epistles of John*, 19–21.

If you imagine that John was the way he was often portrayed in medieval art—a meek, mild, pale-skinned, effeminate person, lying around on Jesus' shoulder looking up at him with a dove-eyed stare—forget that caricature. He was rugged and hard-edged, just like the rest of the fishermen disciples. John was balanced truth and love . . . he was as zealous for the truth as much as he was for doing things in love. Of the New Testament writers he is the most black and white in his thinking. He thinks and writes in absolutes. He deals with certainties. Everything is cut and dried with him. There aren't many grey areas in his teachings because he tends to state things in unqualified, antithetical language . . . in his Gospel it is light against dark, life against death, God vs. Satan . . . in his epistles this pattern continues: we are either walking in the light or in the darkness, we have the Son and life or we do not.[5]

On the flipside, John was also a tender-hearted man, known as "the apostle of love." John refers to himself in his own Gospel five times as "the disciple that Jesus loved" (John 13:23, 19:26, 20:2, 21:7, 21:20). On one occasion in John 13:23 he is said to be resting his head on the bosom of Jesus. John was a delicate balance of grace and truth, just like His Master. He had a rough exterior but a heart of gold.

John was one of the few disciples who did not forsake Jesus during His crucifixion. John was there when they whipped and beat Jesus beyond recognition (John 19:1). John was there to see the Roman soldiers nail iron spikes through Jesus hands and feet (John 19:17–19). John was there until the bitter end when the spear was driven through Jesus' side issuing forth blood and water (John 19:31–37). One of the most tender moments in John's Gospel happens at the foot of the cross where Jesus entrusts the care of His mother Mary over to John (John 19:25–27). Three days later, on that resurrection morning, it is John who outran Peter to the empty tomb of Jesus (John 20:1–10). To his credit, out of all the male disciples John is the last to leave Calvary and the first to arrive at the empty tomb.

John's life was utterly changed by his three-year boot camp experience with Jesus. Only Paul and Luke wrote more of the New Testament than John. He is accredited with one Gospel, three epistles and the Revelation, which he wrote while exiled on the island of Patmos. While all of the other apostles suffered a martyr's death, John was allowed to live eight or nine decades. In 1 John we have a piece of personal correspondence from a credible eyewitness to the life of Jesus.

---

5. MacArthur, 12 *Ordinary Men*, 111–114.

AUDIENCE: TO WHOM WAS 1 JOHN WRITTEN?

You will notice that peppered throughout the epistle is the phrase "my little children." In the literal Greek, the phrase means "my little born-again ones." You will count the phrase eight times (2:1, 2:12, 2:13, 2:18, 2:28, 3:7, 3:18, 5:21). This is John's endearing term for the church members he was addressing.

We know very little about the people that John was writing to. Presumably, they were Greek speaking gentiles scattered throughout the Roman Empire. This epistle has no quotations from the Old Testament, so clearly this was meant to be received by non-Jews. Its elementary syntax and repetition means that the letter could easily be understood by baby believers as well as mature saints.

John did not specify the recipients of this letter, but given his addresses in Revelation 2–3 to seven churches in the immediate vicinity of Ephesus—the city where John ministered late in his life—he likely had those same churches in mind for this letter. This letter offers little in the way of specifics, so pinpointing the date of its composition can be difficult. However, its similarity with the Gospel composed by John means it was probably written near the same time. A date of about AD 90, with John writing from his exile on Patmos, ends up being the best proposition.

AIM: WHY WAS 1 JOHN WRITTEN?

It will be easier to see John's purpose for writing this epistle if we first compare it to the Gospel of John. John gives his purpose statement in the Gospel that bears his name at the backdoor of the book. John 20:30–31 says, "Now Jesus did many other signs in the presence of the disciples, which are not written in this book; but these are written *so that you may believe that Jesus is the Christ*, the Son of God, and that by believing you may have life in His name." In other words, John writes his Gospel to elicit an initial belief in Jesus. The author's intent in the Fourth Gospel is evangelistic; he assumes the main audience will be unbelievers discovering the life and ministry of Christ for the first time.

However, John writes his epistle for another reason and to a different audience. In this epistle John is not looking to get his readers to faith in Christ, but he is trying to get them to live out their faith in Christ. Thus, the Gospel of John is directed toward unbelievers, while the epistle of 1 John was written for believers.

The Message of 1 John

So we could say that the Gospel of John and 1 John are complementary in their design. In many respects, 1 John acts as a practical commentary or supplement to the Gospel of John. The Gospel of John introduces the person of Christ, while the epistle of 1 John teaches us how to live in fellowship with Christ. Examine the chart below to see how these separate documents dovetail together.

The Gospel of John	1 John
Theological	Ethical
Evangelistic purpose	Pastoral purpose
Biographical	Polemical
How to be saved	How to know we are saved
Leads to faith in Christ	How to live in faith with Christ
Focused on the life of Christ	Focused on the life of the Christian
Salvation	Sanctification
The deity of Christ	The humanity of Christ

There are many scholars (myself included) who support the theory that the Upper Room Discourse and 1 John are thematically connected. After careful study it is evident that most of John's practical lessons for Christlike living were born out of his last hours with Jesus in the Upper Room. John 13–17 is the longest teaching block in the Gospel of John, known as "the Upper Room Discourse" and "the High Priestly Prayer." John was there when Jesus stooped down like a servant, took up a basin of water and a towel, and began washing the dirt off the disciples' feet. Think of this—the God of the universe performing the lowliest of all tasks reserved for only house servants and slaves! This experience had a profound influence on John and it opened his heart to the unforgettable lessons Christ taught around the dinner table.

When John sat down as an elderly man to write his epistles, the passage of time had not eroded his memory for the teaching of Christ was still fresh on his mind. The same themes and principles that Jesus taught in the Upper Room became the inspiration and content for 1 John. Examine the chart below and take note how the seed for this epistle was planted in the mind of John as a young man listening to the Savior talk about love, truth, and abiding with Him:

Living in the Light

Theme	Upper Room Discourse (John 13-17)	1 John
Little Children	13:33	2:1, 2:12 2:18, 2:28, 3:7, 4:4
New Commandment/Love	13:34-35, 15:12-13	2:10, 3:1, 3:11-16, 4:7-21
Obeying Christ	14:23-24, 15:10	2:3-6, 3:24, 5:2-3
Truth	14:6, 14:17, 16:13, 17:17	1:8, 2:21, 2:26-27, 4:1-6, 5:6
Abiding/Fellowship	15:1-10, 16	1:3, 1:6-7, 2:6, 2:17, 3:6, 3:24
Joy	15:11, 16:20, 22, 24, 17:13	1:4
Overcoming the World	15:18-25, 16:33	2:15-17, 5:4-5
Holy Spirit	14:26, 15:26, 16:7-15	2:20, 2:27, 3:24, 4:2, 4:6, 5:6-9
Prayer	14:13-14	3:21-22, 5:14-15

John states four reasons for writing his letter. The first is a *personal reason* and it is found in the prologue, "And we are writing these things *so that our joy may be complete.*" John wrote because he wanted believers from every generation to experience the sublime fulfillment that comes from knowing Christ. Jesus said, "These things I have spoken to you, that my joy may be in you, and that your joy may be full" (John 15:11, 16:24).

Years ago a Sunday School teacher gave me an acrostic for remembering how to find joy. She said, "Joy is when you put Jesus first, Others second, and You last." By putting Jesus at the center of life joy is a natural by-product. A professor of mine once said, "Never trust the theology of a man who doesn't laugh." If the Christian life doesn't give you enduring and unending contentment then something is wrong—either you've left Jesus on the sidelines or perhaps you don't have Him in the first place.

There is also a *moral reason* behind the writing of 1 John. John says, "My little children, I am writing these things to you *so that you may not sin*" (2:1). John wanted Christians to be aware of the dangers of sin, so that we can ultimately experience spiritual victory. John wrote with the purpose that his readers would have a safeguard against sinning. The practice of sin destroys our testimony with others and disrupts our fellowship with Christ.

This means that John is going to get into your personal life. He's going to follow you home, go to work with you, and get into your inner thought life. John is going to ask, "Are you walking in the light or in the darkness?" He has much to say about the nature of sin. The apostle discusses the sin of self-deception (1:8), he gives a clear definition of sin (3:4), he explains the origin of sin (3:8), the consequences of a persistent lifestyle of sin (5:16), the prime source of temptation leading to sin (2:16–17), and the cure for sin (1:7).

John also has a *doctrinal reason* for writing. He warns, "I write these things to you *about those who are trying to deceive you*" (2:26). At the close of the first century a pernicious cult had splintered off the main church. They were known as the Gnostics. The Gnostics were a hodge-podge of

Christian theology, mysticism, and Platonic thought. Although Gnosticism was diverse, New Testament scholar N.T. Wright says Gnostics historically have held four basic ideas in common: the world is evil, it was the product of an evil creator, salvation consists of being rescued from it, and the rescue comes through secret knowledge or *gnosis*, in Greek.[6] Wright adds:

> This special gnosis is arrived at through attaining knowledge about the true god, about the true origin of the wicked world, and not at least about one's true identity . . . What is needed, in other words, is a "revealer" who will come from the realms beyond, from the pure upper spiritual world, to reveal to the chosen few that they have within themselves the spark of light, the divine identity hidden deep within.[7]

The Gnostics' beliefs led them down the slippery slope into all kinds of strange aberrations, like the idea that Jesus was not fully human (a subtle heresy known as docetism). They borrowed the dualism of Plato and argued that matter was evil and reasoned that Christ could not have had a real human body because that would mean God would be in union with that which was essentially evil.

In other words, the Gnostics were saying that Jesus only appeared to be a human—His body was a phantom. This presented all kinds of theological problems because if Jesus was not fully human then the world does not have a Savior. Humanity needed a representative that was 100 percent God and 100 percent man—someone who could represent man to God, and at the same time, someone who could represent God to men. Taken together, the humanity and deity of Christ built a bridge from heaven to earth. Only the God-man could reconcile the two estranged parties. If Christ was not fully God then He was a bridge broken at the furthest end and if He was not fully man then He was a bridge broken at the nearest end. Therefore, one reason why John wrote this epistle was to respond to the Gnostic heresy and diffuse a theological bomb waiting to explode.

Lastly, John also had a *spiritual reason* for writing. He wanted all believers to have certainty concerning their salvation. He wrote in 5:13, "I write these things to you who believe in the name of the Son of God *that you may know that you have eternal life.*" This letter gives readers a spiritual litmus test to see if they bear the true marks of a believer or not. John is interested in the spiritual fruit produced by faith. Throughout the letter

---

6. Wright, *Judas and the Gospel of Jesus*, 31–34.
7. Ibid., 33.

Living in the Light

John gives us several tests by which we can examine ourselves and have assurance that we are truly born again. In fact, one of the words that John uses the most in this letter is *know* (39x). Look at the following examples of how we can have certainty of our fellowship with Christ:

- "Now by this we know that we know Him, if we keep His commandments" (2:3).
- "We know that we have passed from death to life, because we love the brethren" (3:14).
- "By this we know that He abides in us, by the Spirit who He has given us" (3:24).
- "We know that whoever is born of God does not sin" (5:18).

ARRANGEMENT: HOW IS 1 JOHN STRUCTURED?

I once had an English teacher who taught us how to write essays in the following manner—she said, "In the opening paragraph tell them what you're going to tell them. In the body of the essay tell them. Finally, in the conclusion tell them again what you've already told them." That simple, straightforward writing style doesn't keep the reading audience scratching their heads wondering where you are going with your ideas.

As you read through 1 John you will notice that the apostle also adopted that simple method. In some places John sounds like a broken record player because he continually repeats the same messages over and over again—"love one another," "keep His commandments," "believe that Jesus is the Christ." Many scholars have attempted to organize 1 John into a systematic outline but with great difficulty. The trouble comes for the exegete because John was not a methodical writer like Paul. Reading through the Pauline epistles it's clear that he was professionally trained because he marshals evidence like a lawyer. Paul was a logician who built his airtight arguments into the heavens.

John writes more like a musician. He is content to touch on a theme, float off in another direction, and come back later on and revisit the original theme again. With that in mind, we can better understand John's writing style by first identifying his main themes that blend together like the melodies in a symphony. John's favorite themes were abiding in the truth (a doctrinal test), loving one another (a social test), and keeping God's commandments (a moral test). John R.W. Stott referred to these as "the tests of life," and they are "three cardinal tests by which we may judge whether we possess eternal life or not."[8] John argues that when believers abide in these three principles then they maintain close fellowship with God. If we base our understanding of John's epistle by the repetition of these themes then we can see a pattern emerge in the flow of the text. Most of John's content is a variation on the themes of love, obedience, and abiding in the truth. Below is a proposed outline:

1. The Basis of Fellowship with God (1:1–2:27)
    A. The Conditions for Fellowship (1:1–2:14)
        - The Apostolic Witness (1:1–4)
        - Walking in the Light (1:5–7)
        - Confession of Sin (1:8–2:2)
        - Obedience to Christ (2:3–6)
        - Love: The New Commandment (2:7–14)
    B. The Cautions to Fellowship (2:15–2:27)
        - Love for the World (2:15–17)
        - Spirit of the Antichrist (2:18–27)

2. The Behavior of Fellowship with God (2:28–5:21)
    A. The Characteristics of Fellowship (2:28–4:21)
        - Purity of Life (2:28–3:3)
        - Practice of Righteousness (3:4–10)
        - Love One Another (3:11–18)
        - Confidence by Obedience (3:19–24)
        - Test the Spirits (4:1–6)
        - God is Love (4:7–21)
    B. The Consequences of Fellowship (5:1–21)
        - Victory over the World (5:1–5)
        - Assurance of Salvation (5:6–13)
        - Answered Prayer (5:14–17)
        - Freedom in the truth (5:18–21)

8. Stott, *The Letters of John*, 58.

2

Foundations of the Faith
(1 John 1:1–4)

When I was boy my dad and I would take regular fishing trips on Saturday mornings. However, there is one trip that stands out in my mind more than any other. The stream we were fishing in wasn't very deep. In fact, I can remember it being up only a few inches above my ankles. At first glance you would think that a tadpole would have trouble living in the stream, much less a trout.

But we went out with our dough balls, corn niblets, and night crawlers and casted our lines in the cold waters. We fished for some time and caught nothing—anybody that's ever been fishing knows that dreadful feeling. Then I remember we came to a little clearing in the stream and my dad was just a few feet ahead of me. I cast my line and the baited hook landed right between my dad's legs. This was a total accident on my part and that I'm sure I could not do it again if I tried.

The instant my hook hit the water I felt a tug on my rod. I reeled as fast as I could and fought the whopper with all of my strength. About that time my dad looked down and saw a fish thrashing about under his legs and he started to dance around. I can remember laughing so hard and I was so excited that I could barely hold the rod in my hands. Right there out of that little shallow stream I pulled out the biggest fish I had ever seen in my young life. What made it even better was that I could actually say that I caught it from under my dad's feet!

At first glance the letter of 1 John is like that little mountain creek I was telling you about. It appears shallow, but there is big stuff just below the

Foundations of the Faith (1 John 1:1-4)

surface. In fact, it's quite deceptive. Don't be fooled by the simple vocabulary and by its short length because some of the most profound Biblical truth is right there just waiting to be pulled out.

In our previous chapter we did a complete overview of the book and we saw that the same John who wrote the Gospel of John also wrote this letter. Each work has its specific purpose: the Gospel of John shows us how to have eternal life; 1 John shows us how to know that we have eternal life.

We saw that this little letter was written for a number of reasons. One purpose was to correct false teaching that had infiltrated the infant church. Already in the first century a mutant form of Christianity had emerged called Gnosticism. The basic worldview of the Gnostics was a cosmic dualism which divided the universe into a battle between good and evil, matter and spirit, darkness and light. Because matter was seen as essentially evil, the Gnostics denied the humanity of Jesus. They reasoned that it was impossible for God to unite himself with an evil, material body. Therefore they taught that Jesus' body was an apparition which gave the appearance of being physical. Somehow, they reasoned that when Jesus walked the earth He left no footprints and felt no real pain.

John begins his little letter the same way he began his Gospel—with a profound prologue. He explores some deep theological concepts partly to dispel the Gnostic heresy and partly to lay the basic foundations for the Christian life.

THE FACT OF CHRIST'S INCARNATION (1:1-2)

John opens up by introducing the uniqueness of Christ. Notice the balance between the humanity and deity of Christ. This is called the doctrine of the incarnation. It refers to the eternally existent second person of the Trinity adding to His divine nature the nature of humanity. As Athanasius eloquently said, "The incarnation is not the subtraction of deity, but the addition of humanity." Jesus is the God-man, one person with two natures.

Now you may ask, "Why is all of this theology important?" Because if you believe in a counterfeit Jesus, then that will give you a counterfeit salvation. Right doctrine is the difference between truth and error, life and death, heaven and hell.

The cults and false religions of the world always have a distorted view of Christ. The Mormons teach that Jesus is the spirit-brother of Lucifer. The Jehovah's Witnesses hold that Jesus was the appearance of Michael the archangel. Islam says that Jesus should be revered as one of the five great prophets but not the Son of God. *The Da Vinci Code* claimed that Jesus was married to Mary Magdalene and they had a child. Everyone wants to shape Jesus into their mold. They want a Jesus that makes them feel comfortable, doesn't offend their personal brand of morality, and makes no demands. In short, man wants a god no different from himself.

Ironically, none of these spurious claims come from people who actually lived and walked and talked with Jesus. That's where John enters the picture as a credible eyewitness. He's not giving us hearsay or second-hand information. Old grandpa John is saying, "Let me tell you about the real Jesus. I know what these others are saying, but let me give you the facts, not the fiction."

First, John focuses on *the deity of Christ*. He uses a phrase here that is unique only to his writings when he refers to Jesus as the "Word of Life." If you are a student of John's Gospel, you'll notice that in the prologue he refers to Jesus as "the Word" there too. John writes, "In the beginning was the Word and the Word was with God and the Word was God . . . and the Word became flesh and dwelt among us" (John 1:1, 14).

Why does he refer to Jesus as the Word of Life? The Greek word for "word" is *logos*. It means a "thought or an expression." The Greek philosophers embraced *the Logos* as the ultimate creative mind behind the order of the universe. *The Logos* was the impersonal, rational force which kept the laws of the universe running with precision. John hijacked this nebulous and cerebral notion of a divine architect that the Greek thinkers pondered and applied it to Jesus.

Moreover, words are the means of communicating concepts and thoughts. Words are ideas clothed in language. You know you cannot see ideas, they are immaterial and invisible. The only way I can know what you are thinking is if you express that idea through the vehicle of language. John is saying that Jesus Christ is the language of God. Christ is the noun of God; He's the adjective of God; He's the verb of God. Jesus is the Alpha and Omega of God's alphabet (Rev. 1:8). Jesus spells out God to us in a way we can understand. The way that the invisible and immaterial God revealed His character was by clothing the second person of the Trinity in human flesh (John 1:14, 18). Jesus Christ is the revelation of God with skin on. So to know Jesus is to know God and to know God is to know true life (John 17:3).

Foundations of the Faith (1 John 1:1-4)

Notice in 1:2 that John says "we declare to you the eternal life which was with the Father and was manifested to us." You can find almost the exact same logic in John 1:18, "No one has ever seen God: the only God who is at the Father's side, he has made him known." This is a recurring pattern from the Gospel of John. The apostle was captivated with the entry of the eternal Christ into our time and space. Just look at all the instances in which John mentioned that Jesus "came down from heaven."

> "*For God did not send his Son into the world* to condemn the world, but in order that the world might be saved through Him" (John 3:17).

> "*I have come down from heaven* not to do my own will, but the will of Him that sent me" (John 6:38).

> "*I have come into the world as light*, so that whoever believes in me may not remain in darkness" (John 12:46).

> "*I came from the Father and have come into the world*, and now I am leaving the world and going to the Father" (John 16:28).

> "For this purpose I was born and for this purpose *I have come into the world* –to bear witness to the truth. Everyone who is on the side of truth listens to me" (John 18:37).

This is what makes Christ different from all the other religious leaders and self-proclaimed prophets. All other holy men have a man trying to reach up to God—Christ is the only instance in which God comes down to man. The infinite God limited Himself to breathing, to eating and drinking, to sweating and bleeding, and even to death (Phil 2:5–8). Christianity is the only religion in the world that features the self-humiliation of God. C.S. Lewis explained the incarnation in his own inimitable way:

> Lying at your feet is your dog. Imagine, for the moment, that your dog and every dog is in deep distress. Some of us love dogs very much. If it would help all the dogs in the world, would you be willing to become a dog? Would you put down your human nature, leave your loved ones, your job, hobbies, your art and literature and music, and choose instead of the intimate communion with your beloved, the poor substitute of looking into the beloved's face and wagging your tail, unable to smile or speak? Christ by becoming man limited the thing which to Him was the most precious thing in the world; his unhampered, unhindered communion with the Father.[1]

1. Lewis, <http://bible.org/illustration/become-dog>.

Living in the Light

John also describes *the humanity of Christ*. In 1:1 John appealed to the primary modes of sensation—hearing, seeing, and touching—as he emphasized the flesh-and-blood nature of Jesus. Let's break down these verbs:

> Heard: Do you ever wonder what the voice of Jesus sounded like? Perhaps as John wrote he remembered how Jesus' voice reverberated as He taught from the boat on the Sea of Galilee. It could be that he remembered what Jesus sounded like when He desperately prayed in the Garden of Gethsemane. Maybe he recalled Jesus' last cries on the cross.

> Seen: Perhaps John is recalling all the mighty miracles of Jesus. He saw the sick and lame healed. He saw dead raised to life. He saw the nails and the wood which held Jesus to the cross and then he saw Him appear to them in the upper room. John ends his Gospel by stating that if all the things that Jesus did were written in detail the whole world couldn't contain the books (John 21:25)!

> Looked upon: There is a slightly different Greek word used here (*theaomai*) than the one translated "seen." In fact, it is the same word from which we derive our word theater. John looked intently at Jesus and studied him. I'm sure the apostle never forgot the way Jesus' eyes could pierce through any man and see right through the soul.

> Handled: No doubt, John remembered how it felt when Jesus washed his feet. He remembered leaning on Jesus' shoulder. John could easily recall the memory when the resurrected Jesus appeared before Thomas and said, "Reach here with your finger, and look at my hands, put your finger in my side and do not be unbelieving but believe."

Why is John spending so much time describing the humanity and physicality of Jesus? Remember he was combating the Gnostic teachers who were arguing that Jesus did not have a real human body. John is refuting the claims of the Gnostics by saying, "Don't believe these guys. I was there as an eyewitness. I saw Him, heard Him, and touched Him." I like the way one devotional writer explained the staggering reality that God entered our time and space:

> When Apollo 11 neared the moon in July 1969, the editors of The New York Times felt their coverage of the first step on lunar soil should go beyond headlines and photos to embrace an achievement shared by all humanity. So they asked Pulitzer Prize-

Foundations of the Faith (1 John 1:1–4)

winner Archibald MacLeish to write a poem. The day after Neil Armstrong and Edwin Aldrin Jr. walked on the moon, the front page contained these words: You were a wonder to us, unattainable, a longing past the reach of longing, a light beyond our light, our lives—perhaps a meaning to us . . . our hands have touched you in your depth of night. That day, through the hands of others, we touched the moon. The apostle John wrote some memorable words about an even more significant historical event—the visit of God's Son to this planet. John touched Jesus. And today, so can we. As surely as John held Him in the flesh, we can grasp the Son of God through faith. We too can experience the joy of having a close relationship with the Father and the Son.[2]

Jesus is not just a man in a book or a dead historical figure, but He was and is a real, living Savior. Because Jesus came in the flesh then it means that He can identify with our human infirmities (Heb. 4:15). God the Father is a Spirit (John 4:24). He is immaterial and has no body. The Father does not know what it is like to hunger or thirst, or to feel loneliness. He has never experienced what it is like to be sick, to bleed, and to feel pain like you and I. Not so with the Son.

In the incarnation, Christ made Himself susceptible to the frailties of humanity. Through Jesus Christ, the eternal God experienced what it was like to be despised and rejected by men, what it was like to be homeless, and what it was like to taste death. Because of the humanity of Jesus we have someone in heaven who not only knows the facts of what we're going through, but also identifies with the feelings of what we're going through.

THE FELLOWSHIP OF CHRIST'S FAMILY (1:3)

John invites all believers into an authentic community with God and God's people. God is the originator of fellowship. In the Trinity exists a divine community between the Father, Son, and Spirit. God has never been alone or needed anyone to meet His needs for companionship. We can see God's love for community reflected in the creative order. That is why in nature there are swarms of bees, packs of wolves, flocks of birds, and schools of fish. Community is the reason why God instituted the human family and community is the basis of the Church.

---

2. McCasland, "Contact."

Living in the Light

The Greek word that is used in the text for fellowship is *koinonia*. This particular word carries the thought of "being united in a common cause or a shared life." No man is an island in the Christian experience. We are saved to belong to the family of faith as sons and daughters of the Most High. This means that all believers are running a race, but they have others running alongside them. When you fall there is someone there to pick you up. When you lag behind there is someone there to push you forward. When you cross the finish line and enter the gates of glory you will join the ranks of other saints who have finished well and have been cheering you on from the balcony of heaven.

Notice that John identifies two levels of fellowship: Horizontal—"that you may have fellowship with us."—that is the joining of hearts and minds together in the church and vertical—"and truly our fellowship is with the Father and with his Son Jesus Christ."—this is the joining of the soul with God. This is what the early church was known for in Acts 2:42, "They devoted themselves to the apostles' teaching and to *fellowship*, to the breaking of bread, and to prayer."

The fellowship that John is talking about here is not just casual acquaintance. *Koinonia* is not about cookies and coffee once a week for an hour in Sunday school. Neither is Christianity merely a mental assent to a set of abstract theological principles. While doctrine is essential, John is talking about having a personal, daily walk with the God of the universe and getting involved in the lives of other believers.

I remember when I was kid my friends and I thought three-way calling was a modern marvel of technology. For those of you who have never experienced the magic, three-way calling is when you have two people talking on the phone and they invite another person to join in on the phone call. When I was a kid my buddies and I would always do a three-way call on Monday night because Monday night was wrestling night. When Hulk Hogan was fighting the Giant or when Rick Flair was going up against the Macho Man we would always want to call each other and yell and scream and enjoy the wrestling together.

According to John, the Christian life is about a three-way conversation. It's about believers being invited into the tightest community that has ever existed. The Father and the Son have been in conversation for all of eternity—Jesus wants to let us in on the fellowship as well.

The amazing thing about the Church is that she is a collection of people who are united by their mutual love for Christ. It's a living, breathing,

Foundations of the Faith (1 John 1:1–4)

growing organism where each member has their special role. It's a place of unity and diversity with people from all walks of life, all colors, languages, and talents. We may not have much in common on the outside, but when you get into a real fellowship of believers it doesn't matter what walk of life you are from. Ravi Zacharias tells the following story to illustrate how believers from around the world can be united under the banner of Jesus Christ:

> Some years ago a person in Christian ministry from the United States happened to be visiting Romania. It was during the bitterest days of the Cold War. As he trudged slowly through a rather busy but beleaguered section of town, bundled up against the biting cold, he was aware of the somber, grim faces of the people hurriedly brushing past him. Suddenly, as if in a different world, a man walked by, his ragged course coat wrapped tightly around him, a woolen scarf thrown around his neck and a warm cap pulled tightly over his scalp, whistling melody to his heart's content. The veteran Christian worker was caught completely by surprise, for the melody was that of a grand but not too common Christian hymn, "The Great Physician now is here, the sympathizing Jesus." Shocked to hear it on a busy Romanian street, he picked up his pace to match strides with the cheerful whistler. He was aware that he might be under observation, so not wanting to put the Romanian at risk, he cautiously walked alongside of him and whistled the tune with him. The Romanian stopped, looked, and excitedly spouted forth a barrage of words in his own native tongue, his face beaming. Immediately, he knew that the words meant nothing to this stranger, separated as they were by this barrier of language. As if by instinct, simultaneously, they both pointed to the heavens, laid their hands on their chest and clasped one another in an emotional embrace. Not a word was spoken, but two worlds were joined as they bade each other good-bye and went their separate ways, still whistling the same tune. In one memorable moment eternity's resources knit together two spirits, bridging two worlds, because of identical life-transforming experiences—the mending of their lives by the touch of "the Great Physician."[3]

That's why heaven is going to be awesome because it will be unrestricted and unending fellowship with the Savior and with God's redeemed people. The fellowship that John had with Jesus is the fellowship he longs for us to have with Jesus. The mind-blowing reality is that one day in heaven

---

3. Zacharias, *Deliver Us From Evil*, 103.

you and I will be able to walk up to Jesus and touch him just like John did when Jesus was on earth.

THE FULFILLMENT OF CHRIST'S FOLLOWERS (1:4)

John ends his prologue by talking about the great secret of the Christian life—joy. When you are in communion with God then joy is a natural side-effect (Gal 5:22). How can you be in God's presence and be unhappy? David said it like this, "In thy presence there is fullness of joy" (Ps. 16:11). The Westminster Catechism proclaims that the chief end of man is to "glorify God and *enjoy* Him forever." When God is the central focus of our pursuits then life becomes a perpetual novelty of discovering the simple pleasures of God's goodness.

John doesn't want you to have half-joy; he wants you to have fullness of joy. That means that your cup is overflowing and spilling over, like when you pour yourself a soda and it starts frothing over the top of the cup and you must slurp up the fizz before it spills out. The joy that Jesus offers is like a bubbling spring that is continually effervescent and satisfying (John 17:13). Even while Christ faced the horror of the cross He was able to look past Friday afternoon and see the victory of Sunday morning with joy (Heb. 12:2).

The infamous atheist Fredrick Nietzsche scornfully remarked about the Christians of his day, "I would believe in their salvation if they looked a little more like people who had been saved." Sadly, there are too many Christians that look like they have been baptized in lemon juice. The absence of joy either means one of two things—either they never had Jesus in the first place or the Devil has stolen their joy. When we take our eyes off Jesus then joy is supplanted with fear and worry over changing circumstances.

Joy is the flag which flies from the heart's castle to tell the world that the King is in residence. Christianity is not just about about the quantity of life but also the *quality* of life. We experience joy because we have a personal Savior that took away our sin debt. Our heart overflows because Christ offers us unconditional love, a unique purpose for life, and the undeniable hope of a home in heaven. The great fulfillment of evangelism is that we get to lead others to Jesus which only multiplies our joy (Philemon 6).

I think that when John wrote 1:4 his mind went back to the Upper Room moments before Jesus' arrest, trial, and crucifixion. In the midst of that dark scene look at what Jesus talked about three times:

Foundations of the Faith (1 John 1:1-4)

"Truly, truly, I say to you, you will weep and lament, but the world will rejoice. You will be sorrowful, *but your sorrow will turn into joy*" (John 16:20).

"So also you have sorrow now, but I will see you again, and your hearts will rejoice, and *no one will take your joy from you*" (John 16:22).

"Until now you have asked nothing in my name. Ask, and you will receive, *that your joy may be full*" (John 16:24).

In his masterful treatise, *Orthodoxy*, G.K Chesterton wrote, "Joy, which was the small publicity of the pagan, is the gigantic secret of the Christian."[4] He concludes his work by making these powerful remarks about the person of Christ, "There was something that He hid from all men when He went up a mountain to pray. There was something that He covered constantly by abrupt silence or impetuous isolation. There was some one thing that was too great for God to show us when He walked upon our earth; and I have sometimes fancied that it was His mirth."[5]

If you have never read the biography of David Livingstone I would encourage you to do so. He's possibly one of the greatest missionaries that ever lived. In 1871 David Livingstone was dying of sickness in an African jungle. He had been preaching to the primitives and nearly lost his life on multiple occasions, once because of a lion attack!

This time he had contracted a terrible malady and badly needed medicine. A New York magazine sent a reporter, Henry Stanley, to bring him medicine and to write a journal of the missionary-explorer's expeditions up the Nile River. When Stanley found Livingston, the only other white man in the African Congo, he gave those immortal words, "Dr. Livingstone I presume." As Stanley and Livingstone developed a relationship he told the missionary, "Don't even try to convert me. I am the biggest swaggering atheist on the face of the earth." Stanley lasted only four months. The power of Livingstone's testimony was irresistible. Later on Stanley recorded these words in his journal:

> In 1871 I went to him as prejudiced as the biggest atheist in London . . . But there came for me a long time for reflection. I was out there away from a worldly world. I saw this solitary old man there, and asked myself, "How on earth does he stop here—is

---

4. Chesterton, *Orthodoxy*, 153.
5. Ibid., 154.

he cracked, or what? What is it that inspires him?" For months after we met I found myself wondering at the old man carrying out all that was said in the Bible—"Leave all things and follow Me." But little by little his sympathy for others became contagious; my sympathy was aroused; seeing his piety, his gentleness, his zeal, his earnestness, and how he went quietly about his business. I was converted by him, although he had not tried to do it."[6]

When Christ rules from within you don't have to pretend to be different—you just are. It is the joy of Christ which the world so desperately longs for and which we have the privilege of sharing with others. When we walk with Christ in intimacy and fellowship the world takes notice and they ask, "How can I have that?"

---

6. Phillips, *Exploring The Epistles of John*, 29.

3

Walking in the Light
(1 John 1:5–7)

ON A TRIP TO Philadelphia my tour guide explained that during the colonial days of America much of the city lay in darkness after sunset. That was until an ingenious young man by the name of Benjamin Franklin had the bright idea of hanging lamps out on the street poles. Franklin tried to convince the citizens of Philadelphia to light the streets at night, but few bought into his outlandish idea. Undeterred, Franklin bought an attractive lantern, polished the glass, and placed it on a long bracket that extended from the front of his house. Each evening as darkness descended, he lit the wick. His neighbors soon noticed the warm glow in front of his house; passersby found the light helped them avoid tripping over protruding stones. Soon others placed lanterns in front of their homes, and eventually the city recognized the need for having well-lit streets.

The apostle John teaches us that life devoid of fellowship with God is like being shut away from the light. Like the shadowy streets of Philadelphia without Franklin's lanterns, life bereft of intimacy with God is dark, cold, depressing, and filled with illusions. In this epistle John has given us several tests by which believers can determine if they are in fellowship with God or not. One of the tests given in 1 John is if we are walking in the light or the darkness.

John is calling us today to examine ourselves not in comparison to other Christians, but to bring our life out into the eternal light of God's truth where it can all be exposed. Remember that one of the themes in John's epistle is intimate fellowship. The thesis of these verses before us is simply this: if we desire fellowship with God then we need to walk where He is; we need to walk in the light. If we do not walk in the light then we forfeit fellowship with God and true joy. In this section John explains what we must do if we desire to have fellowship with God.

THE CHARACTER OF GOD'S LIGHT (1:5)

John begins by describing the moral nature of God. The apostle makes one of the most profound theological statements with the simplest of words. This is one of three great "God is" statements that appear in this letter. In 1:2 God is *life*, in 1:5 God is *light*, and in 4:8 God is *love*.

The quality of light tells us at least three things about God: physically, light represents the glory of God; intellectually, light represents the knowledge of God; morally, light represents the holiness of God. In this context, when John says, "God is light," he is referring to God's sinlessness, righteousness, holiness, and purity. Just in case you didn't understand it, John tags on that little phrase at the end of verse five, "in Him there is no darkness at all." Darkness is merely the absence of light. Where there is light, there is no darkness. In other words, John is saying, "Sin is as far away from the person of God as darkness is from light."

According to the Bible, light is associated with two things: *illumination* and *revelation*. Illumination is the process of expelling the darkness. God dwells in unapproachable light (1 Tim. 6:6) and James calls God the "Father of lights" (James 1:17). At the dawn of time God created light on the first day (Gen. 1:3). Jesus claimed to be "the light of world" and whoever followed Him would not walk in darkness (John 8:12). If it were not for the illuminating power of God's holiness we would not know what sin is and we would be utterly doomed to walk in the shadows. John Phillips comments:

> A wonderful property of light is that it cannot be defiled. Even though it passes, say through a glass of muddy water, light is not defiled. Moreover, light can and most certainly does, reveal defilement. Also life as we know it craves light. A plant will always turn toward the light and struggle to reach it. Such are the characteristics of natural created light. Many of these properties reflect the One who reveals Himself as the Light. He is always the same, He is immaculate and beyond the reach of darkness, He reveals Himself

to us in all the diverse beauties of His being. And beneath the sunshine of His smile life can flourish, take root, and grow.[1]

Revelation is the process of exposing what is concealed in the darkness. Physics tells us that light, whether understood as a wave or a particle, is invisible. We don't actually see the light, but we see the objects which the light reveals. I like the way C.S. Lewis put it when he said, "We believe that the sun has risen not because we see it, but because by it we see everything else." In the same way light reveals our reality, God's moral character exposes our impurity. When we walk with God, the light of His truth shows us what we really are. Jesus said to Nicodemus, "For everyone who does wicked things hates the light and does not come into the light lest his deeds should be exposed" (John 3:20).

Christians who are living in sin usually avoid the light at all costs. It's a downward cycle: first, they sin and then they avoid the light to retreat deeper into the darkness. One of the first things that people do when they choose a lifestyle of sin is avoid the Bible because God's Word is like an x-ray beam that shows the depravity of our hearts. As their Bible collects a thick layer of dust they also stop going to church. When we are walking in darkness the last thing we want to hear is a man preaching the Word of God heaping on more guilt and conviction. Pretty soon their fellowship with God is non-existent and their faith has nearly evaporated.

This passage always reminds me of when I wash the windows around my house and the frustration that follows. I find that no matter how many times I wash the windows I can never get them totally clean. Without fail at about five or six o'clock in the evening the rays of the setting sun come beaming in through the windows. When the light passes through that glass I can see every smudge mark, every streak, and every place that I missed. The light shows that I am a poor custodian. My best efforts are never good enough to remove the dirt and grime.

Similarly, if we desire fellowship with God then we are going to be in a place that is going to make us uncomfortable. Why? Because God is light and if we are going to have fellowship with Him then we are going to be in the presence of holiness. The Spirit of God will light up the dark places of our hearts. If we try to hide our sin issues then we only set ourselves up for greater frustration. His light will uncover our best hiding places and bring things to our attention that we never noticed before.

---

1. Phillips, *Exploring The Epistles of John*, 32.

Living in the Light

THE CONFRONTATION OF SIN IN GOD'S LIGHT (1:6)

A few years ago I heard a new phrase that caught my attention—"practical atheist." This is when a person believes intellectually that God exists but behaves practically like there is no God. John addresses the duplicitous nature of Christians who publically profess Christ in word, but privately deny Christ in deed.

I imagine that if John were alive and preaching today he would expound on this verse like this, "If you've got your hands raised up in the worship service on Sunday morning then on Sunday night you've got pornography on your laptop then you're a liar." He then turns to the topic of money and says, "If you say you love Jesus and care for the poor, yet you don't give and tithe to the church then you love money more." He would say, "If you drive around with a Jesus fish on your bumper, yet during the week you spread gossip and slander then you are not walking in the light." I grow weary of the fact that people can attend church for ten to twenty years and never change. We believe in Jesus enough to get us out of hell, but we don't desire Him enough to change the way we live.

When I was a kid, during the summer nights my friends and I would play flashlight tag. This is basically hide-and-seek in the dark. The point of the game was simple. One person was "it" and they had the flashlight. Everyone else would try and find a hiding spot somewhere in the darkness. If you were hiding, the goal was to find a place that was so dark and concealed that you would be the last person to be found.

There are lots of Christians who spend a majority of their life playing flashlight tag with God. They have gotten really good at finding hiding places for their sin in the darkness. They spend their life running away from the light. John argues that this way of life is the opposite of fellowship. John says if you want God then you've got step out of the darkness and into the light. Yes, it will be painful, like when you come out of a dark movie theater in the middle of the day and the sun hurts your eyes. However, confronting sin issues head-on is the only way you can find freedom, joy, and peace in Christ.

I can remember stepping into my cheap college apartment and flipping on the light, only to watch the cockroaches scatter in the light. The light exposed an infestation that had been growing in the darkness. Now at that point I had a couple of options: I could ignore it and continue to live with the roaches, or call an exterminator to deal with the problem. When we walk in the light of God's holiness He's going to expose the infestation of sin in our hearts so that it can be eradicated. We can choose to ignore it and live in filth or deal with it and live in fellowship. I think that Adrian Rogers said it best when he commented, "We can understand children who are afraid of the dark, but we cannot understand adults that are afraid of the Light."

THE COMPANY IN GOD'S LIGHT (1:7A)

When we decide to walk in the light, John says that two things will happen. First, we will experience the fellowship of God. Notice that word "fellowship" again. That is the fourth time it has been used in the first seven verses. Remember the Greek word is *koinonia* and it means "a shared way of life." It is one of the major themes in this epistle. John advocates that if we conform our lives to the light then we can enjoy some benefits, namely, *koinonia* with God and God's people. Walking in the light means transparency. Walking in the light allows everything about your life to be clearly displayed and seen before God and man because you have nothing to hide.

Perhaps it's best to illustrate this with two biblical examples: Adam and Moses. One of the inevitable consequences of sin is always separation. Sin ruptures and breaks our fellowship with God. Just after Adam and Eve sinned in the Garden what did they do? According to Genesis 3:7–8, they suddenly realized their nakedness and ran from God in fear.

> Then the eyes of both were opened, and they knew that they were naked. And they sewed fig leaves together and made themselves loincloths. And they heard the sound of the Lord God walking in the garden in the cool of the day, and the man and his wife hid themselves from the presence of the Lord God among the trees of the garden.

The unimpeded fellowship that Adam and Eve had with God in Eden was forever broken. That is what happens when we walk in darkness; God becomes our enemy rather than our friend.

Now look at the case of Moses in Exodus 34:29. Moses is coming down from the mountain after being in the presence of God. The text says, "When Moses came down from Mount Sinai, with the two tablets of the testimony in his hand as he came down from the mountain, Moses did not know that the skin of his face shone because he had been talking with God." Spending time in the fellowship of God brings about transformation. In other words, when you are living in the light with God it changes you from the inside out. Moses' face radiated with the glory of God because he had been in such close proximity to God that it had begun to rub off on him.

This reminds me of the times when my wife (Caitlin) and I were still dating. We would go out for a night on the town and have a wonderful evening together. We would enjoy a great meal, hold hands, and revel in being in each other's company. Then the time would inevitably come when we would have to say goodbye and I would take her back to her parents' home. After the date many times I would be riding back in my car and I could still smell her perfume. On several occasions I realized that the scent of her perfume had actually rubbed off on my shirt. Every time I inhaled I would get a sweet waft of her perfume and think back on our evening.

The whole point of living in the light of God is that we look less like ourselves and more like Jesus. Being in the company of God is life-changing. As you spend time in fellowship with God you begin to notice that you're not the same person anymore. God changes the way you talk, think, and act. He changes the affections of your heart and gradually you are formed more into the image of His Son (Rom. 8:29). In short, God rubs off on us like my wife's perfume.

THE CLEANSING IN GOD'S LIGHT (1:7B)

John gives us a beautiful reminder in the last half of verse seven of what happens when we sin while walking in the light. Thankfully, there is cleansing of our sins through the blood of Jesus. The Greek verb in 1:7 is in the present tense which means that it is a continual process. Simply put, this means that the blood of Jesus cleanses us and goes on cleansing afterward.

The blood of Christ—that is, the effects of His death on the cross—have a perpetual cleansing effect on those who are walking in fellowship with Him. We are cleansed from all our sins even though we are too immature or ignorant to know all our sins. The reason why we can stay in the light of God is not because we are good in ourselves, but it is because the blood of Jesus continually scrubs us and removes the iniquity that would otherwise hinder us from fellowship. The Bible is clear that the blood of Christ is what makes our fellowship with God possible:

> ". . . knowing this that you were not redeemed with corruptible things like silver or gold, for the aimless conduct received by traditions from your fathers, but with *the precious blood of Christ as a lamb without blemish and without spot*" (1 Peter 1:18–19).

Walking in the Light (1 John 1:5–7)

"Come now, let us reason together, says the Lord: *though your sins are like scarlet, they shall be as white as snow;* though they are red like crimson, they shall become like wool" (Isaiah 1:17).

"In Him *we have redemption through his blood*, the forgiveness of our trespasses, according to the riches of his grace" (Eph. 1:7).

The shedding of Jesus' blood on the cross was no small thing. Every drop that was splattered on Calvary's hill was the most precious offering ever made. His blood would satisfy the demands of a holy God and make it possible for you and me to be cleansed of A-L-L sins.

A skeptic once challenged a believer: "How does blood cleanse sin?" The believer replied with a counter-question: "How does water quench thirst?" The skeptic replied, "I don't know, but I know that it does." "In the same way," said the believer, "I don't know how blood cleanses sin, but I know that it does—God says so."[2]

Since God required the life of an innocent substitute, Jesus' blood perfectly fit what God demanded. According to Hebrews 9:23–28 when Jesus ascended back to the Father in heaven, He took His own blood, entered into the tabernacle of heaven, sprinkled it on the mercy seat, and made a one-time payment for the sins of the world. Because the blood is still there today speaking on our behalf we have the penalty of sin removed and the promise of heaven reserved.

When evangelist John Wesley (1703–1791) was returning home from a service one night, he was robbed. The thief, however, found his victim to have only a little money and some Christian literature. As the bandit was leaving, Wesley called out, "Stop! I have something more to give you." The surprised robber paused. "My friend," said Wesley, "you may live to regret this sort of life. If you ever do, here's something to remember: 'The blood of Jesus Christ cleanses us from all sin!'" The thief hurried away and Wesley prayed that his words might bear fruit. Years later, Wesley was greeting people after a Sunday service when he was approached by a stranger. What a surprise to learn that this visitor, now a believer in Christ and a successful businessman, was the one who had robbed him years before! "I owe it all to you," said the transformed man. "Oh no, my friend," Wesley exclaimed, "not to me, but to the precious blood of Christ that cleanses us from all sin."

Let us not trample underfoot the blood of God's Lamb by living in the darkness, but by living in the light. It is the blood that brings us into the light and it is the blood that keeps us in the light.

2. Ibid., 35.

4

Total Confession
(1 John 1:8–10)

THE STORY IS TOLD of four preachers who were out fishing and having a moment of candid transparency. As the conversation got more personal the moment came when they confessed their various vices, failures, and hang-ups. One preacher said, "Well, you know fellas, sometimes I watch movies I shouldn't be watching." Another preacher said, "I have a guilty pleasure as well. I go to the casino and gamble occasionally." The third preacher said, "When I am by myself and the wife and kids are out, I like to smoke cigars." The fourth preacher, who had been listening to all of this, said "Well, my sin is gossip and I can't wait to get out of here!"

The area of confession is one which we must all deal with in the Christian life. Because we are all sinners not only by nature but also by choice that means we need frequent confession and cleansing. However, the key to unlocking the forgiveness of God is found in confession. Don't expect God to cover what you are unwilling to uncover. In the words of John Stott, "Before we see the cross of Jesus as something done for us, we must first see that the cross is something done by us. Indeed, only the man who is prepared to own his share in the guilt of the cross may claim his share in its grace and forgiveness."[1]

The recurring theme of 1 John is fellowship with God. In order to maintain fellowship with God there has to be the acknowledgment and total confession of sin. Intimacy cannot be experienced between two parties when there is a breech in the relationship. Sin is always that barrier that

---

1. Stott, *The Cross of Christ*, 60.

separates us from God. This can be explained by using a simple illustration of two concentric circles, the outer named "relationship" and the inner named "fellowship" like what is pictured below:

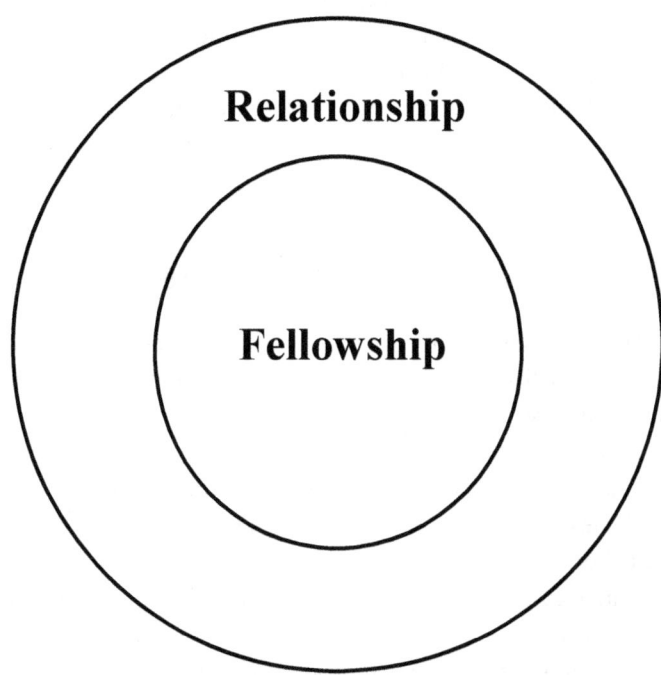

Through Christ's work on the cross we enter into a permanent relationship with the Father; however, when we sin we break fellowship with the Father and we are moved from the center of the inner circle to the periphery of the outer circle. Our sins do not move us out of the relationship circle, but they do remove us out of the fellowship circle. We do not lose our place in the family of God, but our fellowship with God is broken until we repent and confess.

In my daddy's wood shop he has a tool called a square. It is a rigid, inflexible piece of metal that is formed into a perfect ninety degree angle. If I am working with a piece of wood and I want to see how close to square it is or if it is warped, all I have to do is compare that wood to the standard of the square and it will always give me an accurate picture. When building a piece of furniture, it's vital that the various pieces be in square or else the parts will not fit together. Even if one piece is out of alignment, it can affect the others: corners will not join together flush, doors will not shut properly, and drawers will not slide smoothly. The square is brutally honest; it always exposes my problem. Yet, without its correction, carpentry would be impossible.

The light of God's truth, as spelled out in His Word, is like that unbending square. Its purpose is to correct and guide so that areas of life "fit together" properly. When the light of God's truth exposes our sin problem we should not ignore it but confess it. When we confess sin the process of correcting the course of our spiritual lives begins and our fellowship with God is restored.

THE PERILS OF CONCEALED SIN (1:8, 10)

John explains what dangers result from not confessing our sins before God. The first is that we live in a state of self-deception, "If we say we have no sin, we deceive ourselves . . ." Notice that in 1:8 John uses the term "sin" in the singular. What John is talking about here is the denial of original sin—that man is inherently born a sinner by nature. According to the Bible, the person who denies that he is a sinner is a person that is least in touch with his own heart (Rom. 3:23).

I am amazed that when you step into the halls of academia today or if you listen to the so-called experts in psychology, you will hear the resounding agreement that man is basically good. They argue that man is in a continual process of discovering his potential. They promote behavior modification and decry the possibility of personal responsibility. Sin is a nasty three-letter word left over from the archaic thinking of the dark ages and the sooner we abolish ourselves from the doctrine of depravity the sooner we are to become enlightened.

I remember sitting in a college psychology class when the professor said, "The reason why people make bad choices is because of society. In other words, the problem with man is his socialization. The reason why people do bad things is because the culture around them engenders them to kill, steal, and lie." At that point another student raised his hand and said, "But isn't society made up of people?" There was a moment of awkward silence, because in a brief moment this PHD just had his whole worldview undercut by a single question. Malcolm Muggeridge said it years ago, "The doctrine of depravity is the most debated doctrine in society, but it is also the most empirically verifiable."

Total Confession (1 John 1:8-10)

I was witnessing to a man not long ago and he told me what would change the state of society. He said, "If people had better education then that would solve many of our social ills." The major problem with this solution is that education only makes man more sophisticated in his evil. Education only makes us more clever and proficient at committing sin. Teddy Roosevelt once quipped, "A man who has never gone to school may steal from a freight car; but if he has a university education, he may steal the whole railroad." Man's condition is not just ignorance, but the fact that he is bent towards the darkness rather than the light.

Second, John also tells us that the person who denies their own sin is not only living in a lie, but they are a liar, ". . . and the truth is not in us" (1:8b). Besides outright denial, I have found that in general humans lie about their sin problem in one of four ways.

> *Minimize sin*—meaning that they make light of their own sin by comparing themselves to another person. The common objection is, "Well, I haven't killed anyone or robbed a bank so I'm really not a bad person." This is what the Rich Young Ruler did in Mark 10:17-31. When Jesus confronted him with the law he said, "All these I have kept since I was a boy."

> *Move sin*—this means that when people are confronted with sin they transfer the blame of their actions on to another person. "I cheated on my wife because my father cheated on my mother." "I do the things I do because no one ever told me they loved me." This is what Adam did in the Garden of Eden. God confronted Adam and Eve after they ate the forbidden fruit and Adam said, "The woman whom you gave to be with me, she gave me fruit of the tree, and I ate" (Gen. 3:12).

> *Mask sin*—this is when we try to cover up and conceal our sin problem so that everyone will think that we have got it all together. David did this after he slept with Bathsheba and she got pregnant. To cover up the sin David brought Uriah, her husband, home from war and tried to get him to sleep with his Bathsheba so that it would look like it was their child. When that didn't work out David engineered a plan to have Uriah killed on the front lines of battle. In the end, not only was David an adulterer but also a murderer (2 Sam. 11:1-27).

> *Manage sin*—this is when we try to hold on to our sin as long as possible because we think that we can actually control it. We rationalize sin and say, "It's not really that big of an issue; I can give it up

anytime I want to." This was Samson's problem. Samson thought that because he was so strong he could handle the little seductress Delilah. However, she wore the brute down. Three times she asked him, "Where does your strength lie?" and finally he caved in (Jud. 16:1–31).

John argues that when we refuse to deal with sin and call it what it really is then we live a lie and pretty soon when you lie to yourself enough times, you begin to believe it.

Third, when we refuse to confess sin we declare God a liar, "If we say we have not sinned, we make him a liar" (1:10a). Denying sin is not only lying to ourselves, but is tantamount to committing blasphemy. D. Edmond Hiebert commented on this verse:

> It is one thing to reveal that we ourselves are liars, but it is a far more serious thing to make a liar out of God. Such a claim is a direct attack upon the character of God and impugns His whole program of human redemption . . . The noun "liar", not merely charges God with telling lies, but also declares that in character He is a liar, false in His very nature. It reduces God to the level of the Devil, who is the father of all lies."[2]

I can remember when I was about twelve years old and I went through this stage where I hated taking showers. I would try and go for days on end without taking a shower. I was convinced in my mind that I really didn't need to take showers because I wasn't dirty. So I would try and sneak around my mom. One sweltering summer day we had been to a funeral service. As the sun bore down on us at the graveside, the sweat began to run down by neck and back profusely. After we moved indoors for refreshments my mom found me. The first thing she noticed was the collar around my nice white dress shirt. Where I had been sweating all the dirt and grime that built up on my body had made its way onto the inside collar of my shirt; it was a classic case of ring-around-the-collar. Finally, my true condition came out. It was at that moment that I realized that Mom was right. I was nasty.

When we say to God, "I don't have a sin problem"—we lie; when we say to God, "but I'm a Christian and I don't struggle with sin anymore"—we lie. It isn't until we see what our sin actually looks like that we realize God was right all along and we are living in self-denial.

Lastly, when we deny sin we demonstrate that the Word of God is not in us (1:10b). I have learned over the years that there is no way you can

---

2. Hiebert, *The Epistles of John*, 68.

Total Confession (1 John 1:8-10)

spend time in the Word of God and feel absolutely good about yourself all the time. Don't take me the wrong way—God's Word is spiritual food, it's encouraging, and it's full of wonderful promises. However, there are days when I get up and I don't feel like studying the Bible because I know that when I do I will be looking into a mirror that shows me warts and all. D.L. Moody said it best, "The Bible will either keep you from sin, or sin will keep you from the Bible." God's Word is like a surgeon's scalpel. It cuts us only to heal us (Heb. 4:12–13).

THE PROCESS OF CONFESSING SIN (1:9A)

When we get to the point of confession, the first step to releasing our sin is to agree with God. John uses an interesting Greek word here in the text for "confess." It is the word *homologeo* which literally means "to say the same thing as" or "to agree." Confession in the Biblical sense is not simply making a mental assent to the idea of sin, nor is it praying a simple prayer like, "God forgive me of all the bad things I've done." Confession is much more than that. Not only is there an intellectual component, but there is also an emotional component that comes from a broken and contrite heart.

Many times we approach confession very flippantly like the man who wrote an anonymous letter to IRS. His letter said, "Gentlemen: Enclosed you will find a cashier's check for $150. I cheated on my tax return last year and have not been able to sleep ever since. If I still have trouble sleeping I will send you the rest."

I once heard about an old farmer who had a conscience that troubled him. At last he went to his neighbor and said, "Sir, I'm sorry. I stole a rope from you a while back." The neighbor was gracious enough to forgive the thieving farmer. However, he still had no peace of mind. Later he told his wife, "Maybe I should have told him that there was a cow tied to the end of that rope when I stole it."

The confession that John is talking about is agreeing with what God says about our sin and calling it what He calls it. The world wants to clean up sin and put a designer label on it so it doesn't sound so bad. What we call an "affair," God calls adultery. What we call an "alternative lifestyle," God calls an abomination. What we call a "credibility gap," God calls lying. What we call "pro-choice," God calls murder. What we call, "social drinking," God calls drunkenness. We may legalize sin and give it the highest level of approval by endorsing it in the supreme courts of our land, but it still doesn't change God's opinion.

Confession is simply this—*it's letting God know that you know what He already knows about you.* David was a man who knew what it was like to weep bitterly after he quit playing games and broke down before God. He said, "For I know my transgressions, and my sin is ever before me. Against you, you only, have I sinned and done what is evil in your sight, so that you may be justified in your words and blameless in your judgment. Behold, I was brought forth in iniquity, and in sin did my mother conceive me" (Ps. 51:3–5).

Confession is not for God; it's for us. When we feel the depths of our sin, then and only then can we understand the depths of God's grace. When we see our sin as it really is, then it makes the forgiveness of God that much more amazing and the blood of Jesus that much more precious to us.

The next step in confession is admitting your sin to God and calling it out to Him. After you have agreed with what God has said about who you really are, what happens next is a spiritual inventory needs to be taken, whereby you allow the Spirit of God to examine your life with a fine-toothed comb. Notice in 1:9 that John uses the word "sins" in the plural not the singular. In other words, confession is not only something that deals with sin in general, but sins in particular. When we confess our sins God wants us to be specific in our confession. Therefore, we don't say "God forgive me of my sin," but instead we say, "God forgive me for my lust, my gossiping tongue, my resentful attitude, my pride, etc."

When I was in college I had to learn how to do laundry for the first time. The first few times I tried to wash my clothes it was a disaster. Instead of separating all my dirty clothes into distinct piles related by color I just took all my laundry and put it in the machine all at once. I began to notice something, when I lumped all my clothes together nothing really got clean. My gym shorts and socks still came out smelling rank. Finally, I figured out my problem was that I was cramming all the clothes in at once. Later someone suggested that instead of dumping all the clothes in at once, I should put the garments in one-by-one. The point is this—many times when we confess sin we try and lump it all together and get it done quickly like a dirty chore. What God wants us to do is slow down and individually deal with our sins one at a time.

Total Confession (1 John 1:8–10)

THE PROMISES OF CONFESSED SIN (1:9B)

After we have confessed our sins we should accept God's forgiveness based on His nature. In other words, God promises to do what He says He'll do, because of who He is. Notice that John gives us a couple of divine attributes to back up God's promise of pardon—God's faithfulness and God's justice.

God's faithfulness means that it is impossible for God to act any other way than is consistent with His moral perfection. Paul said in 2 Tim. 2:13 that "Even if we believe not, yet He remains faithful, He cannot deny himself." God is faithful to His promise to forgive us unconditionally. If God does not forgive us when we come to Him the way He has prescribed then He is not God. Tony Evans puts it this way: "I love that Motel 6 commercial. It says, 'We're gonna leave the light on for you.' That's quite a statement about the faithfulness of Motel 6 to be up and waiting on you. Guess what? God's light of forgiveness is always on, welcoming those sinners home who want to repent and ask for forgiveness."[3]

God is also just, which entails that He will give us exactly what we deserve. Because Jesus went to the cross and died in our place and shed His blood, the wrath of God has been turned away. The fact that Jesus Christ paid the full penalty for our sins means that God will not demand a second payment. Jesus appeased the demands of the Father once and for all.

Do you remember some of the last words of Jesus uttered from the cross? In John 19:30, Jesus said, "It is finished" or "*tetelestai*" in Greek. In the days of the Roman Empire when a debt was paid the buyer would be given a receipt with the word "*tetelestai*" written across it meaning "paid in full." In antiquity when a prisoner had served his sentence and he was released from jail he was given a certificate called a "writ of ordinances" that outlined what his crime was and verified that he had served his time. Across this certificate was the word, "*tetelestai*" meaning that his sentence had been paid in full and he could not be made to serve the same sentence twice or called into a situation of double jeopardy.

Paul expressed this idea in Colossians 2:14 when he said that Christ ". . . wiped clean the handwriting of requirements that was against us, which was contrary to us. And he has taken it out of the way, having nailed it to the cross." When Jesus Christ died on the cross, the payment for our crimes was made in full. Therefore, when John says that God is just to forgive us, what he means is that the righteousness of God requires

---

3. Evans, *Tony Evans Book of Illustrations*, 111.

Him to forgive because the debt has been fully met. We are not required to pay for our sins all over again because Jesus already accomplished that.

George Woodall was a missionary to London's inner city. One day a young woman he had led to the Lord came to him and said, "I keep sinning. Has God really forgiven my past?" Mr. Woodall replied, "If this is troubling you, I think I know what He would say to you. He would tell you to mind your own business." "What do you mean?" she inquired with a puzzled look. The missionary replied, "When Christ went to the Cross He made your sins His business. When He took them away, He put them behind His back, dropped them into the depths of the sea and posted a big sign with bold red letters that reads, "No Fishing!"

God doesn't just forgive, He forgets. He erases the board. He destroys the evidence. He burns the surveillance video. He clears the memory from the computer. He throws it all into the sea of His forgetfulness (Ps. 103:12).

5

Looking for a Good Attorney?
(1 John 2:1–2)

ONE OF THE MORE fascinating TV shows over the years has been the show *COPS*. It gives you the opportunity to ride shotgun alongside the officers of local law enforcement. Every time you watch it there is either a stake-out, a domestic disturbance, or a SWAT team is busting down the door of a drug dealer. You are almost guaranteed to see an exciting foot chase, a stumbling drunk being hogtied in his underwear, or some belligerent gangster getting pistol whipped. *COPS* is a show that will never go out of style, and programmers will never have to resort to re-runs because it could air from now until the end of time and never lose its audience or a cast.

Because of humanity's sinful and fallen condition there will always be cops and robbers and because of our fascination with the stupidity of criminals there will always be people watching. In almost every episode someone gets arrested and the deputy slaps the cuffs on the criminal and then begins to recite to the offender their Miranda rights: "*You have the right to remain silent. Anything you say can and will be used against you in a court of law. You have the right to speak to an attorney, and to have an attorney present during any questioning. If you cannot afford a lawyer, one will be provided for you at government expense.*"

In the first two verses of 1 John chapter two we are told that we are entitled to certain rights as believers. As sinners we stand convicted and condemned before the justice bar of God. All who appear before God's heavenly courtroom plead guilty. In this situation, defending your own case or representing yourself is not a good idea—so you and I desperately need a good lawyer.

Living in the Light

John reminds us that we have the right to an attorney. In case you fear that the legal fees for such a lawyer are too costly, John would say "Fear not little children for one has been supplied at the expense of heaven—the name of this divine defense attorney is Jesus Christ, the righteous, and He's never lost a case."

As we have been exploring the book of 1 John we have learned that fellowship is the essence of the Christian life. God desires intimacy with us. However, our intimacy with God is often times broken by the effects of sin. God is holy and if we are going to be where He is then we have to deal with this ugly fact of sin in our lives.

Sin is such an affront to the holiness of God that the Father broke fellowship with the Son over it. You will remember that while Jesus Christ hung on the cross He cried out "Father, Father, why have you forsaken me?" (Matt. 27:46). As the burden of humanity's sin was placed upon Jesus, even the Father in heaven could not look upon His beloved Son (Hab. 1:13).

Our sin issue presents quite a problem. How can guilty criminals have fellowship with an unimaginably holy God? What rights does a convict have before the righteous Judge of the universe? Only one—the right to an attorney who makes a case on our behalf.

As we read the opening verses of the second chapter of 1 John you must imagine yourself in God's courtroom. Picture yourself in the throes of a legal drama where you're on trial, but in the midst of this scene there steps Jesus Christ. He has been appointed to represent you. There are some things you need to understand about the credentials of this attorney.

JESUS ADVOCATES FOR US (2:1)

John opens by giving one of his purpose statements for writing, "I am writing these things to you so that we may not sin." There are many in the church who have the opposite view of sin. They think, "Well if I'm going to sin, I might as well sin boldly because I know that God will forgive me." Paul says in Rom. 6:1, "What shall we say then? Are we to continue in sin that grace may abound? By no means! How can we who died to sin still live in it?" The grace of God is not a license to sin, but grace is supposed to make us more sensitive to the dangers of sin. A driver's license gives you the privilege to drive safely, not the right to exceed the speed limit. In a similar way, God's grace and promised forgiveness doesn't mean we can live any way we want. Instead grace gives us the privilege and ability to live the way we are supposed to live.

Looking for a Good Attorney? (1 John 2:1-2)

John continues, "But in the event that you do sin there is an Advocate." Salvation does not eradicate our ability to sin. We still have the potential to sin and we will sin. In that case, when you do make a mess of things there is someone in your corner. The Greek word used in the text is *parakletos*, and is translated "Advocate." The word means, "one who is called to our side." John uses this word in his Gospel to refer to the Holy Spirit (John 14:16, 26, 15:26, 16:7) and it's also translated as "Comforter" or "Helper." The Holy Spirit is our advocate on Earth, but Jesus Christ is our advocate in heaven. He is our divine defense attorney before the Father.

The second person of the Trinity and the third person of the Trinity are two different advocates working together in perfect harmony to accomplish the completion of our salvation. The Holy Spirit enables us to live the Christian life, empowers us to resist sin, and walk in the light. Because we are like sheep, prone to wander, Jesus Christ and His shed blood cleanse us from all sin in the event that we stumble.

Some of my all-time favorite movies are the *Rocky* movies. It's a classic underdog story where Rocky advances from being a nobody on the tough streets of Philly to a championship prize fighter. In the movies Rocky has a crotchety old trainer named Mickey. Mickey's favorite term of endearment for Rocky is "you bum." Yet without the guidance and direction of Mickey, Rocky would have never become "The Italian Stallion." Mickey practiced tough love, but he was always there in Rocky's corner of the ring cheering him on, bandaging his wounds, and giving him advice in the ring.

That's an Advocate! One who is in our corner at all times. One who is called alongside, who not only encourages us but loves us unconditionally. Even when you fall down into sin, you have an Advocate who sticks closer than a brother.

The reason why we need an Advocate is because we have an accuser. In Rev. 12:10 it says that the Devil stands before God day and night as the accuser of the brethren. Satan stands as the prosecuting attorney before the Judge condemning you for all your sins. He knows all your faults and all your failures and he loves to bring them before God. Satan is still bitter after God booted him out of heaven for his rebellion. Satan knows he can't defeat God, but he can get back at Him by going after His children. That's why the Devil wants fellowship between you and God broken. He hates God and he hates you.

Believers often wonder, "Now that Jesus is in heaven, what is he doing?" He's not taking it easy. Just because Jesus is in heaven doesn't mean

Living in the Light

that He's quit working. The Bible says that Jesus who has now ascended to the Father has become our intercessor, mediator, and go-between. He is taking up for us in the midst of Satan's accusations.

Paul describes it like this in Rom. 8:33–34, "Who will bring any charge against those whom God has chosen? It is God who justifies. Who then is the one who condemns? No one. Christ Jesus who died—more than that, who was raised to life—is at the right hand of God and is also interceding for us." The writer of Hebrews says in 7:24–25, "... because Jesus lives forever, He has a permanent priesthood. Therefore, He is able to save completely those who come to God through Him, because He always lives to intercede for them." John Phillips says it like this:

> When Satan comes before God, he comes as the accuser. This is one instance in which he does not come to tell lies about us, even though he is the Father of all lies ... Sad to say he comes to tell the truth about us. He gets nowhere, however. The Accuser is met by the Advocate and all He has to do is raise His pierced hands and Satan is silenced.[1]

There is one critical difference in this courtroom from all others—the Judge is your Heavenly Father, the defense attorney happens to be the Judge's Son, and the defendant (that's you) happens to be loved by the Judge and His son. Are you beginning to see the picture here? The courtroom is stacked in your favor. If God be for us, who shall be against us?

JESUS APPLIES HIS RIGHTEOUSNESS TO US (2:1)

When Jesus is advocating for us, what evidence does He present to plead our case? Did you notice the little phrase tagged on here to the end of 2:1? "We have an advocate with the Father, Jesus Christ *the righteous*." Christ, as our divinely appointed defense attorney, has impeccable credentials. He has something that no other lawyer can claim—sinlessness.

In God's courtroom you need a representative who doesn't have the same sin problem we do. Jesus, as our defense council, is uniquely qualified to stand in God's presence to represent us because He is the only one who has perfectly fulfilled God's law on behalf of all believers. This attorney doesn't have what we have (sin), but He does have what we don't have (righteousness).

---

1. Phillips, *Exploring the Epistles of John*, 41.

Looking for a Good Attorney? (1 John 2:1-2)

This courtroom also operates under a different method. Most lawyers try to prove the innocence of their victim. Most attorneys plead "not guilty" for their clients. Jesus, on the other hand, acknowledges our guilt before the Father. He never says we are innocent; He agrees totally with the charges brought against us. However, our defense attorney presents some compelling evidence in our favor—namely Himself. 1 Peter 3:18 says, "For Christ also suffered once for sins, the righteous for the unrighteous, that He might bring us to God, being put to death in the flesh but made alive in the spirit."

The reason why Jesus can get you acquitted is not because you're so good; it's because He's so good. It's not because you kept the law; it's because He kept the law. Through His death on the cross, the perfect life that Jesus lived is credited to you and the terrible sinful life that you lived is credited to Jesus. This is what theologians call the doctrine of imputation. The word "imputation" is an accounting term and it means to deposit or credit something into someone's account that may or may not be his. The Bible identifies three great imputations:

- Adam's sin was transferred to the entire human race after the Fall (Rom. 5:12, 3:23).
- The sin of humanity was transferred to Jesus when He died on the cross (2 Cor. 5:21).
- The righteousness of Christ is transferred to the believer when he/she accepts Him as Savior (Rom. 4:1-8).

At the cross a great exchange took place. Jesus Christ got your sin and when you trusted in Him you got His righteous life. God treated His Son as the worst sinner who ever lived and He treats the worst sinners as the sons and daughters of God.

Let's say that before me I have two books. Both of these books are biographies which record every thought, every word, and every deed of a person's life. One book is entitled *The Life of Jesus Christ*. This book is beautiful and perfect. This book never records one sin in the life of Jesus. Its pages tell the story of a wonderful life and the illustrations are amazing.

The other book is *The Life of Derrick McCarson*. This book is ugly, tragic, and filled with terrible sinning of all verities. It's filled with lustful thoughts, lies, cursing, and lots of things I'm not proud of. However, when I trusted in Jesus Christ as my Savior, He took the pages out of His book and He took the pages out of my book. Then Christ took the pages from His life story and placed the cover with my name on it over His life story. The cover of the book reads *The Life of Derrick McCarson*, but when you open the book up it tells of the righteous deeds of Jesus. Then Christ took the pages from my book and put the cover with His name on it over my life story. The righteousness of Christ is credited to my name, and the sin of my life is credited to Jesus Christ.

As my divine defense attorney Jesus takes the book with my name on the cover and His sinless record and places it on the bench of the Judge and says "Here is my client's record." When the Father looks at your life He sees Jesus. The very righteousness that God demands is the very righteousness that Jesus provides for us. Or as the songwriter says—"My hope is built on nothing less that Jesus' blood and righteousness."

JESUS APPEASES GOD'S WRATH FOR US (2:2)

John uses a unique term in 2:2, *propitiation*, to refer to the sacrifice of Christ. It's one of those ten dollar theological words that you just can't leave home without. The word means "an appeasement" or "a satisfaction." It's used four times in the New Testament (here and in Rom. 3:25, Heb 9:5, 1 John 4:10).

In order to fully grasp the theological significance of this term we must have a working knowledge of the Old Testament sacrificial system. On the "Day of Atonement" (Yom Kippur) the high priest was to take two male goats before the congregation of Israel and cast lots (which was sort of the equivalent of flipping a coin) to determine the fate of each goat. When the lot revealed which goat was to be killed the condemned animal would be prepared as a sin offering (Lev. 16:9–10).

Having sacrificed a bull on behalf of himself and his family, the high priest entered the Most Holy place of the tabernacle, where the Ark of the Covenant resided. There on the mercy seat of the Ark, the glory of God emanated in strange cloud called the *Shekinah*. The high priest would then sprinkle the blood of the sacrificed goat on to the mercy seat, thus appeasing the wrath of God against the sins of the people.

With the sacrifice administered, the high priest would then exit the tabernacle and lay his hands on the head of the remaining goat, symbolically transferring the sins of the community to the "scapegoat." This goat was then set free into the wilderness as it carried away the sins of people under a barrage of hisses, boos, and hateful remarks from the crowd (Lev. 16:22). It is this imagery that John is drawing on to convey the idea that Christ became the universal propitiation for humanity's sin.

Looking for a Good Attorney? (1 John 2:1-2)

First, John highlights *the satisfaction of the sacrifice*. The blood of Jesus satisfied the inscrutable demands of a holy God and totally paid the sin debt levied against humanity. Because of Christ's sacrifice believers are no longer objects of God's wrath. Jesus bore the judgment of the Father in His body when He was whipped and nailed to two pieces of timber. The punishment that we rightfully deserve for our sins has been turned away and placed on Christ.

It's important that we understand that the Son and the Father are not in opposition to each other. The concept of propitiation does not mean that the Son wants to forgive us and the Father desires to condemn us. Jesus does not turn the wrath of the Father into love. Instead the Father and Son are working in unity; both desire mercy and justice. The mercy of God could not be fulfilled unless the justice of God was fulfilled first. The love of God could not be experienced until someone first took the wrath of God. On the cross Jesus satisfied both the justice and mercy of God. Christ became the object of God's wrath and through His sacrifice God offers pardon to those who will accept His son. In his book *Totally Saved*, Tony Evans explains:

> God's intolerance towards sin is the same intolerance of a surgeon who insists on sterile instruments for an operation. A surgeon's demand for a pure operating environment is not an angry peevish reaction to the presence of bacteria but a settled conviction because he knows that bacteria will contaminate the patient . . . None of us gets upset if our surgeon insists on absolute cleanliness in the operating room, where even a speck of dirt could lead to infection. In fact, we demand that our surgeon be completely intolerant of impurity. If you can understand a surgeon's "wrath" against bacteria in the operating room then you can understand God's wrath against sin . . . God looked into our spiritual bank account and saw that we had nothing with which to pay the bill of sin. So in the person of Jesus Christ, God made himself the answer to our problem. Since we could not satisfy God's wrath against sin, He decided to satisfy His wrath by turning it on His own Son.[2]

As our divine defense attorney, not only does Jesus supply us with His righteousness, but He also serves our sentence. Not only does He argue our case, but He takes our punishment. Case dismissed!

Next, John draws our attention to *the scope of the sacrifice*. John gives an overall appraisal of the effect of Christ's sacrifice. He says that Jesus' sacrifice is not only good enough for you, but also for the whole world. He

---

2. Evans, *Totally Saved*, 66.

is not only a personal savior, but He is a universal savior. There are many Calvinists who will argue for a limited atonement—that is that Jesus died only for the elect or those that God predestined for salvation. However, this verse and many others offer a strong refutation of that kind of thinking.

> "Behold the lamb of God, who takes away *the sin of the world* "(John 1:29).

> "For God so loved *the world* that He gave His only begotten Son..." (John 3:16).

> "God is not willing that any should perish but *that all may come unto repentance*" (2 Peter 3:9).

> "This is good, and it is pleasing in the sight of God our Savior, *who desires all people to be saved and to come to the knowledge of the truth*" (1 Tim. 2:3–4).

Don't get confused on this. The Bible does not teach that everyone is going to be saved (universalism); however, it does teach that everyone *can be* saved. First John 2:2 does not mean that everyone is actually saved by the sacrifice of Jesus. It means that everyone can potentially be saved by the sacrifice of Jesus. *Christ's death is sufficient for all, but efficient only for those who believe in Christ.* Not everyone chooses to be saved, but everyone is given the offer.

You could think of the offer of salvation in terms of a check. When someone writes you a check the money is yours as long as there is money in the bank to cover it and as long as you endorse the check. In other words, the money doesn't become your money until you appropriate the gift by signing your name. God has written the world a check for salvation. The amount of the gift is unlimited—God has enough grace in the bank of heaven to cover everyone on Earth. However, the gift doesn't become yours until you endorse it and make it your own.

I am told that Martin Luther, the Great Reformer, had a dream one night. In this dream he died and went to heaven. When he got there Satan was waiting to meet him outside the gates. In his hands the Devil had a book. Satan opened the book and it had every sin that Martin Luther had ever committed. So Satan began to point his fiery finger at Martin Luther and he accused him of every sin imaginable. You might say he threw the book at him.

Satan said, "How can you expect to get into heaven, Martin Luther? You are a terrible, depraved sinner." Luther said, "Can I see the book one more time?" The devil handed it over and Luther opened it up to the last page. Luther said, "Satan, you forgot one important entry." He pointed to a line written in blood, "He is the propitiation for our sins, and not for ours only but also for the sins of the whole world."

Satan exploits our sin, but the blood of Jesus expels our sin. Satan accuses you, but Jesus cleanses you and then argues your case. He shuts up Satan because He is our divine defense attorney and our perfect propitiation.

6

Birthmarks of the Believer
(1 John 2:3–11)

IN HIS CLASSIC WORK, *The Cost of Discipleship,* Dietrich Bonhoeffer wrote, "Cheap grace is the preaching of forgiveness without requiring repentance, baptism without church discipline, communion without confession, absolution without personal confession. Cheap grace is grace without discipleship, grace without the cross, grace without Jesus Christ, living and incarnate."[1]

As a man who spent his last days rotting away in a Nazi prison, Bonhoeffer knew what it meant to truly follow Christ. Bonhoeffer became known for his resistance against the Nazi dictatorship and his outspoken condemnation of Hitler's "final solution" for the Jews. After he was arrested Nazi officials discovered that he had been connected to a failed assassination plot to take Hitler's life. That was all the S.S. needed to hang him from the gallows of Flossenburg concentration camp. On April 8, 1945 Bonhoeffer, at the age of 39, was executed just a few weeks before the German army would surrender to the Allies.

The camp doctor who witnessed the execution wrote: "I saw Pastor Bonhoeffer . . . kneeling on the floor praying fervently to God. I was most deeply moved by the way this lovable man prayed, so devout and so certain that God heard his prayer. At the place of execution, he again said a short prayer and then climbed the few steps to the gallows, brave and composed. His death ensued after a few seconds. In the almost fifty years that I worked

---

1. Bonhoeffer, *The Cost of Discipleship,* 44–45.

as a doctor, I have hardly ever seen a man die so entirely submissive to the will of God."[2]

Discipleship is more than walking a church aisle, signing a membership card, or muttering a quick prayer of forgiveness under your breath. Discipleship is anything that causes what we believe in our hearts about Jesus to have demonstrable consequences in our daily life. Like Bonhoeffer, the Apostle John was not interested in living a life of "cheap grace," but one which centered on the lordship of Christ.

In 1 John 2:3–11 the Apostle writes about the tests of true discipleship. These are traits of the twice-born and birthmarks of the believer. Essentially, John is giving us three ways we can know that we have true fellowship with Jesus. His simple argument—if Christ is our Lord then it will show up whether we are suffering behind bars or working a regular nine to five job.

A TRUE DISCIPLE SUBMITS TO THE LORDSHIP OF CHRIST (2:3–5A)

The first test that John gives is the test of obedience. Obedience to God's commands is proof of our love for Him. In typical fashion, John states this principle both positively and negatively. Notice that John is not saying that we keep God's commands in order to be saved, but we keep God's commands because we are saved. We do not keep Christ's commands to merit His love; we keep His commands as an expression of love. We are not working to salvation, but we are working from salvation. Keeping the commands of Jesus should be a joy because the more you obey His commands the deeper the relationship goes.

Most of what John is preaching concerning obedience came directly from Jesus' own mouth in the Upper Room Discourse:

> "If you love me, you will keep my commandments" (John 14:15).

> "Whoever has my commandments and keeps them, he it is who loves me. And he who loves me will be loved by my Father, and I will love him and manifest myself to him" (John 14:21).

> "If anyone loves me, he will keep my word, and my Father will love him, and we will come to him and make our home with him. Whoever does not love me does not keep my words" (John 14:23–24).

2. Bethge, *Dietrich Bonhoeffer*, 927.

Living in the Light

> "If you keep my commandments, you will abide in my love, just as I have kept my Father's commandments and abide in His love" (John 15:10).

There are three motives for obedience. We can obey *because we have to, because we need to, or because we want to*. A slave obeys because he has to. If he doesn't obey, he will be punished. An employee obeys because he needs to. He may not enjoy his work, but he does what his boss asks so he can get a paycheck. However, a child who is in a loving relationship with his/her father obeys because they want the approval and blessing of the parent. This is the kind of motivation behind the believer's obedience to Christ. Only those who obey can believe and only those who believe can obey.

I once heard about a little boy who got in trouble and his mother told him to go sit in the corner. After a few minutes, his mother asked him from another room, "Are you sitting down?" The little boy said, "I'm sitting down on the outside, but I'm standing up on the inside." That's the opposite of Christian obedience—outwardly compliant but inwardly rebellious. Jesus wants our heart and our will to align with His purposes.

A true disciple obeys Christ because the relationship between him and Christ is not out of duty but rooted in love. There is a story of a woman who had a husband who kept a long list of chores. This list contained twenty five things he wanted her to do in order for her to be a good wife for him. Every day he took out the list and checked off the things she completed. Cooking—check! Cleaning—check! Taking care of the kids—check! At the end of the day, he would let her know how well she scored. One day it was twenty-three out of twenty-five, another day it was twenty out of twenty-five, etc. This housewife was miserable. She was miserable because she didn't marry to be tied to a checklist. She was tired of feeling like she was the slave of an overbearing chauvinist.

After a number of years, the husband died. The woman felt a weight lifted off her shoulders because she had been performing to meet this unrealistic standard for years. She had been doing her duty and hated every minute of it even though the duties were necessary.

Soon afterward this same woman fell in love with a new man, but this man had no lists, just love. He told this woman that all he wanted to do was love her. He wanted her to wake up in the morning knowing that he loved her. So he left her love letters and flowers frequently. He took her on a romantic date every Friday night and he said "I love you" every night before retiring.

Birthmarks of the Believer (1 John 2:3-11)

One day as she was cleaning the house she opened up a drawer and saw a piece of paper. Folded up in this drawer was the old list from her dead husband. She began to giggle when she realized that everything written down, all twenty-five duties, were happening effortlessly in her new marriage. Everything she hated doing out of requirement by the first husband she was doing for the second husband and loving it! The difference was that her relationship to the new husband was rooted in love rather than duty. For the Christian, obedience to Christ is not a burdensome task but the outworking of a loving relationship.

A believer obeys the commands of God because he knows that in obeying God he is actually rewarding himself. God's commands are given with our best interest in mind, so when we obey the commands of God we set ourselves up for blessing. I read a story one time of General George Patton. One day he took three men and he told them to dig a ditch exactly eight feet long, four feet deep and three feet deep. Then the General went around the corner and listened to the men complain. One questioned, "What is the point of all this?" Another said, "This ditch is useless. It's too small to serve a purpose." The third guy said, "Who cares, let's just get the job done." After the men were done Patton came back. He pointed to the man who didn't complain and said, "You're promoted." Then as he walked away he said, "Men, in this army I'm looking for soldiers who will dig ditches, not ditch responsibility." The lowly buck private was promoted because of his attitude and his dependability to get the job done with no questions asked.

When we obey God we get promoted. We get promoted to a deeper fellowship with Him, and we reap the blessings that come along with making a good decision. When John says in 2:5, "The love of God is perfected in him," it means we are in process. We are not perfect yet, but God's love is being perfected in us. Daily obedience to Christ brings us to maturity. The more we grow in obedience to Him the more perfect our love becomes. Like the housewife who was transformed by love, we too are transformed by Christ's love and the proof of our love is our loyalty.

A TRUE DISCIPLE SEEKS THE LIFESTYLE OF CHRIST (2:5B-6)

The second test that John gives is an outworking of the first. If the first test dealt with your will, this second test deals with your walk. This makes sense because if we are keeping the word of Christ then we will have a walk like Christ. Notice that John uses a word in verse 2:6 that is particular to his writings—"abide." The word means "to stay or remain." Abiding in the sense that John is talking about means that you rely on Jesus for your spiritual life the way that an infant relies on its mother for food, the way that a sunflower relies on the sun for photosynthesis, or the way a light bulb must be screwed into the socket if it is to illuminate. Abiding speaks of a deep, permanent connection to a source of life.

Again, if we go back to the Upper Room discourse we can see where John got the seed thought for this statement. Jesus said, "Abide in me, and I in you. As the branch cannot bear fruit by itself, unless it abides in the vine, neither can you, unless you abide in me. I am the vine; you are the branches. Whoever abides in me and I in him, he it is that bears much fruit, for apart from me you can do nothing" (John 15:4–5). There are two thoughts connected to this imagery of abiding. *Vitality*—just as the branch needs to be connected to the vine for life, we too need to be connected to Jesus if we are going to have spiritual life. *Productivity*—there can be no fruit if there is no root. When a branch is grafted into a tree it becomes part of the tree, bearing the tree's fruit, the same is true for everyone who is united to Christ. Not only do they have the life of Christ flowing through them, but they also produce spiritual fruit (Matt. 7:16–20, Gal. 5:22).

This principle of abiding is so simple that the profundity of it glosses over us. Abiding means that all our ability to live for Christ comes totally from Him. If you desire to live the Christian life, it will not be you living it. It will be Jesus living it through you. You become the vehicle through which Christ expresses Himself. The Christian life isn't reduced to stale rule keeping, but the power of Christ being manifested through the Holy Spirit.

Perhaps a simple illustration of abiding will suffice. A few years ago I was introduced to making coffee in a French press. I must confess that this revolutionized my coffee drinking experience. I could not believe the explosion of flavor that the coffee took on when it was made with this method. Previously I had been making coffee in a regular coffee maker where the water drips down through coffee filter and into the pot. That way is good if you like weak coffee because the water doesn't have much time to interact with the coffee beans.

However, the French press method is totally different. A French press is basically a glass jar that comes with a filter that acts like a stopper. You grind the coffee beans and put them in the bottom of the jar. Then you take the hot water and you pour it into the jar with the grinds. You slightly push

Birthmarks of the Believer (1 John 2:3-11)

down the press and let the water soak in the coffee for 4 or 5 minutes. To use a biblical word, you let your coffee "abide" in the water. That way the coffee grinds have unrestricted access to permeate the water and more time to transfer flavor from the beans into the water. Then you take the plunger and push the grinds to the bottom of the jar, pour a cup and enjoy.

That's the way abiding works. Jesus desires for believers to spend time resting and abiding in Him. The more time you spend in the fullness of His presence the deeper your spiritual relationship is going to be. As you abide with Christ your spiritual life becomes stronger and more robust. The intimacy of your walk with Christ is determined by your level of abiding.

When John says that "we are to walk just as He walked," what he means is that we are to mirror Christ. Usually in the New Testament the word "walk" is a metaphor for the daily conduct of believers. How did Jesus walk? Remember in 2:3-4, how John stressed the importance of obedience? He did that because Jesus walked in complete and total obedience to the Father. Study these verses which underscore how Jesus abided with the Father:

> "I can do nothing on my own. As I hear, I judge, and my judgment is just, because *I seek not my own will but the will of Him who sent me*" (John 5:30).

> "For I have come down from heaven, *not to do my own will but the will of Him who sent me*" (John 6:38).

> "And He who sent me is with me. He has not left me alone, *for I always do the things that are pleasing to Him*" (John 8:29).

> ". . . *but I do as the Father has commanded me*, so that the world may know that I love the Father" (John 14:31).

> "I glorified you on earth, having *accomplished the work that you gave me to do*" (John 17:4).

Here is the secret to how Jesus walked in this world: He walked in total obedience and dependence upon His Father. Jesus didn't set His own agenda, develop His own plans, or make His own schedule and then ask the Father to bless it. Christ was completely submissive to the Father and if we are walking like Christ then we must totally surrender our own life to His authority.

Living in the Light

A TRUE BELIEVER SHARES THE LOVE OF CHRIST (2:7-11)

This last test flows from your heart and into your hands. If you are abiding in Jesus and allowing Him to express His life through you, then a natural side effect is love for the brothers and sisters in the family of faith. John gives his readers a bit of a paradox in 2:7-8. He tells us that the command to love is both old and new. Now how can something be old and yet new at the same time?

In order to understand what John is talking about it's important to realize that Greeks used two different words to refer to something as "new." The word *kairos* refers to something as chronologically new, while the word *kanios* refers to something as new in essence or quality. The term John uses twice here in the text to refer to the "new" commandment is *kanios*.

You might want to think about this in terms of phones. When cell phones came out it was something old but presented in a new way. The idea of talking to someone through a communication device was not new. Phones had been in use for years. However, cell phones were new (*kanios*) in the sense that now you could talk to anyone anywhere and you didn't need a landline. Furthermore, the smart phones are totally revolutionary in that they can access the Internet, text, download apps, and make calls. This kind of "new" (*kanios*) is utterly life changing.

What John is saying here is this, "The command to love is both old and new. The command to love God and love your neighbor as yourself has been around for years, but we really didn't understand what it meant to love until Jesus came around and gave us the purest example of *agape*, self-sacrificial love. Jesus showed us the fullest expression of love." Thus, the commandment to love is not new in time (*kairos*), but character (*kanios*).

Remember the scene in Matthew 22 when a lawyer came up to Jesus and asked him, "What is the greatest commandment in the Law?" Jesus replied, "You shall love the Lord your God with all your heart and with all your soul and with all your mind. This is the great and first commandment. And a second is like it: You shall love your neighbor as yourself. On these two commandments depend all the Law and the Prophets" (Matt. 22:36-40). The love of Christ was made up of a horizontal and a vertical component. Loving God spills over into loving people. It took Jesus to flesh out the real meaning of the old commandment in a new way.

Again John is repeating the command to love which he heard in the Upper Room. Jesus had just finished washing the disciples' feet, modeling before them what it meant to be a humble servant. Jesus said, "A *new commandment* I give to you, that you love one another: just as I have loved you, you also are to love one another. By this all people will know that you are my disciples, if you have love for one another" (John 13:34–35).

The word for "love" used in both the Upper Room and here is the word *agapao*. It is the strongest word in the Greek language to express love. It is a self-sacrificing kind of love, a love that seeks the highest good of the other no matter the cost. John could still remember the feeling of the water between his toes and the words of Jesus. Jesus heightened the expression of love to a new degree. Jesus doesn't love us because we're lovely; Jesus loves us in spite of ourselves. John 15:12 reads, "This is my commandment that you love one another as I have loved you. Greater love has no one than this, that someone lay down his life for his friends."

This is the kind of love that bids a man or a woman to die for another. You might say "I don't know if I can have that kind of love." I say, "You're right; you can't and I can't either. But Christ in you can." So you have to pray what I have to pray, "Lord I can't love these people the way you commanded me, but you can. So, Lord, you love them through me."

E. Stanley Jones, the famous missionary to India, once told a story about a conversation he had with a Hindu man. Jones asked the Hindu why he decided to come to one of his meetings to hear the Gospel. The man replied, "Years ago when I was boy we heckled a missionary preaching in the bazaar where I lived. We jeered at him and threw tomatoes at him. He simply wiped the tomato juice off his face and then after he was done preaching he took us to the sweet shop and bought us treats. I saw the love of Christ in that man we scorned and that's why I'm here today." Love speaks louder than any sermon. It is love that gains us an audience with an unbelieving world.

In 2:9–11 John returns to his light and darkness motif. In chapter 1 light was associated with holiness, truth, and fellowship with God. Darkness was associated with sin, lies, and worldliness. John touches on that theme again and connects light with love and darkness with hate. In other words, John says to us, "Someone who is walking in the light is full of love and someone who is in the darkness is full of hate." There is no middle ground. In the heart of the Christian there can be no prejudice, malice, or racism. Fellowship with God and hatred toward others are mutually exclusive.

Living in the Light

In verse 2:10 notice that the man who loves like Christ has "no cause for stumbling." What John means is that when the world sees how you love others they find no reason to reject the Gospel because your walk and talk line up. Unbelievers taking notice of your life don't "trip" over the fact that you say you love Jesus and at the same time harbor hatred toward someone else. Christians are to be walking advertisements for the Gospel, and a believer who is full of love doesn't send conflicting signals.

By contrast, the one in 2:11 who hates his brother is blinded and fumbles around in the dark. This means that the man or woman who does not love has his/her vision obscured by the hate within them. They cannot see clearly because they are consumed with a root of bitterness (Heb. 12:15).

I remember in my high school chemistry class my teacher did a demonstration with the effects of acid on metal. On a Friday afternoon she took a tin can and placed a small amount of sulfuric acid in the bottom. Then she instructed us to wait until Monday afternoon after it had a weekend to work its corrosive powers. When she unveiled the can the following Monday the base of the tin can was eroded away and the acid had slowly gnawed away at the integrity of the vessel containing it. Hate is like acid. It can damage the vessel in which it is stored as well as destroy the object on which it is poured.

The only antidote for hate is love. A tragic result of hatred is that it retards a believer's progress and destroys their witness. Years ago Francis Schaffer wrote a book called *The Mark of the Christian*. In it he made an insightful comment about the necessity of love for the Christian life:

> Through the centuries Christians have displayed many different symbols to show that they are Christians. They have worn marks in the lapels of their coats, hung crosses around chains fastened to their necks and even had special haircuts . . . However, Jesus has given us a badge to label a Christian not just in one era or in one locality, but at all times and in all places until Jesus returns. It is the badge of love. If we expect non-Christians to know that we are Christians we must wear the badge of love. It is how they will know Christ through us.[3]

When my little sister was growing up she had a blanket that she carried around everywhere. It was ragged and dirty. It was not much to look at, but she loved it. She would wrap her baby dolls in it, sleep with it, everywhere she went the blanket went. When she got married she took the

---

3. Schaffer, *The Mark of the Christian*, 13–14.

Birthmarks of the Believer (1 John 2:3–11)

blanket with her. The man who married her got the blanket too. In fact, the other day I saw that green baby blanket folded up on her bed. Now her child has adopted the blanket. You see, the blanket and my sister are inseparable. If you loved my sister then you also loved the blanket—it was part of the package. John says if you love Christ then you must also love others—it's part of the package. Dirty and ugly as they may be, we must love others as Christ loved us.

7

How is Your Worldview?
(1 John 2:12–17)

IN 2004 AN INTERESTING and charming movie entitled *The Terminal* hit theaters. The movie starred Tom Hanks in the role of the eccentric but loveable traveler named Viktor Navorski. The basic plot of the film is about a man who becomes trapped in a terminal at New York's JFK International Airport. In a strange turn of events, Viktor Navorski is denied entry into the United States because while he was en route to America, a revolution started in his fictional home nation of Krakozhia. Due to the civil war, the United States no longer recognized Krakozhia as a sovereign nation and denied Viktor entrance to the United States. As a result Navorski is unable to leave the airport, but he is also unable to return to Krakozhia. Thus, he becomes a refugee with no country and no home.

  The movie chronicles Navorski's resourcefulness as he must learn how to adjust to living in an airport for months on end. He sets up a make-shift bunk out of old chairs in a section of the airport that is being renovated. Navorski learns how to scrounge for money so he can buy food. He notices one day that he can receive a twenty-five cent reward for every baggage trolley that he returns to the collection machine. He survives on cheeseburgers from the fast-food vendors in the airport food court. He learns how to speak English by reading travel guides he finds in the airport gift store. He shaves and bathes in the airport bathroom. It's all quite comical to see the adventures Navorski gets into all while trying to make an airport terminal his home.

How is Your Worldview? (1 John 2:12-17)

As it turns out the film is partially inspired by the seventeen year stay of an Iranian man, Mehran Karimi Nasseri, who actually lived in the Charles de Gaulle International Airport in Paris, France from 1988 to 2006.

Can you imagine a more unnatural home than an airport? It's bustling and interesting, but it's certainly no place to unpack and settle down. The airport is never the final destination but rather the place that connects us from point A to point B. In much the same way, the believer is never to assume that this world is home. Like Viktor Navorski, the Bible argues that we are refugees in a foreign land just passing through to our final destination (Phil 3:20, Heb. 11:13-16). Our destination is heaven, but in the meantime we have to learn how to adjust to living on the sin-cursed earth. Warren Wiersebe writes:

> The world is not a natural habitat for a believer. The believers' citizenship is in heaven and all his effective resources for living on earth come from his Father in heaven. The believer is somewhat like a scuba diver. The water is not man's natural habitat, for he is not equipped for life in (or under) it. When a scuba diver goes under, he has to take special equipment so that he can breathe. Were it not for the Holy Spirit's living within us and the spiritual recourses we have in prayer, Christian fellowship, and the Word, we could never "make it" here on earth.[1]

John reminds his readers in this passage that believers should be *in* the world, but not *of* the world. In his characteristic manner, John talks to us in opposites—black and white, light and darkness, life and death, love and hate. In this passage he continues this pattern by setting up the polar opposites of worldliness vs. godliness. John argues that you cannot serve God and the world system at the same time.

When John uses the term "world" in this passage, what does he mean? The word "world" is used three different ways in the New Testament and it's important to understand which "world" John commands us not to love. The term "world" is often used to express the physical earth (Acts 17:24), or the idea of mankind (John 3:16); however, in this passage John has another idea in mind. John uses the Greek word *kosmos*. We derive our English words "cosmopolitan" and "cosmetics" from this word. The usage of the term "world" here refers to the way of life that we see operating around us every day—the morals, values, philosophies, schemes, undercurrents, and man-centered activities that take no account of God.

---

1. Wiersbe, *The Wiersbe Bible Commentary: New Testament*, 974.

The reason why the kingdom of God and the kingdom of this world are mutually exclusive domains is because they have different masters. Christ is the undisputed King-of-Kings of heaven; however, the world system has been given over to Satan for a time (1 John 5:19). Jesus said that Satan is "the prince of this world" (John 12:31). Paul referred to Satan as the "prince of the power of the air" (Eph. 2:2) who goes about "blinding the eyes" of people from the Gospel (2 Cor. 4:4). Satan has an organization of well-trained demons working for him and influencing the affairs of men (Eph. 6:11-12). If we could gain a peek behind the scenes of what goes on in this world, we would be shocked to find an invisible network of Satan's minions trying to sabotage and counter God's people.

In this text John gives us four reasons why the Christian cannot maintain fellowship with God and the world at the same time. John draws the battle lines in the sand and tells each one of us that we must choose a side.

LOVE OF THE WORLD THWARTS OUR GROWTH IN GOD (2:12-14)

The first reason why a Christian cannot fellowship with the world is because it stifles our progress towards spiritual development and maturity in the faith. Notice that John begins by defining different levels of Christian maturity. He talks about three different kinds of Christians in different stages of spiritual development—children, young men, and fathers.

"Little children" refers to the baby Christians or the ones who are just taking their first steps in the faith. Young men are the adolescents who are progressing in their walk but are not yet totally independent. Fathers are those who have reached a level of spiritual maturity; they have begun to reproduce and educate others in the faith. Just as an earthly father has children, a spiritual father is a mature believer in the faith who has passed on their "spiritual DNA" to another generation. You are a spiritual father if you now can teach and raise-up other believers to be disciples of Christ.

The problem is that most Christians get saved and stay spiritual infants their whole lives. Either because of lack of discipline or lack of discipleship they never move out of the spiritual nursery. The New Testament gives us several markers for identifying spiritual immaturity:

- No appetite for the "meat" of God's Word (Heb. 5:11-14)
- Easily deceived by false teachers (Eph. 4:14)

How is Your Worldview? (1 John 2:12-17)

- Carnally minded and an elementary understanding of spiritual matters (1 Cor. 3:2, 13:11, 14:20)
- Struggles with "youthful lusts" (2 Tim. 2:22)

What is it that keeps Christians from growing? Jesus tells us that part of the reason why spiritual growth is stunted is because a believer gets entangled in the cares of the world. In the Parable of the Sower, Jesus related the Word of God to a seed (Matt. 13:1-23). As a farmer sowed seed, some of it fell into thorns and weeds. Consequently, the seed could not grow because it was choked out and starved for nutrients. Jesus explains in Matt. 13:22: "As for what was sown among thorns, this is the one who hears the word, but the cares of the world and the deceitfulness of riches choke the word, and it proves unfruitful."

Many believers never develop into fruit-bearers because they have no root into God by which they draw spiritual sustenance, so they simply wither and die. They are so caught up with money, entertainment, job promotions, and the myriad of trendy diversion that the world has to offer that the Word of God never takes hold in their life. Then when things fall apart they wonder why their religion isn't working.

Years ago, as a teenager I geared up one Saturday afternoon to do some weed-eating for my dad. I got the weed-eater out and I filled it full of gas, then I went through the directions to start it up. I primed it, I choked it, I had the throttle set on low—it was all ready to go, or so I thought. I pulled the rip-cord and it wouldn't start. So I pulled it again and again—nothing. I must have pulled that cord for ten minutes trying to get that weed-eater to start up. Then I noticed something critical, in big bold letters written on a sticker on the side, "TWO STROKE ENGINE—GAS/OIL MIXTURE NEEDED." Like a dummy, I had put the wrong fuel in the tank expecting it to run.

Many Christians are trying to run their life on the wrong kind of fuel. They have more of the world in them than the Word of God in them and that's why they are sputtering along in their spiritual life. John reminds us that we will never go' from spiritual childhood to reaching full maturity if you love the world over the Word.

LOVE OF THE WORLD TAKES AWAY OUR LOVE FOR GOD (2:15)

Secondly, John maintains that love for the world nullifies our ability to love God. Notice that John does not say "Don't live in the world," nor does he say "Don't use the world," nor does he say "Don't benefit from the world," but he says "Don't love the world." To love the world means that it determines your decisions and values because it has your affections. Being "in" the world means we can enjoy the things of the world, such as the beautiful creation God has given us, but we are not to immerse ourselves in what the world values, nor are we to chase after worldly pleasures. Eugene Peterson's paraphrases 2:15–17 like this:

> Don't love the world's ways. Don't love the world's goods. Love of the world squeezes out love for the Father. Practically everything that goes on in the world—wanting your own way, wanting everything for yourself, wanting to appear important—has nothing to do with the Father. It just isolates you from Him. The world and all its wanting, wanting, wanting is on the way out—but whoever does what God wants is set for eternity."[2]

When you fall in love with the world, then you fall out of love with the Father. Why? Love is exclusive. When you get married to your spouse, you are saying "Yes," to them and "No," to every other potential partner. When you are wedded to Christ, it's the same way; you say "Yes," to Him and "No," to the things that oppose Him.

In the Upper Room discourse, Jesus told His disciples, "If the world hates you, know that it has hated me before it hated you. If you were of the world, the world would love you as its own; but because you are not of the world, but I chose you out of the world, therefore the world hates you" (John 15:18–19). There is not enough room in the human heart for both God and the world.

The best illustration of worldly intrusion into the life of a believer can be found in the Old Testament example of Lot (Gen. 13:5–13, 14:8–14, 19). Lot's downward spiral can be traced in several steps. After he and Abraham separated, Lot pitched his tent looking toward Sodom. The temptation of the cosmopolitan city was too much for him as Lot moved closer to the city and the well-watered plains of Jordan. Finally, Lot moved into Sodom and made it his home. Inside that ancient city of sin Lot's righteous soul was

---

2. Eugene Peterson, *The Message: The Bible in Contemporary Language*, 1 John 2:15–17.

How is Your Worldview? (1 John 2:12–17)

vexed because of the wickedness he saw daily (2 Peter 2:6–8). Eventually everything that Lot lived for went up in a mushroom cloud because God nuked the city with fire (Gen. 19). Bit-by-bit Lot's love for the things of God was edged out by the intrusion of Sodom.

Growing up as a kid I was a rabid Duke fan. I vividly remember the heyday of Duke basketball when Christian Laettner, Grant Hill, and Bobby Hurley won back-to-back NCAA championships in the early 1990s. To say that I loved the Blue Devils basketball team was an understatement. Blue Devil posters were on my walls. Duke t-shirts and caps adorned by body. Every year I would attend Duke basketball camp in the summer. I even owned an old piece of the hardwood floor from Cameron Indoor Stadium.

However, when I went to college I had some serious allegiance issues. Ironically, when it came time to apply to colleges I was not accepted to Duke, but I was accepted to their arch rival and nemesis UNC. When I first arrived in Chapel Hill I still loved the Dookies. I was a closet Cameron Crazy living in the camp of the enemy. I had been a student for only about a week when I decided I was going to go play in the basketball gym one afternoon. Even though I had a UNC student ID, my heart still belonged to Duke. In my conflict I wore my last pair of Duke shorts to the gym that hot August day. As I arrived at the entrance of the gym the security guard looked me up and down. I handed him my UNC student ID and he said, "Wait, something's wrong with this picture. A UNC student wearing Duke shorts. I'm sorry, but I can't let you into my gym wearing those shorts. You're gonna have to go home and change if you want to play in my gym." It was at that moment that I had to make the decision as to which team I was going to be loyal to. Since all of my time and money was going to UNC I had to do the unthinkable and change sides. I went back to my dorm and changed my shorts, never to wear another piece of Duke clothing.

In a small way, that struggle I had between which team to love is indicative of the choice each believer must make between Christ and the world. James 4:4 adds, "Do you not know that friendship with the world is enmity with God? Therefore whoever wishes to be a friend of the world makes himself an enemy of God." Just as I couldn't carry a UNC student ID and wear Duke shorts, so too a believer cannot carry a Bible under his arm on Sunday and a Playboy on Monday. Love of God and love of the world are contradictory desires. The heart of a Christian cannot be divided between heaven and earth. As Augustine once said, "I must love the love which loves the good and hate the love which loves the bad."

Living in the Light

LOVE OF THE WORLD TEMPTS US TO TURN FROM GOD (2:16)

John's third reason why we cannot buddy-up with the world is because what the world offers is set on turning our passions away from devotion to God. John delineates a three-fold pattern of temptation—the lust of the flesh (physical), lust of the eyes (mental), and the pride of life (emotional). The word "lust" refers to a natural appetite or desire that resides within each one of us. Hunger and thirst are the body's natural desires for food and drink, just as physical attraction to the opposite sex is a biological drive that is innate to our makeup. There is nothing wrong or sinful about these appetites since we have been hard-wired by God to experience these sensations.

However, the problem arises when we try to fulfill these legitimate appetites in illegitimate ways. The drive for sex is natural, but when it masters us and becomes fornication then we have fallen victim to the lust of the flesh. There is nothing wrong with wanting nice things, but when that desire turns into greed and materialism, that's the lust of the eyes. There is nothing wrong with the desire to be successful, but when we use people and manipulate them to get what we want then it turns into the pride of life.

James also describes temptation in terms of a multi-step pattern, "But each person is tempted when he is lured and enticed by his own desire. Then desire when it has conceived gives birth to sin, and sin when it is fully grown brings forth death" (James 1:14–15). James and John make it clear that spiritual failure is always an inside job. The world, the flesh, and the Devil are always working in tandem from within and without to bring us down. None of us is immune to temptation. Just as Superman who was vulnerable to kryptonite, Satan knows our weakness and is quick to exploit it so he can leverage it against us.

This three-fold pattern of temptation that John presents is the same rubric that Satan has been using for all of history. When the Devil entices us he will inevitably assault us on one of these three fronts. Satan used this strategy in the Garden against Eve and he used it against Jesus in the wilderness. Examine the chart below to see these parallels:

How is Your Worldview? (1 John 2:12-17)

Three-Fold Temptation		
Genesis 3:6	*1 John 2:16*	*Luke 4:1-13*
"... saw that the tree was good for food ..."	"lust of the flesh" *(Physical)*	"... turn these stones into bread ..."
"... and a delight to the eyes ..."	"lust of the eyes" *(Mental)*	"... the Devil showed him all the kingdoms of the world ..."
"... was desired to make one wise ..."	"the pride of life" *(Emotional)*	"... throw yourself down from here ..."

I once read about an interesting method used by natives in Africa to catch monkeys. A hunter hollows out a gourd and makes a hole in its side just large enough for a monkey to insert his open hand. The gourd is then filled with nuts and tied to a tree. The curious monkey is attracted by the smell of the nuts and reaches inside and grasps them. However, the hole in the gourd is too small for the animal to withdraw his fist as long as it is tightly closed around the nuts. Because he refuses to release his prize, the unsuspecting monkey falls prey to his captor. Unwilling to relax his grasp, he actually traps himself!

Satan uses a similar method to ensnare us. Satan has been studying human nature for thousands of years so he knows what makes us tick. He tempts us to grasp after more and more, knowing that our insatiable desires will never be fulfilled. As long as we tenaciously hold on to forbidden fruit, we are enslaved.

LOVE OF THE WORLD IS TEMPORARY COMPARED TO GOD (2:17)

Lastly, John says that the world cannot be enjoyed by the believer because it is transient and passing away. Satan is aggressively working to get believers to confuse time and eternity and to lose sight of what has temporary value and what has eternal value. However, we must remember that one day everything in this world is all going to be burned up and refined by fire. According to 2 Peter 3:10-12, the world so many love and build their lives upon is actually scheduled for demolition:

Living in the Light

> But the day of the Lord will come like a thief, and then the heavens will pass away with a roar, and the heavenly bodies will be burned up and dissolved, and the earth and the works that are done on it will be exposed. Since all these things are thus to be dissolved, what sort of people ought you to be in lives of holiness and godliness, waiting for and hastening the coming of the day of God, because of which the heavens will be set on fire and dissolved, and the heavenly bodies will melt as they burn!

Have a blast while you last because all that you see around you is one day going up in smoke! God has hung a sign on this earth that says, "Condemned: Plans in place for radical restoration to begin soon. Come back and see."

I am reminded of this every time I take a trip to an amusement park. Inevitably, you will spend hours in line waiting to ride a rollercoaster for a thirty-second thrill. Then you get in another line to do the same thing over again. Then you pay inflated prices for hotdogs, soda, and other treats which you will inevitably vomit up on the next ride. By the end of the day you have spent all your money on junk food and all your time waiting for the next big thrill. Eventually what happens, no matter how much fun you had that day, at closing time the park shuts down and you must leave. Worldliness is when you are so enamored with the ride that you do not acknowledge that the ride is going to end soon. Those who love the world fail to see the brevity of life and the futility of investing themselves in something that will have no eternal value.

When I travel and I stay in a hotel I am always surprised by the fact they have dressers in the rooms. When I go into a hotel room I never unpack my suitcase. I operate out of my luggage. I never open the drawers, pull out my clothes, and put them away. Why? Because I know I'm not going to stay there very long. I'm visiting for just a day or two. I don't unpack all my stuff because that room is not my home. I enjoy the amenities of the hotel room, but I don't get too comfortable. John says to us, "Don't get too comfortable down here. Remember this world is not your home. The world is passing away and you're just passing through."

8

Living in the Last Days
(1 John 2:18–27)

RAVI ZACHARIAS HAS CRISSCROSSED the globe defending the Gospel against the most hardened skeptics and diehard atheists. As an apologist Ravi often encounters the ivory tower academic who is educated well beyond his intelligence. With clarity and wit Ravi always finds a way to make his point to those who try to challenge the claims of Christianity. What makes Ravi so effective in his approach is his multi-cultural background. He was born and raised in India but lived his adult life in North America, so he has the unique perspective of someone who has lived in both hemispheres.

One of Ravi's most colorful stories came after he did a presentation on a college campus regarding the uniqueness of Christ. Ravi was assailed by one of the university professors for "not understanding the basic nature of truth and logic." During the Q & A session, the professor charged, "Dr. Zacharias, your presentation about Christ claiming and proving to be the only way to salvation is wrong for people in India because you are using 'either-or' logic. In the East we don't use 'either-or' logic—that's Western. In the East we use 'both-and' logic. So salvation is not *either* through Christ *or* nothing else, but *both* Christ *and* other ways."

Ravi found this very ironic because, after all, he grew up in India. Yet here was a western-born, American professor telling Ravi that he didn't understand how things really worked in India! This was so intriguing that Ravi accepted the professor's invitation to lunch to discuss it further.

Living in the Light

One of the professor's colleagues joined them for lunch, and as Ravi ate, the professor used every napkin and place mat on the table to make his point about the two types of logic—one Western and one Eastern.

"There are two types of logic," the professor kept insisting. "No, you don't mean that," Ravi kept replying. "I absolutely do!" maintained the professor. This went on for the better part of thirty minutes: the professor lecturing, writing, and diagramming. He became so engrossed in making his points that he forgot to eat his meal which was slowly congealing on his plate.

Upon finishing his own meal, Ravi interrupted, "Professor, I think we can resolve this very quickly with just one question." Looking up from his furious drawing, the professor paused and said, "Okay, go ahead."

Ravi leaned forward, looked directly at the professor and asked, "Are you saying that when I'm in India, I must use *either* the 'both-and' logic *or* nothing else?" The professor looked blankly at Ravi, then down at his congealed meal and mumbled, "The *either-or* does seem to emerge doesn't it." Ravi added, "Yes, even in India we must look both ways before crossing the street because it's *either* me *or* the bus, not both of us!"[1]

The simple point is that truth is truth no matter where you are on the globe. Yet if you were to ask the average man on the street today if truth matters when it comes to faith and spirituality they will probably say something like, "It doesn't matter what you believe as long you're sincere." However, when you allow feelings to be the measuring stick of truth you end up with all kinds of disastrous results. Randy Alcorn critiques postmodern views of truth when he writes:

> *Truth is whatever you sincerely believe.* You can walk off a ledge sincerely believing you won't fall, but gravity cares nothing about your sincerity. We're not nearly as sincere as we imagine, but even when we are, we're often wrong. '*What's true for you and what's true for me is true for me.*' So, if we step off the roof at the same time, I'll fall because I don't believe in gravity, but you'll hover in the air because you don't?"[2]

The notion that our feelings of sincerity will somehow rewrite the laws of physics and cause the universe to realign with our wishes is a fantasy for adults. Certainly engineers wouldn't build bridges based on what they felt, nor would a heart surgeon perform surgery because of a burning in the

1. Geisler & Turek, *I Don't Have Enough Faith to Be an Atheist*, 54–55.
2. Alcorn, *The Grace and Truth Paradox*, 57.

Living in the Last Days (1 John 2:18-27)

bosom. If truth didn't really matter then a pharmacist could issue arsenic or aspirin interchangeably because both come in tablet form.

Truth is not determined by what we believe, by popular opinion, by what's convenient, or by majority vote. Truth is not invented but discovered. What is truth? Truth is simply what corresponds to reality. The Apostle John was a champion for discovering and knowing the truth. Truth and light were two sides of the same coin. In the apostle's mind, those that walk in the light also abide in the truth of God. John has already warned his readers about the conflict between light and darkness (1:5-10) and between love and hatred (2:7-17). Now he warns his audience about a third conflict—the battle between truth and error.[3] In the first part of this chapter, John applies a character test; now he applies a doctrinal test to indicate the genuineness of his reader's spirituality. In the last major section of chapter two, John gives us three commands for living within the parameters of truth.

BE AWAKE IN THE FINAL DAYS (2:19)

John begins by introducing a new term into our theological vocabulary—"last hour" or "last days." Technically, the Apostle is not talking chronologically, but theologically. When the Bible uses the term "last days," it refers to the undetermined period of time between the two comings of Christ. The last hour began with Christ's incarnation and will end with His revelation in the skies (Rev. 1:7-8). The "last days" is the current period of time that we are living in, also known as the "Church age."

Since Jesus ascended into heaven and the Holy Spirit descended to earth the Church has been living in "the final hour" of God's time-table in which a bride is being prepared for Christ. John is writing to us with urgency here so that believers will realize what prophetic time period we are in. Just as you can look at a blossoming tree and discern the season (Matt. 24:32-33), so too we can look at spiritual signs around us and know that we are living in an evil age of deception, apostasy, and false teaching.

Jesus, in the Olivet Discourse, urged believers to be on guard for the appearance of "false prophets" just prior to His Second Coming (Matt. 24:11, 24). Likewise, the apostle Paul spoke of the "last days" as "perilous times" (2 Tim. 3:1) in which "some will depart from the faith, giving heed to deceiving spirits and doctrines of demons" (1 Tim. 4:1). If ever there

---

3. Wiersbe, *The Wiersbe Bible Commentary: New Testament*, 979.

were a time when every Christian needed to know what they believed and why they believed it, it's right now!

One of Satan's primary modes of attack is to infiltrate the church with false teachers who pronounce a false gospel leading people to a false salvation. The apostle identifies these false teachers as "antichrists." John is the only author in the New Testament to use this word "antichrist" and the term carries two meanings. It refers to a final world despot and to deceptive charlatans who teach false doctrine. In the Greek way of thinking the prefix *anti-* can mean both "against" and "instead of." Thus, an antichrist is anyone who opposes Christ, seeks to supplant Him, or falsely represent Him through deceptive doctrine.

John reminds his readers that the world stage is being set for *the* Antichrist (capital A) to make his appearance. Both the Old and New Testament prophets speak of this final world dictator using 27 different titles to reveal his diabolical personality. This Satanic superman is also referred to as "the man of sin" (2 Thess. 2:3), "the son of perdition" (2 Thess. 2:3), "the beast" (Rev. 13:1), "the little horn" (Dan. 7:8), "a king of bold face" (Dan. 8:23), and "the one who makes desolate" (Dan. 9:27). This tyrannical oppressor will set up a political, religious, and economic system during the seven year tribulation period. His reign will be worse than the regimes of Hitler, Stalin, and Saddam Hussein combined.

John wants his "little children" to know that in the last days preceding the emergence of this world leader there will be little antichrists that will prefigure and exhibit the same characteristics as Satan's CEO. Just like the Antichrist, these false teachers will be deceivers with counterfeit religious systems that distort the true Christ. Looking back over the 20th century many of these antichrists come to mind:

- Sun Myung Moon was the founder of the Unification Church in South Korea. As a teenager, Moon claimed that Jesus appeared to him and asked him to complete the work of redemption that God began nearly 2,000 years ago. Moon accepted the call, realizing that Korea was the new Israel and that God chose him as the Second Advent of Christ.[4] The Unification church is not some fringe cult in the backwoods, but it is believed that there are five to seven million "Moonies" worldwide.
- In 1955 Jim Jones started the People's Temple headquartered in San Francisco, CA. Jones claimed to be the reincarnation of Jesus and he

---

4. Rhodes, *Find It Quick: Handbook on Cults and New Religions*, 210.

Living in the Last Days (1 John 2:18–27)

preached that one day humans would see a new age of "Apostolic Socialism," where true racial and economic equality would be achieved. In November of 1978, he and over 900 followers committed mass suicide by drinking cyanide-laced, grape Kool-aid, while Jones shot himself.

- David Koresh was the leader of the Branch Dravidians in Waco, Texas. Koresh claimed to be the "final prophet, the Son of God, and the Lamb." His extreme interpretations of the Bible set a near date for the end of the world. In 1993, 54 adults, including Koresh, and 21 children died when their compound burned down.

- Marshall Applewhite was the organizer of the Heaven's Gate cult based in San Diego, CA. Applewhite claimed he was "the Son of God" and in 1997 he and 38 other members of Heaven's Gate committed mass suicide in order to rendezvous with a spaceship hiding behind the Hale-Bopp comet.

- Jose de Jesus Miranda is alive today and his church, Growing in Grace, is located in Miami, FL. His followers pray to him, worship him, and give him extravagant gifts of money. He claims, "The resurrected Christ has integrated himself in me." At the same time he wears a "666" tattoo and claims to be the Antichrist. Interestingly enough, Miranda was once a member of the Southern Baptist Convention.[5]

BE AWARE OF FALSE TEACHERS (2:19, 22–23, 26)

In John's day, the antichrists that he probably had in mind were the Gnostic heretics of the late first century that had crept into the church. According to John, the Gnostics were not to be trifled with because they denied the truth of the incarnation and taught that salvation was obtained by gaining secret knowledge about God. His warning to the church was to be on the lookout for these wolves in sheep's clothing. The apostle also identifies several characteristics by which we can identify false teachers today.

First we see that *antichrists depart from the fellowship*. John argues in 2:19 that antichrists are those who break fellowship with the family of faith. False teachers have to leave the church because the truth of God is like sandpaper on their soul. They chafe under the undiluted preaching of the

---

5. Zarrella and Oppmann, "Pastor With 666 Claims to Be Divine," <http://articles.cnn.com/2007-02-16/us/miami.preacher_1_cult-leader-followers-tattoo?_s=PM:US>.

Word of God. The antichrists in the first century formed splinter factions which taught strange aberrations of Christian doctrine.

I wonder if John paused and thought back with feelings of sadness to Judas when he wrote this verse? Judas spent three years in the presence of Jesus and the other disciples. He saw the undeniable miracles, heard Jesus' sermons, and was even given charge over the finances of the ministry (John 12:6). However, Judas' heart was far from the truth. Judas broke fellowship with Jesus and the disciples on the night when Christ washed their feet in the Upper Room. John describes this event in almost the same terms as he describes the behavior of the antichrists:

> Then after he had taken the morsel, Satan entered into him. Jesus said to him, "What you are going to do, do quickly." Now no one at the table knew why He said this to him. Some thought that, because Judas had the moneybag, Jesus was telling him, "Buy what we need for the feast," or that he should give something to the poor. *So, after receiving the morsel of bread, he immediately went out. And it was night.* (John 13:27–30)

In fact, you could make the case that Judas was a type of the Antichrist to come. In the same way that Satan entered Judas, so too Satan will possess and control the Antichrist.

Perhaps the most popular example from our day of this kind of apostasy can be seen in the example of Oprah Winfrey. Oprah describes herself as a "freethinking" Christian who turned against the traditional teachings of Christianity when she heard a pastor say, "God is a jealous God." She couldn't accept that, she says, because she always thought God was a God of love.[6] Now Oprah is one of America's most respected spiritual gurus. Her brand of mysticism is a hodge-podge of New Age spirituality infused with traditional religions from the East. She describes her journey like this:

> I believe that Jesus came to show us the Christ consciousness. Jesus came to show the way of the heart and to show us the higher consciousness that we are all talking about here. Jesus came to say, "Look, I am going to live in a body, in the human body, and I'm going to show you how it's done." These are some principles and some laws that you can use to live by . . . I don't believe that Jesus came to start Christianity . . . I am a Christian who believes that there are certainly many more paths to God other than Christianity.[7]

6. Lutzer, *Oprah, Miracles and the New Earth*, 14.
7. Ibid.

Living in the Last Days (1 John 2:18–27)

John would call a testimony like this the calling-card of an antichrist. It has been said that there are three kinds of people in the church: believers, unbelievers, and make-believers. The Bible warns us that those who depart from truth to seek man-made religion prove that they were never truly born-again in the first place.

Second, *antichrists deny the faith.* John states positively and negatively in 2:22–23 that the litmus test for true Christianity is belief in Jesus as the Son of God. To deny the Son is to deny the Father also. It is impossible to separate God the Father and God the Son since both are members of the Trinity. Jesus said, "I and my Father are one" (John 10:30) and He told Philip, "I am the way, the truth and the life, no man comes to Father except through me . . . whoever has seen me has seen the Father" (John 14:6, 9).

In John's day the antichrists were Christians who were swept into Gnosticism and denied the central teaching of the incarnation. Remember, the Gnostics believed that physical matter was inherently evil and because matter was evil then it was inconceivable that God would take on a human body. Thus, the Gnostics denied the full humanity of Jesus, claiming that His body was merely a phantom.

The great apostasy of our day is the reverse of what John was dealing with. In our time, people have no trouble admitting the humanity of Christ, but what they don't like is the deity of Christ. The antichrists of this generation come up with all kinds of ways to say that Jesus was not the God-man but merely a good man. Consider the following examples:

- The Muslims believe that Jesus is one of the five respected prophets—along with Adam, Noah, Abraham, and Moses. According to the Koran, it is utter blasphemy for a Muslim to say that Allah had a son. The Koran states in Sura 5:72–73 and 75, "They do blaspheme who say: 'God is Christ the son of Mary.' They do blaspheme who say: God is one of three in a trinity: for there is no God except one God Allah . . . Christ the son of Mary was no more than a Messenger; many were the Messengers that passed away before him."

- Joseph Smith, the founder of Mormonism, referred to Jesus as "the first-born spirit child of the Father" meaning that Jesus was the product of the sexual union of the Heavenly Father and Mother. Jesus was the highest of God's begotten children and the "spirit brother of Lucifer." According to Mormons, Jesus progressed by obedience and devotion to the truth in the spirit world until he became a God.[8]

8. Rhodes, *Find It Quick: Handbook on Cults and New Religions*, 68.

- Jehovah's Witnesses teach that Jesus was created as the archangel Michael billions of years ago. Michael (Jesus) was allegedly created first and then God used him to create all other things in the universe. Through Michael, Jesus existed in his pre-human state then at the appointed time he was born on earth as a human being—ceasing his existence as an angel.[9]
- Mahatma Gandhi once said, "I cannot say that Jesus was uniquely divine. He was as much God as Krishna, or Rama, or Mohammad, or Zoroaster."
- The Dalai Lama claimed, "Jesus was either an enlightened being, or a *bodhisvatta* (a being who aids others to enlightenment) of a very high spiritual realization."[10]
- In a 2010 interview, rock-star and pop icon Sir Elton John provocatively stated that Jesus was "a compassionate, super-intelligent gay man who understood human problems."[11]

It's obvious that we are a living in a day in which everybody has their personal opinion about Jesus. While they may be entitled to their own opinion, they are not entitled to their own truth. One day all of man's speculation will be swept aside when Jesus comes with the clouds of heaven. Then "every knee shall bow and every tongue shall confess that Jesus Christ is Lord" (Phil 2:11).

Third, *antichrists deceive those in the faith.* The adversaries of Christianity are evangelists for their own heretical beliefs. Not content with leaving the church never to be heard from again, the antichrists that John encountered were vigilant in siphoning off believers from the pews of the church. It's a troubling fact that most people who join cults have a previous background in some mainstream Christian denomination. Ron Rhodes, an expert on cultic activity, and one of my former seminary professors writes:

> Numerous cult authorities have noted that a key factor giving rise to the cult explosion in the United States is that churches have failed to make Bible doctrine and Bible knowledge a high priority ... Tragically, many people who attend church have not been given biblical discernment skills, and they end up joining a particular

9. Ibid., 101.
10. Dalia Lama, "The Karma of the Gospel."
11. Dotson Rader, "Elton John: There's a Lot of Hate in the World," <http://www.parade.com/celebrity/celebrity-parade/2010/elton-john-web-exclusive.html>.

Living in the Last Days (1 John 2:18-27)

cult without realizing that its teachings go against the Bible. Such people are unable to distinguish cultic doctrine from biblical doctrine. Among the many real-life examples that illustrate this, the one that stands out in my mind relates to David Koresh and the Branch Davidian cult that met a fiery end in Waco, Texas. One news publication indicated that two of the girls who died there had formerly attended a Christian church. If these girls had become biblically literate in their former church, enough to detect the Scripture-twisting antics of David Koresh, perhaps they would be alive today. The consequences of biblical literacy can be deadly in certain contexts.[12]

Several years ago I took a trip to Washington, DC and spent an afternoon touring the Holocaust museum. If you have ever been there then you know the images and artifacts haunt you long after you leave. It is the only museum I know of that has more exits than entrances. Because people are so assaulted emotionally by the experience many cannot make it all the way through. I remember seeing people weep as I made my way from one exhibit to another. One display that stood out in my mind was a document that was passed around by the Nazi officials in a concentration camp. This particular pamphlet gave the Nazi officials rules for how they were to conduct themselves with prisoners who would soon be headed to the gas chambers. Translated from German, one part of the pamphlet read, "The rule of the camp is that those going to their death should remain deceived until the end."

The sad reality is that many who veer off course spiritually and fall into apostasy do not realize that they are being deceived by Satan and his demons. The spirit of the Antichrist is already at work in this world and the Enemy is willing to do anything to see that those going to their death stay ignorant and blinded of the truth until the end.

BE ABIDING IN OUR FAITHFUL GOD (2:20, 24-25, 27)

Fortunately, in the midst of this chaos John reminds us that we are not helpless. As believers we have been given everything that we need to survive in a world that is against Christ. John explains two ways that his little children can stay on track with the truth.

True believers abide in the Spirit of God. John reminds us twice in 2:20 and 2:27 that we have been anointed and equipped by the Holy Spirit, our

---

12. Rhodes, *The Challenge of the Cults*, 39.

teacher who will guide us into all truth. One of the ministries of the Holy Spirit is discernment—meaning that the Spirit will sensitize believers to the difference between the truth and a lie. Perhaps John drew inspiration for these verses from the words of Jesus when He told His disciples, "When the Spirit of truth comes, He will guide you into all the truth, for He will not speak on His own authority, but whatever He hears He will speak, and He will declare to you the things that are to come" (John 16:13).

In your house you probably have a carbon monoxide detector affixed to the wall. The simple machine is designed to send off an ear piercing alarm when it picks up the presence of CO—a tasteless, odorless, colorless gas. This silent killer enters the bloodstream and robs the body of oxygen. Without a CO detector it's very possible for someone to be slowly poisoned to death in their sleep. By analogy, God has given each believer a truth detector—it's the Holy Spirit. The Holy Spirit does what a CO detector does in a home—it alerts the believer to the presence of danger. When a believer comes across some doctrine or teaching that doesn't comport with the Spirit of Truth, an alarm goes off inside. It's the Spirit of God saying, "Get out now!"

True believers abide in the Word of God. In 2:24–25 John says that in concert with the Spirit, believers should also hold fast to the Word. John uses "abide" three times in this section. The idea is that believers continuously assimilate God's truth to everyday experience. Paul says in Colossians 3:16, "Let the word of Christ dwell in you richly," and in Titus 1:9 he says that an elder in the church "must hold firm to the trustworthy word as taught, so that he may be able to give instruction in sound doctrine and also to rebuke those who contradict it."

It's interesting that John ties together the Spirit of God and the Word of God. It was the Holy Spirit who inspired the writings of the Scriptures (2 Tim. 3:16, 2 Peter 1:20–21) and it is the Spirit of God which teaches us the Word of God. Thus, true believers have two safeguards against error, the internal Spirit and the external Word. The Spirit inspired the Word and the Word is illuminated by the Spirit. The way you stay true in these last days is to internalize the truth of the Bible so that when you hear some preacher on television, or when a cultist knocks on your door handing you a different Gospel you can compare what they are saying with Scriptures.

Every once in a while I will buy a new watch. When the watch comes out of the package the time is never set correctly. The face is usually blinking "12:00." My first objective when I get a new watch is to set the time so that it is synchronized with the actual time. I could use somebody else's watch and go by the time on theirs, but what if it's wrong? I need to go to an unchanging standard that I know I can trust. So I log onto the official website for the atomic clock in Greenwich, England. The atomic clock in England is the most accurate clock in the world, and it is the clock by which all the different time-zones around the world go by.

When you are operating in a world of antichrists where people have the theological consistency of Jell-o, you need a standard that will never change. The only book that has an origin which transcends time and space is the Bible. The Bible is the standard by which believers should measure everything else. When you abide in the Word of God you are staying with a timeless, unchanging standard.

In 2:25 John reminds us of the final reward that believers are striving for—eternal life. While living in the last days it's easy to forget that heaven is the ultimate goal. If we stay in fellowship with Christ through the Spirit and the Word then the hope of eternal life will renew our minds day by day. Fellowship with Christ in time is a foretaste of fellowship with Christ in eternity. Every believer possesses God's pledge of eternal life witnessed by the Spirit and reinforced by the Bible. John's comment on the primacy of God's Word reminds me of a quote that was written on the flyleaf of one of my first Bibles:

> This Book is the mind of God, the state of man, the way of salvation, the doom of sinners, and the happiness of believers. Its doctrines are holy, its precepts are binding; its histories are true, and its decisions are immutable. Read it to be wise, believe it to be safe, practice it to be holy. It contains light to direct you, food to support you, and comfort to cheer you. It is the traveler's map, the pilgrim's staff, the pilot's compass, the soldier's sword, and the Christian's character. Here paradise is restored, heaven opened, and the gates of hell disclosed. Christ is its grand subject, our good its design, and the glory of God its end. It should fill the memory, rule the heart, and guide the feet. Read it slowly, frequently, prayerfully. It is a mine of wealth, a paradise of glory, and a river of pleasure. Follow its precepts and it will lead you to Calvary, to the empty tomb, to a resurrected life in Christ; yes, to glory itself, for eternity.[13]

---

13. Source Unknown

9

Rapture Ready?
(1 John 2:28–3:3)

IN HIS AUTOBIOGRAPHY, *JUST As I AM*, Billy Graham, writes about an encounter he had with the late President of the United States, John F. Kennedy. The story goes that JFK had just been elected as president and he invited Rev. Graham down to Palm Beach, Florida to play a round of golf. As they were riding in the car on the way back from the golf course, President Kennedy asked that the car be pulled over to the side of the road. The engine was turned off and then the president turned to Billy and this exchange occurred:

> "Do you believe in the Second Coming of Jesus Christ?" the president asked unexpectedly. "I most certainly do." "Well, does my church believe it?" "They have it in their creeds." "They don't preach it," he said. "They don't tell us much about it. I'd like to know what you think." I explained what the Bible said about Christ coming the first time, dying on the cross, rising from the dead and then promising that He would come back again. "Only then" I said, "are we going to have permanent world peace." "Very interesting," he said, looking away. "We'll have to talk more about that some day." And he drove on.[1]

Tragically, we all know that a few years into his term at the White House JFK was assassinated on November 22, 1963. According to Graham he never got to finish that conversation with the president. Billy said that on the day of Kennedy's funeral he was haunted by their roadside conversation

1. Billy Graham, *Just As I Am*, 468.

Rapture Ready? (1 John 2:28–3:3)

as Cardinal Cushing read from 1 Thessalonians 4:16, "For the Lord himself will descend from heaven with a shout, with the voice of the archangel and with the trump of God: and the dead in Christ shall rise first."[2]

As I thought about that story it occurred to me that it's not enough to simply know about the Lord's coming, but to be ready for His coming. As the old preachers would say, "Whether by clod or by cloud we shall all meet the Lord." At the outset of chapter 3, John turns our attention to the inescapable fact that Christ will return at an hour we cannot know. The Bible teaches that the return of Christ happens in two stages, first at the Rapture of the Church and then secondly, seven years later at the Second Advent. Moreover, the Rapture is a future event on God's prophetic calendar that has no sign attached to it. The Scriptures are clear that the return of Christ is imminent and that believers should be encouraged and motivated by this truth every morning when their feet hit the floor (Matt. 24:36, 42, 44, Rev. 3:11).

In the passage before us, John is writing about being prepared for the moment when Christ finally appears at the Rapture. Although we have fellowship with God right now through His Spirit and in His Word, John wants us to be looking forward to the day when we actually get to see Jesus face-to-face. If you think fellowship with Christ is good now then just wait because the best is yet to come. John answers three basic questions in this passage about the appearing of Christ:

1. "What should we do until He comes?"
2. "How do we know that He will come?"
3. "When He comes, what will it be like?"

ANTICIPATING HIS APPEARING (2:28–29, 3:3)

I once heard about a young lady who was getting ready for a blind date. The gentleman suitor told the girl that this was not just going to be the typical dinner and a movie. Instead he told her that he had reservations at an exclusive downtown restaurant, then he arranged for a carriage ride through the park, and finally their evening would culminate at an extravagant hotel where there would be ballroom dancing and live music. Based on what she knew, the girl thought her prince charming had arrived. Naturally, the girl wanted to make a good impression so she took the day off from work.

---

2. Ibid., 475.

Living in the Light

She cleaned her apartment, went to the beauty salon for a haircut, facial, pedicure, and manicure. Then she made her way to her favorite department store where she bought a new dress and matching handbag. After hours or primping in front of the mirror she looked gorgeous!

The date was to begin at 6:00 sharp, but the minutes ticked away and there she sat all dressed up and nowhere to go. By 7:00 she was beginning to get worried. He hadn't called, so she touched up her make-up once more and flipped through a magazine. By 8:00 she concluded that she had been stood up, so she took off her dress, let her hair down, washed off the cosmetics and nestled into her most comfortable pajamas. About the time she got cozy on the couch, surrounded by her favorite junk food, there was a knock at the door. It was her date and she was not impressed by his tardiness. His remarks didn't help either. The inexperienced young man looked at her surprised and said, "Wow! I gave you two extra hours and you're still not ready to go!"

That silly story does illustrate a kernel of spiritual truth as Christ said, "Therefore, stay awake, for you do not know on what day your Lord is coming" (Matt. 24:42). In connection with the imminent return of Christ, John argues that His unexpected arrival should act as an incentive for believers to live pure and holy lives. Even though the Lord may tarry, we should be prepared at all times lest we are caught unawares.

According to John, we can be ready for the return of Christ by abiding in Him. If you haven't figured it out yet, John loves to start a theme and then revisit it multiple times in his writings. We have already learned about the importance of continually staying close to Christ (2:6, 10, 14, 17, 24, 27). In John's theology abiding is a three-fold process of obeying the commands of Christ, loving others, and believing the truth. Obedience, love, and knowing the truth act as safeguards against falling out of fellowship with Christ and bringing shame to ourselves. Eugene Peterson paraphrases John's commands like this:

> And now, children, stay with Christ. Live deeply in Christ. Then we'll be ready for Him when He appears, ready to receive Him with open arms, with no cause for red-faced guilt or lame excuses when He arrives . . . All of us who look forward to His Coming stay ready, with the glistening purity of Jesus' life as a model for our own.[3]

---

3. Eugene Peterson, *The Message: The Bible in Contemporary Language*, 1 John 2:28, 3:3.

Rapture Ready? (1 John 2:28-3:3)

If Jesus were to come back this afternoon what would He find you doing? It's a powerful thought isn't it? I have often thought it would awesome to be raptured out of this world while preaching. Talk about an unforgettable sermon illustration! However, the flipside is a sobering thought as well. No doubt Christ will return and catch some believers entangled in lewd and shameful actions—like the school teacher who returns to her classroom only to see the students shooting spit wads at each other and flying paper airplanes.

A few years ago I decided it was time to test the trustworthiness of our puppy. Instead of keeping her in a crate while I was gone, I decided I would let her have free reign of the basement. I was only going to be gone for a few hours and I thought, "How much trouble could a puppy get into while I'm away?" I was not prepared for the warzone that awaited me. As the garage door opened I could see the dog had been busy while I was out. I thought she was house-trained, but the surprise in the floor proved otherwise. The bed I made for her was totally destroyed. She yanked the stuffing out of the pillow and fluffy puff-balls were strewn everywhere. Empty cardboard boxes that were stacked neatly in the corner had tiny teeth marks imbedded in them. The trash can was turned over and the contents had been pilfered through.

Immediately when she saw me coming her doggy demeanor changed. Normally every reunion was met with jumping, barking, and uncontrollable tail-wagging, but this time was different. "Did you do this!?" I demanded sternly with a vein popping out of my neck. Even though she couldn't speak her body language said it all. Her tail tucked between her legs, she dropped her head, and didn't make eye contact. Her master was very disappointed and she was too.

If the rapture were to happen today would you be embarrassed to stand before Jesus? The Bible teaches that immediately after we are taken the Church will be judged by Christ at the Bema Seat, not for our sins, but for how we conducted our lives as His followers (1 Cor. 3:12-15, 2 Cor. 5:10). Those things that are of no eternal value will burn up like wood, hay, and stubble, while those things that are worthy of Christ will be refined in fire like gold, silver, and precious stones. I am convinced that at our final job review there will be tears of joy and tears of shame.

John's message is simple—when we have heard and understood the promised return of Christ then we cannot keep living our lives the same old way. Like the news of an incoming hurricane or an ultrasound that shows a baby in the womb, future events have present implications that we cannot ignore. In fact, the New Testament writers argue that the coming of Christ should impact our daily conduct drastically.

Not only should we renounce sin in our lives as John advocates, but the return of Christ should keep us from judging others (1 Cor. 4:5), motivate us to love others (1 Thess. 3:12–13), give hope to those in grief (1 Thess. 4:18), inspire us to fervently pursue ministry opportunities (2 Tim. 4:1–2), remind us to worship frequently with other believers (Heb. 10:24–25), encourage us to remain faithful (James 5:7–8), and give us a renewed vigor for evangelizing the lost (Jude 21–23). Ian Hamilton, in his commentary on 1 John, has a wonderful statement concerning this:

> Think of a bride who looks forward eagerly to her wedding day. More than anything else, she wants to look her best when the day comes. Why? She wants to please her husband and gladden his heart. Only her best will do for the one who has chosen her and loved her. She has even kept herself a virgin and reserved herself only for the groom, pure in all her white array. To arrive at the day unprepared would be to indicate that in some measure her love for him was less than total.[4]

As the Church, we are the Bride of Christ (Eph. 5:25), and how we look on the day the Groom appears to take us away matters immensely. Our lives tell Him how much we longed for Him and how much we loved Him.

ASSURANCE OF HIS APPEARING (3:1)

John moves on to talk about how we can have certainty that Jesus will come for us. Let's face it, preachers have been preaching this same message for 2,000 years and Jesus hasn't come yet. What sort of guarantee do we have that Christ will keep His word? For John the answer is a simple four letter word that never fails—love. For where there is love there is faithfulness and if God loves us nothing can separate us from Him (Rom. 8:38–39).

In the first part of 3:1 John is amazed by the love that God has for us. It's almost as if He cannot find words to express the height and the depth and the breadth of God's love. God did not love us secretly from heaven. Christ's love for us compelled Him to leave heaven and live where we live,

---

4. Ian Hamilton, *Let's Study the Letters of John*, 31.

Rapture Ready? (1 John 2:28–3:3)

walk like we walk, and die like we die so that He might adopt us into His family. John Phillips adds:

> There are three ways that one can get into a family. You can be born into the family in the usual way, whereby the life of the parent is passed on to the offspring. You can be adopted into the family, whereby an outsider becomes a member of the family through a legal process of obtaining custody. You can be married into the family, whereby your love for another causes you to be wedded and each participant is introduced into the other family. To be triply sure that we are truly assured of our placement in His family, God employs all three principles—we are born again from above, we are adopted in as sons and daughters, and we are married to Christ.[5]

In the second part of 3:1 John contrasts the love of God compared to the love of the world. The world loves only those that love back. It's conditional. The world's brand of love says, "I'll love you if you love me." However, God's love is qualitatively different. God's love is unconditional. He extends His love to all creatures irrespective of whether they will reciprocate love back. God's love says, "I choose you in spite of you."

The reason believers know that Christ is coming back for the Church is not just because He promised He would, but because He loves us so much that He wants us to spend eternity with Him. Christ's love entails that He wills every good thing for us and nothing can be greater or better than the presence of God. Since God is the greatest being in the universe and since He loves us, then the highest thing He can give us is Himself. Jesus cannot stand the thought of heaven without you and me which is why He said, "And if I go and prepare a place for you, I will come again and will take you to myself, that where I am you may be also" (John 14:3).

Some students of prophecy argue that God will make the Church suffer through the tribulation period. Post-tribulation eschatology advocates that the Rapture will take place after the terrible judgment of God levels the earth with a series of unspeakable horrors. However, I could not disagree more vehemently with this view. As the bride of Christ that means we are entitled to certain privileges as objects of Christ's affection. One of the benefits of being in a love relationship with Jesus is that we escape the wrath that is set aside for those that don't love Him.

---

5. John Phillips, *Exploring the Epistles of John*, 89.

In fact, Paul says twice in 1 Thessalonians that God will spare the Church from future judgment set aside for unbelievers. In 1 Thess. 1:10 we are told, ". . . to wait for his Son from heaven, whom he raised from the dead, Jesus *who delivers us from the wrath to come.*" Again in 1 Thess. 5:9 Paul says, "*For God has not destined us for wrath,* but to obtain salvation through our Lord Jesus Christ." Finally, in Revelation 3:10 we read, "Because you have kept my word about patient endurance, *I will keep you from the hour of trial that is coming on the whole world,* to try those who dwell on the earth."

Imagine a beautiful outdoor wedding scene. The crowd waits in anticipation for the appearance of the bride to walk down the aisle. As the music swells, her beauty radiates from within as the bride strides down the path of flower petals towards her prince. Everything is perfect. All of the sudden, the groom breaks wedding protocol and meets the bride in the aisle. To the shock of onlookers he picks her up and carries her over his shoulder to a nearby pond and throws her in. The day she has been planning since she was twelve is totally ruined. The beaming bride is turned into a mud-caked sideshow. Her veil is tangled with green algae and her hair is a soggy mess. I ask you, "What groom would treat his bride that way?" None that I can think of. Therefore, it makes no sense that Jesus Christ would allow His bride to be treated with disgrace when He has pledged His love to her. Based on Christ's promise we can expect to escape the coming judgment.

ASPECTS OF HIS APPEARING (3:2)

Trying to describe what the Rapture will be like is all together exciting and perplexing. Since nothing like it has ever happened before choosing the right words and thoughts to convey the immensity of the moment is difficult. I guess it would be like Lazarus trying to explain to his friends and family what it was like to be dead and then raised back to life again. Sitting around the dinner table the evening after coming out of the tomb, how did Lazarus describe what it was like entering the door of death only to turn around and walk back through?

We face the same mystery when it comes to conceptualizing the Rapture. If you search for the word "rapture" in the Bible you will not find it. That's because the writers of the New Testament never used it. Nonetheless, the concept of the rapture is still there, just as the word "Trinity" is not in the Bible yet we find the doctrine easily in the pages of Scripture. The New

Rapture Ready? (1 John 2:28–3:3)

Testament writers used the Greek word *harpazo* which means "to snatch up" or "to take forcibly" to describe the suddenness of the Rapture. Paul wrote in 1 Thess. 4:17, "Then we who are alive, who are left, will be *caught up* [harpazo] together with them in the clouds to meet the Lord in the air, and so we will always be with the Lord."

To help us picture what will happen to believers at the Rapture, imagine that you have an old box in the attic that contains some nails you want to use. However, since the box has been in the attic a long time, it is also filled with dust and an assortment of other knick-knacks that have been piled in the box over time. The quickest way to retrieve the nails and leave the other stuff behind would be to hold a powerful magnet over the box. All of the objects in the box with magnetic properties would be immediately attracted to it and the nails would be "snatched up" out of the box by an invisible force.

In a similar way, this is what will happen when the Lord Jesus Christ appears in the sky for His children. Everyone with the Holy Spirit indwelling them shares in the nature of Christ and they will be called up from the lowly Earth by His power. Those who have no part with Christ, who do not share in His nature, will be left behind.

John gives two details about the appearing of Christ. First, it will involve *Christ's transformation of us.* John remarks, "Beloved, we are God's children, and *what we will be has not yet appeared*; but we know that when He appears *we shall be like Him* . . ." We are children of God, yet we do not totally understand what that means in our present state. However, when we finally see Christ, He will transform our mortal bodies into His image. The curse will be reversed. Believers both dead and living will be glorified and receive resurrection bodies like Jesus. This is the completion of our salvation. On the cross Jesus took away the penalty of sin—that's justification. As we daily abide with Christ in love, obedience, and truth the power of sin is made impotent—that's sanctification. On the day of the Rapture, when the molecular structure of our bodies is reorganized, the presence of sin will be removed—that's glorification.

Paul described this transformation as an instantaneous change that happens faster than the blink of an eye:

> But our citizenship is in heaven. And we eagerly await a Savior from there, the Lord Jesus Christ, who, by the power that enables him to bring everything under his control, *will transform our lowly bodies so that they will be like his glorious body* (Phil. 3:20–21).

Living in the Light

> Listen, I tell you a mystery: We will not all sleep, *but we will all be changed—in a flash, in the twinkling of an eye, at the last trumpet. For the trumpet will sound, the dead will be raised imperishable, and we will be changed* (1 Cor. 15:51–52).

On that day our bodies will get an unbelievable hardware and software upgrade. God is going to replace the image of Adam, which is fallen and in bondage to sin, with the image of Christ, which is perfect, sinless, and able to defy the laws of physics (1 Cor. 15:49). Never again will you be plagued by the fear of death, the pain of sickness, or the frustration of old age.

It is said that the genius sculptor of the Renaissance, Michelangelo, once had a solid block of marble delivered to his workshop. As his assistants dropped the monolith in front of him, the master smiled and said, "Isn't it beautiful!?" One of his protégés said, "Well I don't see much except a big block of marble." To which Michelangelo replied, "You don't see what I see. I see David in there. He is in my mind and I am going to transfer David into this piece of marble." The student said, "How will you do that?" The master said, "By chipping away everything that does not look like David." We don't know exactly how Jesus is going to do it, but when Christ glorifies us and make us like Himself, He will instantly take away everything that doesn't look like Him.

The second aspect of the Rapture is *Christ's revelation to us*. Notice that John says, ". . . but we know that when he appears . . . *we shall see Him as He is.*" In other words, we will see the glorified Christ with the veil of mystery removed. At the rapture we will not see the Christ that walked around on earth during His incarnation, which was merely deity veiled in humanity. We will see Him in all the fullness and radiance of His glory. We will not see Jesus hanging on the cross writhing in agony. No, we will see Him in His glorified state as the conquering Son of God. Jesus said in John 17:24, "Father, I want those you have given me to be with me where I am, *and to see my glory*, the glory you have given me because you loved me before the creation of the world." Paul also remarked, "For now we see in a mirror dimly, *but then face to face*. Now I know in part; then I shall know fully, even as I have been fully known" (1 Cor. 13:12).

There was only one instance in the Gospels where Jesus pulled back the curtain and showed His true glory to the disciples. On top of the Mount of Transfiguration Jesus appeared with Moses and Elijah (Matt. 17:1–13). The text says that Jesus' clothes became a dazzling white as His glory radiated from within. All that Peter, James, and John could do was fall down on their faces out of fear. The trauma of holiness and the weight of glory were suffocating to these simple men of iniquity. On another occasion during His heavenly vision, John saw the risen Christ and fell down as a dead man (Rev. 1:17).

What John is saying here is this—before you and I can get a full glimpse of Christ as He truly is, we need to be changed. Your sinful body is not properly suited to survive in the environment of Christ's pure and unsullied holiness. Christ is going to give us a new set of eyes to behold Him, a new voice to sing His praises and a new set of hands to embrace our Savior.

As a young man growing up in the early 90s I was a huge basketball fan. Like most young men my age I was enamored with the athleticism and ability of Michael Jordan. Towards the latter part of his career with the Chicago Bulls, I remember a reporter asking him, "What motivates you to win?" By this time Jordan had already won five NBA championships, several MVP awards, and a plethora of scoring titles. He said, "I want to win for my teammates and coaches. There are some guys on this team who have been playing around the league many years but never won a title. My gift to them will be to experience victory so they too can get a ring."

The Lord Jesus has an even greater desire for us. He has promised to carry us over into victory. He wants to see us glorified with Him. He wants us to be partakers in His kingdom and to share in the blessing that He has secured for us. When Christ appears He will reward us with bodies we have always wanted. Christ's resurrection from the dead is the down payment and guarantee of our future resurrection. All of those who are "in Christ" will exchange the image of Adam for the image of Christ.

10

That Nasty Three Letter Word
(1 John 3:4–10)

IN THE NOVEL, THE *Picture of Dorian Gray,* Oscar Wilde describes an exceptionally handsome young man so captivating that he drew the attention of a great artist. The artist asked Dorian to be the subject of a portrait for he had never seen a face so attractive and so pure. When the painting was completed, young Dorian became so enraptured by his own looks that he wistfully commented about how wonderful it would be if he could live any way he pleased so that so no disfigurement would mar his own countenance. He wished that only the portrait would grow old while he could remain unscathed by time and a decadent way of life.

Dorian got his wish. His life of sensuality, indulgence, and even murder left his physical appearance completely unblemished, while the portrait took a beating. Over the years Dorian spiraled downward into greater forms of immorality and debauchery. However, one day Dorian uncovered the portrait he had kept hidden for years. As he uncovered the picture he was taken aback by the hideousness of the portrait which bore the scars of a scandalous life.

Dorian tried to bury the picture from sight, but the charade ended when the artist saw the picture and the grotesque figure. Overcome with grief, the artist realized what it signified and pleaded with Dorian to repent of his sins, ask God's forgiveness, and turn his wasteful life around. In a fit of rage Dorian grabbed a knife and killed the artist, silencing his convicting voice.

There was now only one thing left for Dorian to do. He took the knife to remove the only visible reminder of his wicked life. He raised the knife to slice the painting into ribbons. However, the moment he thrust the blade into the canvas, the portrait returned to its pristine beauty, while Dorian lay stabbed to death on the floor. The ravages that had marred the picture now so disfigured him that even his servants could no longer recognize him.[1]

The story of Dorian Grey is thought by many literary critics to be an unofficial autobiography of Oscar Wilde. The gifted writer was known for his life of excess and his risqué one-liners like, "I can resist everything but temptation," and "The only way to get rid of temptation is to yield to it." Tragically, at the age of forty-six Oscar Wilde died a victim of his own sinful lifestyle. He wrote in *De Profundis*, "As terrible as it was what I had done to others, nothing was more terrible than what I had done to myself." The story of Dorian Gray is a powerful reminder that the wages of sin is death (Rom. 6:23). Even though the soul is invisible, it becomes tarnished with every act of iniquity.

When it comes to the area of sin, the apostle John is very categorical. The apostle bifurcates behavior in rigid absolutes—good or evil, sin or righteousness, light or darkness. For the Christian there is no such thing as moral ambiguity, no grey areas of life. While these distinctions cause many in our culture to cringe, John is absolutely clear that the habitual practice of sin is incompatible with the child of God.

John desires for us to be sensitive to the issue of sin because sin breaks our fellowship with God. The central theme of his letter is how to maximize our level of intimacy with God. Thus, the logic of this passage is very simple. Believers desire fellowship with God. However, a lifestyle of sin disrupts our fellowship with God. In order to have greater fellowship with God we should renounce our sins and walk with Christ. John wants to discuss that nasty three letter word that plagues our every step on Earth, so he give us four reasons why true Christians cannot enjoy sin.

SIN CONTRADICTS THE LAW OF GOD (3:4)

As a boy, Charles Wesley once asked his mother, Suzanna Wesley, "What is sin?" Here is the reply she gave him:

> Take this rule: whatever weakens your reason, impairs the tenderness of your conscience, obscures your sense of God, or takes off your relish of spiritual things; in short, whatever increases the

---

1. Zacharias, *Deliver Us from Evil*, xiii–xiv.

> strength and authority of your body over your mind, that thing is sin to you, however innocent it may be in itself.[2]

I challenge any theologian to give a more apt definition of sin (and this came from a woman who had 19 children!).

John begins by giving a very simple definition of sin as "lawlessness." The Greek word that John uses for "lawlessness" is the word *anomia*, from which we derive our word antinomianism or "no law." In the thinking of John, "lawlessness" refers to the active rebellion against God's standard. The apostle points out that sin a matter of the will. When man knowingly asserts his will against God's that is rebellion and rebellion is the root of all sin. Moreover, John's emphasis is not on sins (plural) but on sin (singular). In other words, sins are the fruit because sin is the root of our being. As R.C. Sproul has said, "We are not sinners because we sin, rather we sin because we are sinners."

A Sunday School teacher once taught my class where the origin of sinful disobedience begins by pointing out that the middle letter in the word "sin" is the letter "i." When we desire our own way rather than God's way we enter into the rebellion of sin. When we defiantly say, "I will" and go against God's moral principles then we are acting like Satan who insolently claimed five times, "I will," usurp the authority of God (Is. 14).

I am reminded of a story from *The Confessions of St. Augustine* which illustrates the defiant behavior that is manifested in each one of us due to our fallen, sinful nature. Augustine writes about his days as a youth when he enjoyed the thrill of sin:

> Near our vineyard there was a pear tree, loaded with fruit, though the fruit was not particularly attractive either in color or taste. I and some other wretched youth conceived the idea of shaking the pears off this tree and carrying them away. We set out that night (having, as we usually did in our depraved way, gone on playing the streets till that hour) and stole all the fruit that we could carry. And this was not to feed ourselves; we may have tasted a few. But then we threw the rest to the pigs. I had no wish to enjoy what I tried to get by theft; all my enjoyment was in the theft itself and in sin. Our real pleasure was in doing something that was not allowed.[3]

---

2. Rhodes, 1001 *Unforgettable Quotes about God, Faith and the Bible*, 201.
3. Augustine, *The Confessions of St. Augustine*, 2.4.

As Adrian Rogers once said, "The heart of the problem is the problem of the human heart." The Bible makes it clear that we are sinners not only by nature (Ps. 51:5, Jer. 17:9) but also by choice. The brand of sin that John is talking about is the sin of commission, but the Bible also defines another kind of sin by omission. James 4:17 reads, "Anyone, then, who knows the good he ought to do and doesn't do it sins." A sin of omission is a sin that is the result of not doing something God's Word teaches that we should do, while a sin of commission is a result of doing something God's Word teaches that we not do.

Imagine that you and I sat down at a table with a glass of cool water before us. I take a dropper filled with black sewage and squeeze just one drop into the liquid. How many drops of sewage would I have to put into the water until it became unacceptable to you? I hope you would say, "Just one." Would you drink this cup of water if it had just one drop of raw sewage in it? Absolutely not! Because all it takes is one drop of waste to ruin the whole glass of pure spring water. Just so, it only takes one sin to render our lives unacceptable to God.

When we sin we break the "law of God" which flows from His perfect and holy character. His laws are a reflection of who He is. When we sin we are not just breaking some abstract law, but it is personal. Sin is an offense against a holy God, we transgress against His character. In this way all sin is relational, because sin violates our vertical relationship with God and our horizontal relationship with others.

John's point is that a person who continues in a lifestyle of sin does not have fellowship with God because sin is the antithesis of God's nature. As Thomas Watson once said, "Sin hath the devil for its father, shame for its companion, loneliness as its sickness, and death for its wages." Lawlessness comes with a high price tag.

SIN COUNTERS THE WORK OF THE SON OF GOD (3:5-7)

The Primitive Quartet recorded a song years ago entitled, "That Soldier Was Me." The lyrics of the song are incredible, especially the first verse and chorus which goes:

> In a dream I was there when they crucified Jesus,
> And in my dream I saw His great agony.
> I ran to the man that was piercing His body,
> And when I pulled Him away that soldier was me.

> Though only a dream, I crucified Jesus.
> T'was my sins He bore on Calvary's tree.
> When He prayed alone in Gethsemane's garden,
> I believe He prayed that night for me.[4]

Whether we realize it or not, it was our sins which drove the nails into the hands and feet of Jesus. Though we were not there in person, we are just as guilty as the Roman soldier who plunged the spear into the side of Christ. John Stott has written:

> This is how the Apostles saw it. Herod and Pilate, Gentiles and Jews, they said, had together "conspired against Jesus" (Acts 4.27). More important still, we ourselves are also guilty. If we were in their place, we would have done what they did. Indeed, we have done it. For whenever we turn away from Christ, we "are crucifying the Son of God all over again and subjecting Him to public disgrace" (Heb 6.6). We too sacrifice Jesus to our greed like Judas, to our envy like the priests, to our ambition like Pilate. 'Were you there when they crucified my Lord?' the old Negro spiritual asks. And we must answer, 'Yes, we were there.' Not as spectators only but as participants, guilty participants, plotting, scheming, betraying, bargaining, and handing him over to be crucified. We may try to wash our hands of responsibility like Pilate. But our attempt will be as futile as his. For there is blood on our hands.[5]

John reminds us of this very purpose why Christ came into the world, "... He appeared in order to take away sins ..." The apostle's argument is that when a believer participates in sin then he undermines the very reason for our Lord's death on the cross! For a Christian to continue in sin is to plunge headlong into the very thing Jesus bled and died to save us from. For this reason alone we should hate our weak, sin-sick flesh which tempts us to trample over the cross of Christ with a cavalier attitude. Because of our sin, Jesus' body was beaten until it was like a bloody piece of hamburger. Because of our sin, six-inch thorns were driven deep into His skull and His face was buffeted by the angry fists of taskmasters. As Isaiah wrote, "... He was pierced for our transgressions; He was crushed for our iniquities ..." (Is. 53:5). The reason why a true Christian cannot bear the thought of sinning is because every time we think about our sin, we hear the ringing of that hammer in the background of our mind.

---

4. Riddle, *That Soldier Was Me.*
5. Stott, *The Cross of Christ*, 63.

That Nasty Three Letter Word (1 John 3:4–10)

John is absolutely clear that walking with Christ and living in sin are mutually exclusive. That is why he writes, "... no one who keeps on sinning has either seen Him or known Him." In other words John asserts that if a person claims to be Christian and finds no problem with dabbling in sin then they are either self-deceived or simply lost all together.

The apostle also makes an argument from the greater to the lesser in these verses. He says, "In Him there is no sin. No one who abides in Him keeps on sinning..." Then he states the reverse of the same principle in 3:7, "... whoever practices righteousness is righteous, as He is righteous." Christ is sinless and if we abide with Him then we will not find the impetus to sin. There is nothing in Christ that can transmit the desire to sin to us. As long as we abide in Christ and the Holy Spirit controls us, we cannot sin. The quickest way we can sin is to grab the reigns of our lives away from the Holy Spirit and act independently of God.

Don't misinterpret what John is saying. The Bible does not teach that a Christian can reach a state of sinless perfection on Earth. Christians are not sinless, but hopefully they do sin less. The new nature goes to war against the old nature. The new nature is completely free of sin while the old nature wants nothing more than to gratify itself with sinful passions. Therefore, every believer is a walking civil war between the Spirit and the flesh (Gal. 5:16–26).

The story is told of a Native American elder who gave his life to Christ. After coming to Jesus, he continuously battled the desire to go back to sinful lifestyle of drinking. A friend who took notice of his changed life asked the old man how he stayed on "the straight and narrow." He described his own inner struggles like this, "Inside of me there are two dogs. One of the dogs is mean and evil. The other dog is good and kind. The mean dog fights the good dog all the time. But the one I feed the most is the one who wins." So it is with every believer who fights the flesh in a daily battle. We must starve out our sin nature by staying close to Christ and nourishing our Spirit with worship and the Word.

SIN COMES FROM THE ENEMY OF GOD (3:8)

C.S. Lewis has written, "There are two equal and opposite errors into which our race can fall about the devils. One is to disbelieve in their existence. The other is to believe and to feel an excessive and unhealthy interest in them. They themselves are equally pleased by both errors and hail a materialist or a magician with the same delight."[6] Ask the average person on the street today if Satan exists and they will shake their head in the negative. Satan has been relegated to the dustbins of mythology by our sophisticated, scientific culture. As one poet quipped, "And so they voted the Devil out, and of course the Devil's gone, but simple people would like to know, who carries his business on?"

John, the eminent theologian, reminds us that Satan is alive and well today. We know this because we see his children run amok in society. They are in lecture halls of universities, in the highest places of government, working on road construction crews, counting money in the banks, shooting up drugs on the street corners, and even sitting in the pews of church. The practice of sin was originated and introduced into the human race by Satan, thus unregenerate men are his children, not merely because they imitate him, but because they are indwelt by the principle of sin of which he is the source.

John's words in 3:8, "Whoever makes a practice of sinning is of the devil, *for the devil has been sinning from the beginning,*" are reminiscent of Jesus' words to the Pharisees in John 8:44, "You are of your father the devil, and your will is to do your father's desires. *He was a murderer from the beginning*, and has nothing to do with the truth, because there is no truth in him. When he lies, he speaks out of his own character, for he is a liar and the father of lies."

Since Satan is the "father" of sin, those who practice sin are in effect his children because they exhibit his nature with their Devil-like behavior. Anyone who habitually practices sin proves that they do not have the nature of Christ in them. John's point is that a true follower of Christ disdains sin because it gives a temporary victory over to the enemy of our soul. Satan loves it when Christians fall because it destroys our testimony and gives him a beachhead in our lives. Later on he can use that failure as a means to bludgeon us with guilt.

It's important to understand that God did not create the Devil. He created Lucifer, a beautiful angelic being. Lucifer became the Devil when he rebelled against God. Before he fell Satan was God's top general over the angelic realm. When Satan declared independence from God, he was booted from heaven and took a third of the angels with him (Rev. 12:4). In an attempt to wage war on God, Satan introduced sin into the human race by tempting Adam and Eve, thus corrupting God's crown jewel of creation.

---

6. Lewis, *The Screwtape Letters*, preface.

However, Satan's fall set in motion a series of unintended consequences that even he could not foresee. In trying to usurp God, Satan actually became God's ultimate servant. God has allowed Satan a temporary reign over the earth, yet God promised that Satan would eventually be defeated by the "seed of the woman" (Gen. 3:15). Eons ago, it was prophesied in the Garden of Eden that Jesus Christ—the Redeemer of mankind—would one day crush the head of the serpent.

Thus, John's grand statement in 3:8, "The reason the Son of God appeared was to destroy the works of the devil." Because of the cross of Christ and His glorious resurrection, Satan is a defeated foe living on borrowed time. Satan's death sentence has been given, but the execution has yet to be carried out. You might want to think of this in terms of lightning and thunder. When a storm is on the horizon we see the flash of lighting first, then we hear the sound later. Because light travels faster than sound, there is a time lag between seeing the bolt of lightning and hearing the crash of thunder. In a similar way, we can say that at the cross of Christ we have seen the flash, but we have not heard the crash of Satan's fall. However, with God, there is no such gap; He regards the judgment and sentence as already complete.

Let's take a moment to trace the defeat of Satan down through the ages:

- Satan was defeated *initially* in Heaven. When he rebelled against God, any power or authority that Satan could exercise had to be given prior approval by God. Satan couldn't even tempt Job without first asking permission from God (Job 1:6–12).

- Satan was defeated *strategically* in the Garden of Eden. In Genesis 3:15, God declared that the Serpent would have his head crushed by the seed of the woman. It's clear from the beginning that God is calling the shots. Not only does God tell Satan *that* he is going to lose, but He tells him *how* he is going to lose! And there is nothing that Satan can do to stop it.

- Satan was defeated *spiritually* in the Wilderness. Three times Satan tempted Christ, but three times he was rebuked with the Word of God (Matt. 4:1–11). Jesus proved that He was spiritually superior to the first Adam, and that there was nothing Satan could throw at Him that would work (Heb. 4:15).

- Satan was defeated *publically* at Calvary. Jesus took the cross, an instrument of death, and turned it into an instrument of life. The curse of death and sin no longer have a hold on believers. Christ turned the cross into a dagger and pointed it at the heart of Satan. Paul remarked that Christ became like a conquering general who, "disarmed the rulers and authorities and put them to open shame, by triumphing over them" (Col. 2:15).

- Satan will be defeated *finally* in Hell. The Bible says in Revelation 20:7–10 that Satan's ultimate end will be the lake of fire. Milton once wrote that "Satan rebelled because he would rather rule in Hell than serve God in heaven." What Satan didn't realize is that there are no kings in Hell. He will forever be banished from the presence of God and have eternity to suffer for his cosmic crimes. So when the Devil tries to remind you of your past, you remind him of his future!

Donald Grey Barnhouse once told the story of a wealthy man who had a great grove of fruit trees. This man loved to walk amongst his trees and admire their beauty, but this man also had an enemy who hated him sorely. His enemy would try to find ways to annoy the master of the estate. At last the jealous enemy devised a plan that he thought would strike at the heart of the master.

He decided to go to the estate at night and cut down one of the master's most beautiful trees. So he made his plans well. He took his hacksaw and axe and began his work—all night long cutting down this tree until his muscles were sore and his hands blistered.

When the morning came, the enemy saw the master riding on his horse with another man out in the grove of trees. He had not yet felled this towering tree so the enemy doubled his efforts. Finally, the trunk gave way and the wood creaked as the tree began to fall over. When the enemy saw this he shouted in victory, but he did not see the branch which twirled over and pinned him to the ground in agony.

As the master of the grove approached his fallen enemy, that man lying under the branches lashed out at him. The owner of the grove called his companion over to his side and he said, "You thought to do me a great harm, but I want to show you what you have done. This man here with me is an architect who has the plans to build a house for me in the midst of these trees. In order to make room for the house it was necessary to cut down one of these trees." He showed the enemy the architect's plans. "The tree which you have toiled on all night, and which now is your death, is the exact tree that had to be removed to make room for my house. You have worked for me and did not know it. Now your work is for my gain and bitterness is your food in death."

So it is with Satan. Lucifer thought he was so smart and clever in working against God, when in fact, the minute he decided to rebel he became a defeated foe who has actually been working for God all along.

SIN CONFLICTS WITH THE SPIRIT OF GOD (3:9-10)

Depending on what translation you read, 3:9 can be a source of contention. Even though the meaning of this passage seems simple enough, there are some who get tripped up in what seems to be an apparent contradiction. John seems to contradict himself when he says, "Whoever has been born of God does not sin, for His seed remains in him; *and he cannot sin . . .*" when back in 1:8 John says, "If we say we have no sin, we deceive ourselves and the truth is not in us."

However, the apparent contradiction dissolves when we realize that John never claims that believers are without sin or never commit sin. The rendering of this verse in many translations is unfortunate because they do not take into account that in the original Greek the verb is in the continuous present tense. Thus, this verse should be rendered, "Whoever is born of God does not continuously practice sin." If a pig and a lamb fall into the mud, the pig wants to stay there, but the lamb wants to get out. Both a believer and an unbeliever can fall into the same sin, but the difference is that a believer cannot stay in it and feel comfortable.

The reason the child of God is sensitive to sin is because of the indwelling presence of the Holy Spirit. John refers to the Spirit as the implanted "seed" which is deposited in every believer the moment they trust in Christ. At the point of salvation every believer receives a perfect spiritual nature from God. This spiritual nature cannot be altered or lost and it comes with a new set of affections and desires. However, when we are saved we do not magically lose the old flesh nature which is enslaved to sin. The flesh desires the things of the world and the Spirit desires the things of God. This battle between the Spirit and the flesh is a constant struggle for every believer until the day we die. Paul writes about this war within in Romans 7:15-20:

> For I do not understand my own actions. For I do not do what I want, but I do the very thing I hate. Now if I do what I do not want, I agree with the law, that it is good. So now it is no longer I who

> do it, but sin that dwells within me. For I know that nothing good dwells in me, that is, in my flesh. For I have the desire to do what is right, but not the ability to carry it out. For I do not do the good I want, but the evil I do not want is what I keep on doing. Now if I do what I do not want, it is no longer I who do it, but sin that dwells within me.

The reason a true believer cannot enjoy sin is because the Holy Spirit, as an act of grace, will not let them. The Spirit will sensitize every born-again child of God to sin and when a believer does sin the Spirit will cut and prick their heart to the point of conviction. Therefore, John wraps up in 3:10 by stating that the difference between a child of God and a child of Satan is their attitude and disposition towards sin.

Many dog owners have installed in their yards what is called an "invisible fence." It's basically a wire that is buried just underground around the perimeter of the yard and it emits a signal. The dog wears a special collar that communicates with the wire underground. When the dog gets too close to the wire it beeps as a warning that he is close to forbidden territory. If the dog goes too far it gives him an electric shock so he will learn to stay away from the danger of the road.

The Holy Spirit is like a Christian's invisible fence. When you get too close to the edge of sin, the Spirit will give you a warning. "Get out! Retreat! Flee!" is what the Holy Spirit screams to our conscious. If you go over the edge and fall into temptation the Spirit will give you an unpleasant "shock" called conviction which is followed by heartfelt guilt. This spiritual protection is intended to lead the wayward believer back to safety and repentance. As the writer of Hebrews says, "the Lord disciplines those He loves, and He punishes everyone He accepts as a son" (12:6). If God does not discipline you, then you're not His child. So praise God if you can't enjoy sin because it means you are one of His!

11

What's Love Got to Do with It?
(1 John 3:11–18)

IT HAS BEEN WIDELY noted among historians that one of the many contributions Christianity made to the development of Western Civilization was the practice of charity and compassion. D. James Kennedy remarks in his book, *What if Jesus Had Never Been Born?*, "The world before Christianity was like the Russian tundra—quite cold and inhospitable. One scholar, Dr. Martineau, exhaustively researched through historical documents and concluded that antiquity has left no trace of any organized charitable effort. Disinterested benevolence was unknown. When Christ and the Bible became known, charity and benevolence flourished."[1]

Perhaps the best example of how Christian charity changed the harsh and barbaric landscape of the Roman Empire was the way early believers responded when ravaging plagues swept through villages and towns like wildfire. The first serious plague devastated the Mediterranean between 165 and 180 AD and the second about on hundred years later. It is estimated that during its fifteen-year duration the first plague decimated one-fourth of the population of the entire Empire. The deadly plague was no respecter of persons, as it even claimed the life of Emperor Marcus Aurelius. Early Christians were wiped out right alongside the pagans.

Imagine yourself caught in the plague. The stench of death surrounds you. Caravans of carts work their way through the streets and out of the city carrying bodies to a communal dumping ground where they are either buried or burned. People all around you are dropping like flies. Yet in the

---

1. Kennedy & Newcombe, *What if Jesus Had Never Been Born?*, 29.

midst of this epidemic, Christians were the only ones who cared for the sick, which they did at the risk of contracting the plague themselves. Meanwhile, pagans and Romans were throwing infected members of their own families into the streets, even before they died, in order to protect themselves from the disease. As the sick lay dying in the streets, caring Christians would come along, pick them up, and tend to them in their final hours.

At the height of the second great epidemic around 260 AD, Dionysius, a church father in Alexandria, wrote a lengthy tribute to the heroic nursing efforts of local Christians, many of whom lost their lives caring for others.

> Most of our brother Christians showed unbounded love and loyalty; never sparing themselves and thinking only of one another. Heedless of danger, they took charge of the sick, attending to their every need and ministering to them in Christ, and with them departed this life serenely happy; for they were infected by others with the disease, drawing on themselves the sickness of their neighbors and cheerfully accepting their pains. Many, in nursing and caring for others, transferred their death to themselves and died in their stead . . . The best of our brothers lost their lives in this manner, a number of presbyters, deacons, and laymen winning high commendation so that death in this form, the result of great piety and strong faith, seems in every way the equal of martyrdom.[2]

This kind of selfless compassion caused the calloused Roman society to take note of the way the Christians cared for the afflicted. In fact, Tertullian, the church father in Carthage, wrote that the common expression among the pagans concerning the Christians was, "See how they love one another!"[3]

That simple message highlights a recurring theme of John's letter. "Love one another." It runs through the Apostle's letter like a scarlet thread connecting and binding all his doctrinal and practical teaching into a unit. Wiersbe insightfully comments:

> John's letter has been compared to a spiral staircase because he kept returning to the same three topics: love, obedience, and truth. Though these themes recur, it is not true that they are merely repetitious. Each time we return to a topic, we look at it from a different point of view and are taken more deeply into it.[4]

---

2. Stark, *The Rise of Christianity: A Sociologist Reconsiders History*, 82.
3. Tertullian, *The Apology*, 39.7.
4. Wiersbe, *The Wiersbe Bible Commentary: New Testament*, 988.

What's Love Got to Do with It? (1 John 3:11-18)

Throughout this epistle, John emphasizes that a distinctive feature of a Christian who has close fellowship with God is the manifestation of love in their daily life. Just like it is impossible to have the flu without having the symptoms show up—runny nose, body aches, fever, etc.—the same is true with fellowship with God. It is impossible to know God intimately and not have the side effect of His love show up. In John's school of ethics the proof of your fellowship with God vertically is your love for people horizontally.

What John wants us to know is this—if you have received the love of God, then you will share the love of God. The love we have for others is a response to the love God has shared with us. We love because we are loved. Thus, true Christian love is a responsibility and a response. If we do not love one another, we cannot walk in the light no matter how loud our profession may be.

THE COMMAND TO LOVE (3:11)

Without a doubt, "love," was the Apostle John's favorite word. In the five short chapters of this epistle, John used the word "love" forty-five times. It's important to understand that the Greek language has several words to express different levels of love, while the English language has just one. In the Greek mindset these different words for the concept of love expressed different kinds of human relationships. *Eros* is the word used to denote erotic love or sexual attraction. *Phileo* is used to refer to a brotherly kind of love that might be shared between friends. However, *agapao* is the word John uses the most in this letter. *Agape* love is the strongest degree of love expressible, as it refers to a selfless, self-sacrificing kind of love.

In our culture we often equivocate on the term "love." In other words, we use the word "love" with more than one meaning or sense in mind. In one breath we say, "I love my spouse," yet with the next breath we say, "Thanks, honey, I love this chocolate cake you made." Obviously the word "love" carries different shades of meaning depending on its context. We all realize that no one loves chocolate cake the way they love their husband or wife.

John uses the precision of the Greek term *agape* to communicate that Christian love is qualitatively different. Christian love is passionate, action-oriented, and flows out of the abundance of our relationship with God. Someone who has the love of Christ continually wills the good of the other and doesn't count the cost. The kind of love John is talking about is unconditional love that gives until there is nothing more to give. Remember that Biblical love is volitionally based, not emotionally based. It is choice-based, not always feelings-based. This is how the Christian can love their enemies, their neighbors, and their fellow believers because they choose love over their present emotional state (Matt. 22:36–40, John 13:34–35).

Love is the supreme ethic because it is universally recognized and desired. God designed us to respond to love. I would submit to you that the one factor which drives human behavior more than any other is the desire to love and be loved. The reason we are commanded to love is because love is the most powerful force that has ever been unleashed on earth. Paul says at the end of 1 Cor. 13:13, "So now faith, hope, and love abide, these three; but the greatest of these is love." George MacDonald put it eloquently, "The love of our neighbor is the only door out of the dungeon of self." The sacred romance of Christianity is being in a love relationship with God and then learning how to love like God.

THE CONVERSE OF LOVE (3:12-15)

John begins honing in on the virtue of love by first defining what it is not. Remember, John writes in contrast—light and dark, love and hate, truth and lie. So he is first going to give us the opposite of what he wants us to do. When I was searching for my wife's engagement ring I noticed that the jeweler's did a very intentional thing when they were showing me a diamond. They would set the diamond against a totally black piece of felt. The contrast between the blackness of the cloth and the sparkling of the diamond helped me see the difference between the two materials and made the diamond that much more brilliant.

John is using a similar approach by drawing our attention to the Old Testament example of Cain in 3:12, "We should not be like Cain, who was of the evil one and murdered his brother." In the opening chapters of Genesis we learn that Cain was the first son born to Adam and Eve and he ended up becoming the first murderer when he killed his brother Abel. Recall that Cain was a farmer and Abel was a shepherd. Both were religious men, both worshipped God, and both made sacrifices to God.

> Now Adam knew Eve his wife, and she conceived and bore Cain, saying, "I have gotten a man with the help of the Lord." And again, she bore his brother Abel. Now Abel was a keeper of sheep, and Cain a worker of the ground. In the course of time Cain brought

What's Love Got to Do with It? (1 John 3:11-18)

to the Lord an offering of the fruit of the ground, and Abel also brought of the firstborn of his flock and of their fat portions. And the Lord had regard for Abel and his offering, but for Cain and his offering He had no regard. So Cain was very angry, and his face fell. The Lord said to Cain, "Why are you angry, and why has your face fallen? If you do well, will you not be accepted? And if you do not do well, sin is crouching at the door. Its desire is for you, but you must rule over it. Cain spoke to Abel his brother. And when they were in the field, Cain rose up against his brother Abel and killed him (Genesis 4:1-8).

Notice that Cain is not pictured as a godless atheist, but someone who went through a religious ritual with the wrong attitude. He was outwardly religious, but inwardly irreverent. According to Hebrews 11:4 the reason why Cain's offering was rejected and Abel's offering was accepted was the crucial element of faith, "By faith Abel offered to God a more acceptable sacrifice than Cain, through which he was commended as righteous, God commending him by accepting his gifts. And through his faith, though he died, he still speaks."

Cain's offering was from the works of his hands and from the ground which was cursed now due to the Fall (Gen. 3:17-19), while Abel's offering was an animal sacrifice. Abel approached God the correct way through faith and by the blood of an innocent substitute. On the other hand, Cain approached God the incorrect way through works and his sacrifice was bloodless, for "without the shedding of blood there can be no remission of sin" (Heb. 9:22).

As a result of Cain's rejection he was destroyed by the green-eyed monster of envy. Cain's murderous attitude came out of his sense of failure before God. He viewed Abel as a rival in spiritual things, or as John says, Cain appraised that ". . . his own deeds were evil and his brother's righteous." Cain's envy led to hate and his hate led to murder. Before Cain mangled his brother in the field, he had already committed fratricide in his heart. Obviously, the reason that hate entered the heart of Cain was because his relationship with God was broken. In fact John makes this clear because he points out that Cain "was of the evil one." The origin of Cain's sin came from Satan. Cain did not become a child of the Devil by murdering his brother. He murdered his brother because he was a child of the Devil. Cain might have had all the external trappings of religion, but he was really lost.

John uses the tragic relationship between these brothers to make a point about our spiritual brothers in 3:13-15. John is saying that if you have envy, jealousy, bigotry, or hatred in your heart towards another then you are in the same condition as Cain. Hatred is the pre-requisite for murder and a bitter heart shows that you are not in fellowship with God. Love springs from God, while hate originates from the Devil. If you are in the grip of hate, you are exhibiting the qualities of Satan. In fact, John is harkening back to the words of Jesus from the Sermon on the Mount:

> You have heard that it was said to those of old, 'You shall not murder; and whoever murders will be liable to judgment.' But I say to you that everyone who is angry with his brother will be liable to judgment; whoever insults his brother will be liable to the council; and whoever says, 'You fool!' will be liable to the hell of fire (Matt. 5:21-22).

God looks at the condition of our hearts and even though we may not drive a knife into our enemy's back, we are still guilty on a spiritual level for murdering them in our hearts. In God's economy hatred is the moral equivalent of murder and if hate is not dealt with it leads to murder. That is why John writes in 3:15, "*Everyone who hates his brother is a murderer,* and you know that no murderer has eternal life abiding in him." Roy Zuck writes:

> London held its breath in June 1987. While working on a building site, a construction foreman thought his workers had hit a cast iron pipe while using a pile driver. After picking up and then dropping the huge object, they realized the pipe strangely resembled a bomb. It was a 2,200 pound World War II bomb, one of the largest the Germans dropped during the Blitz which killed more than fifteen thousand Londoners. After evacuating the area, a ten-man bomb disposal unit worked eighteen hours before finally deactivating the seven foot device. Hatred is like an unexploded bomb. Unless it's deactivated it can detonate and cause great damage.[5]

Don't neglect to see the parallel in 3:13 that John makes by using Cain as a picture of the world and Abel as a picture of the Christian. "Don't be surprised if the word hates you," John reminds us. In other words, he is saying, "What Cain did to Abel and what the Pharisees did to Jesus is what the unbelieving world will do to you."

Like Cain, their ancient forefather, the children of the Devil manifest their character by exacting violence on God's true worshippers. Why does the world hate Christ and the message of the Gospel? Very simply it's because Christianity alone says that man cannot earn his salvation. The

---

5. Zuck, *The Speaker's Quote Book*, 246–247.

What's Love Got to Do with It? (1 John 3:11–18)

Gospel declares that man is a depraved sinner who must be saved by faith in Christ alone. Not to mention that the message of Christ is narrow and uncompromising. Those who desire pluralism, which says all religions lead to God, grit their teeth at the audacity of the believer who preaches that Christ is the only way to the Father. Meanwhile, grace flies in the face of works and all of man's attempts to merit God's favor through religion.

In John 15:18–19 Jesus said, "If the world hates you, know that it has hated me before it hated you. If you were of the world, the world would love you as its own; but because you are not of the world, but I chose you out of the world, therefore the world hates you." Identifying ourselves with Christ automatically signs us up for being misunderstood and persecuted. If the cold, uncaring world nailed Christ to a cross for His radical message of love and grace then we should expect to receive similar indignation.

Sometimes the only way hate is exposed is when the supernatural love of God shines through the lives of suffering saints. Richard Wurmbrand's *Tortured for Christ* graphically tells how persecuted believers in Romania ministered to their taskmasters. In the darkness of a rat-infested dungeon, guards tied prisoners to crosses and smeared them with human excrement. Anyone would think that men capable of such heinous evil were beyond redemption, yet those same guards saw the inexplicable love, devotion, and faith of the Christians they tortured. Wurmbrand wrote:

> I have seen Christians in Communist prisons with fifty pounds of chains on their feet, tortured with red-hot iron pokers, in whose throats spoonfuls of salt had been forced, being kept afterward from water, starving, whipped, suffering from cold—and praying with fervor for the communists.[6]

Wurmbrand even told of guards coming to Christ while beating Christian prisoners, then confessing their faith later and being imprisoned and tortured themselves.

Martin Luther King Jr. once said, "Darkness cannot drive out darkness; only light can do that. Hate cannot drive out hate, only love can do that." The Christian is called to love the unlovable and love them in spite of themselves. John says in 3:14 that love for others is the evidence of a transformed life, "*We know that we have passed out of death into life, because we love the brothers. Whoever does not love abides in death.*" It's easy and quite natural to love our fellow brothers and sisters in the family of faith;

---

6. Wurmbrand, *Tortured for Christ*, 57.

however, when we learn how to love someone who does not reciprocate love, we exhibit the highest kind of Christ-like love.

THE CHARACTER OF LOVE (3:16)

After Napoleon's devastating loss at the battle of Waterloo, the diminutive field marshal was exiled to the lonely island of St. Helena. In an ironic turn of fate, his kingdom, which at its height extended across Europe enfolding Germany, Austria, Italy, and France, was now reduced to a tiny outcrop in the Atlantic. There in his solitude and the ignominy of defeat, Napoleon turned his mind from the battlefield to spiritual matters. In his memoirs he wrote these powerful words about the kingdom of Christ, "Alexander, Caesar, Charlemagne, and myself founded empires; but what foundation did we rest the creations of our genius? Upon force. Jesus alone founded his empire upon love; and at this hour millions of men would die for Him."

John has spent a great deal defining the characteristics of love in reverse; he has told us what love is not, now he is going to tell us what love is. John turns his attention from the model of hate—Cain, to the perfect model of love—Christ. The apostle focuses on three aspects of Christ's perfect *agape* love.

First, John noted the *voluntary nature of Christ's love*. Notice the words of 3:16, "By this we know love, that *he laid down his life . . .*" True love does not have to be coerced. Jesus willingly gave up his rightful place in heaven beside the Father to assume the role of a servant so that He might suffer and die in the most horrific way (Phil 2:5–8). Like the songwriter has sung many times, "It wasn't the nails that held Jesus to the tree, it was His great love for you and me." At any moment he could have called down legions of angels to end His suffering, yet He relinquished His divine power (Matt. 26:53). Jesus literally loved us to death. While His death on the cross looked like a tremendous tragedy, Christ had everything under control because He was a willing victim.

> ". . . just as the Son of Man did not come to be served, but to serve, and to give His life a ransom for many" (Matt. 20:28).

> "I am the good shepherd. *The good shepherd gives His life for the sheep . . .* As the Father knows Me, even so I know the Father; and *I lay down My life for the sheep*" (John 10:11–15).

What's Love Got to Do with It? (1 John 3:11–18)

"For this reason the Father loves me, because *I lay down my life that I may take it up again. No one takes it from me, but I lay it down of my own accord. I have authority to lay it down, and I have authority to take it up again.* This charge I have received from my Father" (John 10:17–18).

"Greater love has no one than this, that someone *lay down his life for his friends*" (John 15:13).

Second, John noted the *vulnerable nature of Christ's love*. Christ did not withhold anything from humanity when He came to earth. He was made vulnerable to persecution, rejection, the cruel elements, false accusation, sadness, and even death. In loving the world Christ paid the ultimate price by making Himself vulnerable to unrequited love. But real love does not count the cost. Love takes wild risks at the expense of the lover and for the benefit of the beloved. C.S. Lewis has written:

> To love at all is to be vulnerable. Love anything and your heart will be wrung and possibly broken. If you want to make sure of keeping it intact you must give it to no one, not even an animal. Wrap it carefully round with hobbies and little luxuries; avoid all entanglements. Lock it up safe in the casket or coffin of your selfishness. But in that casket, safe, dark, motionless, airless, it will change. It will not be broken; it will become unbreakable, impenetrable, irredeemable . . . the only place outside heaven where you can be perfectly safe from all the dangers of love is Hell.[7]

Thirdly, John noted the *vicarious nature of Christ's love*. At the end of 3:16 the text reads, ". . . He laid down His life *for us*." Paul says in Romans 5:8, "But God shows His love for us in that while we were still sinners, Christ died *for us*." At the cross of Calvary Jesus took our place. The hell that we deserved, Jesus experienced as our substitute. An eternity of suffering was compressed into six hours one Friday afternoon.

There is a true story of a little boy whose sister needed a blood transfusion. The doctor explained that she had the same disease the boy had recovered from two years earlier. Her only chance of recovery was a transfusion from someone who had previously conquered the disease. Since the two children had the same rare blood type, the boy was an ideal donor.

"Would you give your blood to Mary?" the doctor asked. Johnny hesitated. His lower lip started to tremble. Then he smiled and said, "Sure, for my sister." Soon the two children were wheeled into the hospital room.

---

7. Lewis, *The Four Loves*, 121.

Mary was pale and thin. Johnny was robust and healthy. Neither spoke, but when their eyes met, Johnny grinned.

As the nurse inserted the needle into his arm, Johnny's smile faded. He watched the crimson liquid flow through the tube. With the ordeal almost over, Johnny's voice slightly shaky, broke the silence. "Doctor, when do I die?" the boy asked. Only then did the doctor realize why Johnny hesitated, why his lip trembled when he agreed to donate his blood. He thought giving his blood to his sister would mean giving up his life. In that brief moment, he made his decision to be like Jesus.[8]

THE CHALLENGE OF LOVE (3:17-18)

John brings his lesson on love close to home by challenging each believer to be a conduit through which the love of Christ passes to a hurting and needy world. Love cannot be silent nor can it sit still. The heart of a person who has been touched by Christ will not wait idly by, but will be motivated to sacrificially give of themselves to others. While we may not be able to give our life on a cross, we can sacrificially give our time and treasure to those who cannot repay us. Love involves more than the great and noble acts, such as sacrificing one's life for another, but also includes the mundane and unseen acts of daily compassion.

A parallel verse to John's challenge is found in James 2:15-16, "If a brother or sister is poorly clothed and lacking in daily food, and one of you says to them, 'Go in peace, be warmed and filled,' without giving them the things needed for the body, what good is that?" Believers are obligated to fill physical needs before spiritual needs. Apathy is not a word that is in the vocabulary of the believer. Lip-service is not enough. Saying "I love you" and demonstrating "I love you" are two different things. It has been said that "a man wrapped up in himself makes for a very small package." The same is true for believers who turn a blind eye to the needs of a hurting world.

Chuck Swindoll once told a story that happened shortly after World War II came to a close and the people of Europe began picking up the pieces. Much of the old country had been ravaged by war and was in ruins. Perhaps the saddest sight of all was that of little orphaned children starving in the streets of those war-torn cities.

---

8. Gray, *Stories for the Heart: The Original Collection*, 131–132.

What's Love Got to Do with It? (1 John 3:11–18)

Early one chilly morning an American soldier was making his way back to the barracks in London. As he turned the corner in his jeep, he spotted a little lad with his nose pressed to the window of a pastry shop. Inside, the cook was kneading dough for a fresh batch of doughnuts. The hungry boy stared in silence, watching every move. The soldier pulled his jeep to the curb, stopped, got out, and walked quietly over to where the little fellow was standing. Through the steamed-up window, he could see the mouth-watering morsels being pulled from the oven, piping hot. The boy salivated and released a slight groan as he watched the cook place them onto the glass-enclosed counter ever so carefully.

The soldier's heart went out to the nameless orphan as he stood beside him. "Son . . . would you like some of those?" The boy was startled, "Oh, yeah . . . I would!" The American stepped inside and bought a dozen, put them in a bag, and walked back to where the lad was standing in the foggy cold of the London morning. The soldier smiled, held out the bag, and said simply: "Here you are." As he turned to walk away, he felt a tug on his coat. He looked back and heard the child ask quietly: "Mister, are you God?"[9] Become a giver and watch God open the hearts of others to Himself.

---

9. Swindoll, *Day by Day with Charles Swindoll*, 278.

12

Becoming a Confident Christian (1 John 3:19–24)

THE STORY IS TOLD of a pioneer in the early days of America who came to the shores of the Great Lakes heading westward. It was deep winter and the surface of the lake was covered with ice. Even though the sub-freezing temperatures and the blowing snow drifts had continued for days, this man did not fully trust that the ice was thick enough to support his body weight. As he stepped out on the ice, the creaking of the frozen floor at his feet gave him an uneasy chill. He thought, "What if the ice broke? There is no one for miles around and surely I will drown or turn into an icicle if I fall through!"

Night was falling and it was urgent that he reach the other side. Finally, after much hesitation and with many fears, he began to creep cautiously across surface of the ice on his hands and knees. He thought that he might distribute his weight as much as possible to keep the ice from breaking beneath him. There he was crawling like an infant at a miserably slow pace across the ice, wondering the whole time if he would ever cross to the other side before sunset.

About halfway across the lake he thought he could hear the faint clunk of horse hooves. As he paused, the weary traveler distinctly heard singing mixed with the sound of the howling wind. He looked behind and scanned the horizon. He couldn't believe what he saw coming toward him. A man driving a horse-drawn load of coal across the ice came flying by him singing merrily as he went his way. There he was—on his hands and knees, trembling, and doubting whether the ice was strong enough to bear him up!

Becoming a Confident Christian (1 John 3:19-24)

In our spiritual pilgrimage there are many believers who are like the pitiful man crawling through life when they could be running and leaping. While many believers enjoy their Christian journey—dancing and singing in freedom on their way with Jesus—there are others who are miserably scraping by. They spend a majority of their time cowering in doubt or stymied by the paralysis of fear. Those unfortunate souls who lack the necessary confidence to push forward make little headway in their spiritual life because they are constantly questioning God. When fear supplants faith, then our Christian growth grinds to a halt.

In the final verses of chapter three, John speaks to his readers about how to live a life of confidence before God. The apostle reminds us that our confidence in God comes as a result of our special relationship with Jesus, in spite of our failures, feelings, or faults. In the preceding context John has been speaking about the way believers ought to love each other in a Christ-like manner. John moves on to explain what benefits are the result of living a life of love. For John, the practice of love must be more than simply a feeling of "warm fuzzies." Instead, "love" is a verb that is displayed in our daily deeds. John explains that when God's love becomes a way of life for us then three very valuable things manifest—assurance, boldness in prayer, and the evidence of a Spirit-filled life.

CONFIDENCE THROUGH AN ASSURED CONSCIENCE (3:19-20)

I once heard a story of a little boy who had lots of pretty marbles. However, he was constantly eyeing his sister's bagful of candy. One day he said to her, "If you give me all your candy, I'll give you all of my marbles." She gave it much thought, and agreed to the trade. He took all her candy and went back to his room to get his marbles. But the more he admired them the more reluctant he became to give them all up. So he hid the best of them under his pillow and took the rest to her. That night she slept soundly while he tossed and turned restlessly, unable to sleep and thinking, "I wonder if she gave me all the candy?"

There is no torment in the world comparable to that of a condemning conscience. Like that little boy, many of us walk through life plagued by the question, "Has God given me His best?" But the question we must first answer is, "Am I giving God my best?" Often we feel the sting of conviction because we have knowingly cheated God out of our full obedience. Other times, conviction burdens our heart when Satan dredges up some sin from our past that we have already asked God to forgive.

An astute reader will notice that John uses the word "heart" three times in these verses. The Greek word for "heart" is *kardia*, and it is where we derive our term "cardiovascular." However, when John speaks of the heart he is not talking about the organ responsible for pumping blood. Instead the heart refers to what we would call the conscience. It is the center or the seat of moral conviction.

The Bible teaches that every human being has some sense of right and wrong, an internal compass that helps us distinguish between good and evil. Theologians have called it "the moral law of God" which is inscribed on every heart. Because we reflect the image of God, humans intuitively know that behaviors such as murder and theft are wrong. Paul refers to this in Romans 2:15 when he says, "For when Gentiles, who do not have the law, by nature do what the law requires, they are a law to themselves, even though they do not have the law. *They show that the work of the law is written on their hearts, while their conscience also bears witness, and their conflicting thoughts accuse or even excuse them.*"

I think that John MacArthur makes some insightful comments about mankind's intrinsic moral nature when he writes:

> The conscience then is God's guilt-producing warning device, given to every person to confront sin. In the same way that pain is a physical warning mechanism that tells people they have a bodily injury or an illness, the conscience is a spiritual warning mechanism that alerts of conduct dangerous to the soul. Of course, to function effectively the conscience must be informed by the right standards, because it is only a reactor to the person's convictions about right and wrong. If ill-informed by falsehoods and lies, the conscience will still react to those untruths that govern an individual's beliefs. Conscience is thus not in itself an independent system of morality. Rather it operates based on whatever knowledge and belief system that informs it, and in response to the cultural conditions surrounding it ... It can be silenced not only by being misinformed, but by being constantly ignored, or overridden, until it is scarred and unresponsive.[1]

Jiminy Cricket once told Pinocchio, "Let your conscience be your guide." However, that is fatal advice because the human conscience has been broken and distorted by sin. Jeremiah the prophet said in Jer. 17:9,

---

1. MacArthur, *The MacArthur New Testament Commentary: 1–3 John*, 142.

Becoming a Confident Christian (1 John 3:19-24)

"The heart is deceitful above all things, and desperately sick; who can understand it?" Therefore it cannot always be taken as a reliable guide—even for a believer.

You might think of our fickle conscience like a compass in relationship to a magnet. Generally, a compass is a pretty reliable guide for determining your direction in travel. The needle almost always points north because it aligns itself with the magnetism of the earth's poles. However, once you introduce another magnet into the equation, the compass needle can be made to point in any direction. Just wave a magnet over a compass and watch the needle spin off course. The same is true of the human heart. Sin has been introduced into the equation and many times the effects of sin, like the effects of that magnet, can cause us to veer off course.

In our context, it appears that John does not necessarily have in mind the general sense of guilt that the Holy Spirit brings to the heart of the believer when he or she falls into sin (John 16:8-9). In fact, He has already dealt with the problem. If we have a guilty heart because we have sinned, there is only one solution: "Confess your sin," John says, "and God is faithful to forgive us our sins and to cleanse us from all unrighteousness" (1:9).

Instead John seems to be talking about condemning feelings brought on by the effects of an overactive sense of guilt. There have been countless times in my ministry when I have felt like a complete and total failure. I have preached my heart out thinking that the Holy Spirit has done His work, and yet when the invitation was given no one responded. Afterwards, I begin to think, "Was it my fault, Lord? Was my message unclear or boring? Was there some secret sin in my life?" At this point, if I'm not careful, I can begin to sink into a pit of self-pity.

Other times the Devil will begin firing his flaming darts trying to assail my joyful spirit. The Enemy loves to bring up past failures or sins that I know are under the blood. Satan, as the accuser of the brethren, is relentless in his mind games. He is an expert at getting us to call into question God's unconditional love for us. If we listen to him long enough we start believing His lies and our security is eroded by his acidic accusations.

However, John has an antidote to the tranquilizing effects of a condemning heart. In 3:20 he writes, "... for whenever our heart condemns us, *God is greater than our heart, and He knows everything.*" God has the ability to overrule doubt, trump feelings of inadequacy, and overcome our guilt. How? Because the Lord can see the total picture of your life and God knows your thoughts and the motivations behind your actions. God's omniscience means that He knows you better than you know yourself.

Living in the Light

Our conscience is fickle and forgetful, but unlike our faulty conscience God does not forget those things we have done in service to Him. God can see that we love Him, and He knows that we fail Him from time to time. Even when you've blown it, God can override your feelings with the fact of His never-changing love. Since God's love for us was not merited on our performance, then there is nothing we can do to make Him love us any more or any less.

Perhaps, the best example of this can be found in the Apostle Peter. The greatest failure in his life was when he denied the Lord three times on the night of Jesus' trial (Matt. 26:69–75). The Bible says that after Peter cussed Jesus for the third time, he heard the rooster crow. Then he remembered the words of Jesus and he went away and wept bitterly. What's unique about Peter's failure is that Jesus knew he was going to deny Him before it ever happened. Christ told Peter, "Simon, Simon, behold, Satan demanded to have you, that he might sift you like wheat, but I have prayed for you that your faith may not fail and when you have turned again strengthen your brothers" (Luke 22:31–32). Even with that knowledge, Peter was powerless to prevent his failure.

However, in John 21, the resurrected Jesus met Peter on the beach. Jesus asked him three times, "Do you love me?" Each time he replied, "Lord, you know I love you." This is the reversal of the denial that happened days earlier. Peter denied Christ three times and now he affirms Christ three times. On the third time, Peter says, "*Lord, you know everything; you know that I love you*" (John 21:17). Jesus was greater than Peter's heart and, in the most loving manner, the apostle who rarely lived up to his nickname of "the rock" was restored.

There is a vast difference between human conscience and divine omniscience. God is the greatest witness to our soul's activities. If we condemn ourselves, we must remember that there is a greater Judge of our souls and He will always be fair with us. God does not want us to wallow in feeling of guilt but rather experience freedom and acceptance in His love. I think we should adopt the theology of the school teacher who wrote the following poem years ago:

> He came to my desk with a quivering lip,
> The lesson was done.
> "Have you a new sheet for me, dear teacher?
> I've spoiled this one."
> I took his sheet, all soiled and blotted,
> And gave him a new one all unspotted,

> And to his tired heart I cried.
> "Do better now, my child."
> I went to the throne with a troubled heart,
> The day was done.
> "Have a new day for me, dear Master?
> I've spoiled this one."
> He took my day, all soiled and blotted,
> And gave a new one all unspotted.
> And to my tired heart He cried,
> "Do better now, my child."[2]

CONFIDENCE THROUGH ANSWERED PRAYER (3:21-23)

Unanswered prayer can be a serious blow to our spiritual growth. When God doesn't come through in a miraculous way the tendency is to doubt His power, love, and overall attentiveness to our request. For C.S. Lewis the struggle over the thorny problem of unanswered prayer caused him to turn away from his Christian faith at the age of thirteen and it was not until some twenty years later that he knelt and prayed, ". . . perhaps, that night, the most dejected and reluctant convert in all of England."[3]

I have discovered in my Christian life that prayer is the most frustrating and difficult routine to build into my daily schedule. On one hand, the act of prayer is as simple as carrying on an open-ended conversation with God, while at the same time it's one of the most mystifying and demanding of all disciplines. In our day of technology that evolves at the speed of light many of us self-reliant go-getters reason, "Who has time to pray?" I will be the first to admit that prayer is an unnatural activity because it flies in the face of the prideful, self-made man. Prayer levels our autonomy and makes us stop to do business with an invisible God.

Perhaps one of the reasons we don't pray is because we don't think there is anyone on the other end who actually cares and will help us in our time of need. However, 1 Peter 5:7 reminds us we should not hesitate to "cast all your anxieties on Him, because He cares for you." The writer of Hebrews has said, "Let us then with confidence draw near to the throne of grace, that we may receive mercy and find grace to help in time of need" (Heb. 4:16).

---

2. Source Unknown
3. Lewis, *Surprised by Joy: The Shape of My Early Life*, 228.

Living in the Light

John makes the point that when we have confidence before God then we can have power in prayer. The confidence of the believer rests on a right relationship with God. John says that when the lines of communication between our heart and heaven's throne room are not blocked by issues in our own heart then "whatever we ask we receive from Him."

Don't misunderstand what John is saying here. Prayer is not a blank check that we get from heaven. God is not a cosmic Santa Claus where we give Him our list of egocentric requests. It has been well said that, "Prayer is not man accomplishing His will in heaven, but God accomplishing His will on earth." Selfishness is a definite prayer buster. James 4:3 says, "When you ask, you do not receive, *because you ask with wrong motives*, that you may spend what you get on your pleasures." I think many of us would be embarrassed if our selfish prayers were advertised on a billboard for the world to see. I have noticed even in my life when I ask for things like "traveling safety" or "good health" I am tacitly asking God to give me a convenient, easy life free of trials. Not only is that selfish, but it's unrealistic because trials, persecution, and suffering are the very things God uses to mold and shape us into stronger servants (James 1:2–4).

Fortunately, God is too loving to say "Yes" to our inappropriate requests. I once saw a Calvin and Hobbes comic strip that illustrated this perfectly. Calvin asked his mother, "Mom, can I set my mattress on fire?" "No!" she says. He implores a second time, "Can I ride my tricycle off the roof?" Again, "No!" is heard from another room. The third time, Calvin sneaks up behind his mom sipping her coffee at the dinner table, "Mom, can I have a cookie?" Undistracted the mother takes another sip from her mug and says, "No, Calvin." He walks away dejected muttering under his breath, "She's on to me."

In the same way, God is wise to the secret motivations behind our prayers. I have often referred back to a simple formula for understanding God's answers to our prayers. If the request is wrong, God says, "No." If the timing is wrong, God says, "Slow." If you are wrong, God says, "Grow." But if the timing is right and you are right, God says, "Go!"[4]

John also attaches a couple of important conditions to our prayers. Notice that the prerequisites for prayer are that "*we keep His commandments and do those things that are pleasing in His sight. And this is His commandment: that we should believe on the name of His Son Jesus Christ and love one another,* just as He has commanded us." In order for our prayers to

---

4. Hybels, *Too Busy Not to Pray*, 86.

be legitimate we need to be living in obedience to the commands of Christ. Along with selfishness, other factors may hinder our prayers from being answered such as ongoing relational conflict (1 Peter 3:7), unresolved sin issues (Ps. 66:18), or unbelief (James 1:5-8). If you have discovered that your prayers are not getting through and the heavens have turned to brass then the problem is on your end, not God's.

One evening all of the TV remotes in my house decided to suddenly quit working. It was really strange as I would press buttons on the remote to turn on the TV and the light would blink on the remote, but the TV wouldn't turn on. So, I looked around to see if there anything wrong with the TV, but I found nothing. Next I checked to see if there was anything obstructing the sensor on the TV; again I didn't find anything amiss. Then I popped the battery cover on the remote and discovered the problem. Around the batteries a nasty corrosion had formed where the end of battery makes contact with the remote. Apparently, the corrosion was not allowing the signal from the remote to travel to the TV with any power. The signal may have been going out, but it failed to make it to the destination. Once I cleaned the gunk away from the battery, the remote worked fine and I was enjoying my favorite program.

Many times in our prayer lives the reason we are not getting through to God is because sin or some other issue has built up and corroded our lives. Everything may look fine on the outside, but like that remote, the problem is really on the inside. If you are tolerating sin in your life, don't waste your time asking for God to work on your behalf until you first clean away the prayer-deadening effects of sin, unbelief, or relational strife.

CONFIDENCE FROM THE ABIDING PRESENCE OF THE SPIRIT (3:24)

Lastly, John ends by reminding us that the third marker for having confidence before God is the indwelling presence of the Holy Spirit. Although John has mentioned the importance of abiding with Christ several times, this is his first explicit mention of the Holy Spirit in his epistle. The ministry of the Holy Spirit is manifold. Not only is He responsible for the act of regeneration (John 3:5), but the Holy Spirit adopts us into the family of God (Gal. 4:6), imparts to us the fruits of the Spirit (Gal. 5:22), illuminates our mind to the truth (John 16:13), convicts us of sin (John 16:8-9), helps us pray (Rom. 8 26), and seals us unto the day of redemption (Eph. 1:13).

Living in the Light

All of these things are evidence pointing to the fact that we belong to God. Paul remarked in Romans 8:16, "The Spirit Himself bears witness with ours that we are children of God." The Holy Spirit initiates our belief in Christ and goes with us daily to assure us that we are property of Christ. The inner promptings of the Spirit to worship, the sharp pain of conviction that prods us when we commit sin, the internal warning bells that ring when we hear false doctrine, and the voice that stirs in us when we cry out in prayer are all tell-tell signs that God's Spirit abides in us.

We have all seen the iconic images of the Golden Gate Bridge stretching across San Francisco Bay. In 1937, the great Golden Gate Bridge was finally completed. It cost $77 million. It was built in two stages: the first slowly, and the second rapidly. In the first stage, twenty-three men fell to their death. And the work ground to a halt because fear paralyzed the workmen as helplessly they watched their companions plummeting from the structure to the water far below. Finally, an ingenious person thought, "There needs to be a net." So they put together, for $100,000 the largest net ever built and hung that net beneath the workmen. When phase two began, ten were saved who fell into that net. The work proceeded twenty-five percent faster until the job was done.[5]

God wants us to have assurance and confidence in the Christian life. That is why He has placed the "security net" of the Holy Spirit in us. As the Spirit abides in us, He assures us that we are safe and sound until heaven. Even though we may stumble from time to time, there is nothing we or Satan can do to take away our salvation. Every time the Spirit stirs within us, we know to whom we belong.

---

5. Swindoll, *Swindoll's Ultimate Book of Illustrations and Quotes*, 509–510.

13

Learn to Discern
(1 John 4:1–6)

IN 1982 PEOPLE IN the Chicago area started dying of a strange and mysterious toxin. The source of the deaths was eventually traced back to local pharmacies where people were buying the ubiquitous pain-killer Tylenol. Unknown to the customers, they were not actually getting medicine, but instead they were getting poison. Later it was discovered that someone had laced bottles of Tylenol with deadly capsules of cyanide. As a result of this dreadful sabotage, seven people died and a massive recall of Tylenol products ensued. The event ended up costing the manufacturer over $100 million. Today when you buy any over-the-counter drugs the bottles are sealed with tamperproof lids to prevent the same tragedy from happening again.

In a spiritual sense a similar thing is happening today. Folks are attending various churches, spiritual seminars, consulting psychics, and dabbling in various forms of New Age mysticism. In an attempt to discover spiritual truth they think they are getting medicine when, in fact, they are being fed deadly poison. Even though they are in a place that purports to be a spiritual hospital, they are getting sicker rather than being healed. The reason is because the truth has been laced with error.

John closed chapter three with some remarks about the Holy Spirit. In his original letter these chapter and verse divisions did not exist, but 3:24 is actually a hinge which connects one section of the letter to the next. After introducing the ministry of the Holy Spirit in 3:24, the apostle launches into a discourse on spiritual discernment in 4:1–6. John wants us to be adept at distinguishing between truth and error because what you believe influences how you behave. You are what you think, and if your thinking is flawed then the whole course of your life will end up shipwrecked (Pro. 14:12).

Since abiding with Christ requires us to know the truth and love the truth, John gives us several doctrinal tests to gauge our adherence to orthodoxy. All truth flows from God and it is His truth which sets the boundaries for right belief and right behavior.

THE CALL FOR DISCERNMENT (4:1)

John begins by sounding the alarm that the world we inhabit is not a playground but a battleground. The spirit of the Antichrist is already at work in the world (2:18). Satan can masquerade as an angel of light and convincingly advertise himself as a harmless guru of user-friendly spirituality (2 Cor. 11:14). In a world of shadows, counterfeits, smoke, and mirrors the truth can be distorted. Although Grandpa John with his years of experience saw everything in terms of black and white, often little children lack discernment and distinct categories can bleed together into grays. That's why John says we need to develop the discipline of discernment.

Notice John uses the word "test" there in the text. In the original language the word carries the thought of a metallurgist testing the purity and value of a precious metal with intense scrutiny. Why? Because not all that glitters is gold. Paul uses the same word in 1 Thess. 5:20–21, "Do not despise prophecies, but *test* everything and hold fast to what is good." Discernment is the intuitive ability to read between-the-lines and perceive beyond what is being said. Discernment involves an insight that goes beyond the obvious. Joe Stowell writes:

> Discernment in Scripture is the skill that enables us to differentiate. It is the ability to see issues clearly. We desperately need to cultivate this spiritual skill that will enable us to know right from wrong. We must be prepared to distinguish light from darkness, truth from error, best from better, righteousness from unrighteousness, purity from defilement, and principles from pragmatics.[1]

John is saying, "Don't just accept what some teacher or preacher is saying. Examine what is being taught with careful consideration." Like one of my seminary professors said, "Christians don't get brownie points for being stupid!" Evaluate what is being taught by comparing it to the Scriptures.

---

1. Stowell, *Fan The Flame*, 44.

Learn to Discern (1 John 4:1-6)

Don't be a gullible Christian that takes in everything just because it has a Jesus-sticker slapped on it or because it's on the Christian TV station, or because you got it out of the Christian bookstore.

Instead imitate the believers at the church of Berea. Observe what Luke says about their pattern of investigation when Paul and Silas rolled into their town and started teaching, "Now these Jews were more noble than those in Thessalonica; they received the word with all eagerness, examining the Scriptures daily to see if these things were so" (Acts 17:11). In other words, they just didn't take Paul and Silas at their word, but they did their own investigation and went back into the Old Testament to confirm their doctrine.

Why is John so adamant about the need for discernment? He gives the reason, ". . . because many false prophets have gone out into the world." There's always a religious crackpot who has discovered some hidden nugget in the pages of prophecy and built a whole following around a scripture taken out of context. Likewise, there are televangelists in fancy suits, wearing gold chains who parade around on TV promising that if you sow a "faith seed" then they will mail you a vial of Mary's tears or Peter and Paul loincloths. Faith healers are going around slapping people on the forehead claiming that they have been "slain in the Spirit." Moreover, there are preachers filling pulpits who are more like entertainers than men of God. They are not concerned for the wellbeing of your soul because they will smile into the camera and preach a prosperity theology of the American dream with a little Jesus sprinkled here and there. John is repeating for his beloved church the same warnings of Jesus:

> Beware of false prophets, who come to you in sheep's clothing but inwardly are ravenous wolves. You will recognize them by their fruits" (Matt. 7: 15-16).

> "Not everyone who says to me, 'Lord, Lord,' will enter the kingdom of heaven, but the one who does the will of my Father who is in heaven. On that day many will say to me, 'Lord, Lord, did we not prophesy in your name, and cast out demons in your name, and do many mighty works in your name?' And then will I declare to them, 'I never knew you; depart from me, you workers of lawlessness'" (Matt 7:21-23).

> "And many false prophets will arise and lead many astray" (Matt. 24:11).

Living in the Light

Discernment is an oft neglected skill, yet it's the difference between ingesting spiritual aspirin or spiritual arsenic. My high school chemistry teacher had a little ditty that she often recited, "Jimmy was a chemist's son, but Jimmy is no more, because what Jimmy thought was H_2O was H_2SO_4"—which is the difference between water and sulfuric acid. The Devil is interested in the details.

Perhaps one of the most prized timepieces money can buy is a Rolex watch. Many people would jump at the opportunity to own such a status symbol. However, these expensive timepieces are often counterfeited and sold on the black market for just a fraction of what a real Rolex would cost. A few years ago I made a trip to Washington, D.C. and along the streets were all kinds of vendors. Snack shacks, t-shirt huts, and presidential memorabilia were lined up like a curbside bazaar. One man had a table set up that advertised, "Rolex watches—Great Deals!" He wasn't kidding, for only $50 I could own a replica of the watch that Donald Trump wears or one of the Omega's that James Bond sports in the movies. The well-dressed Indian man behind the counter assured me that these watches had a lifetime guarantee and that if I ever had trouble with one I could just send it back to the manufacturer. I was already suspicious, but I really knew I was dealing with a fake when I examined the watch face and noticed the spelling of this particular brand—R-O-L-E-X-X.

In the marketplace of spirituality there are numerous fakes, knock-offs, and counterfeits. It has been said that Satan is not a creator, but a great imitator. For every one of God's truths, Satan has concocted ten counterfeits that look right, sound right, and feel right.

This is why knowing true Biblical doctrine is so important. Many believers have left the study of doctrine to the stuffy seminary professors in tweed jackets. However, knowing the truth and becoming conversant in right doctrine is essential for staying wise to the wiles of the Devil. C.S. Lewis has written in *Mere Christianity* about the necessity of knowing doctrine:

> ". . . if a man has once looked at the Atlantic from the beach, and then goes and looks at a map of the Atlantic, he also will be turning from something real to something less real: turning from real waves to a bit of coloured paper. But here comes the point. The map is admittedly only coloured paper, but there are two things you have to remember about it. In the first place, it is based on what hundreds and thousands of people have found out by sailing the real Atlantic. In that way it has behind it masses of experience

just as real as the one you could have from the beach; only, while yours would be a single glimpse, the map fits all those different experiences together. In the second place, if you want to go anywhere, the map is absolutely necessary. As long as you are content with walks on the beach, your own glimpses are far more fun than looking at a map. But the map is going to be more use than walks on the beach if you want to get to America. Now, Theology is like the map . . . Doctrines are not God: they are only a kind of map. But that map is based on the experience of hundreds of people who really were in touch with God experiences compared with which any thrills or pious feelings you and I are likely to get on our own are very elementary and very confused. And secondly, if you want to get any further, you must use the map. In fact, that is just why a vague religion all about feeling God in nature, and so on is so attractive. It is all thrills and no work; like watching the waves from the beach. But you will not get to Newfoundland by studying the Atlantic that way, and you will not get eternal life by simply feeling the presence of God in flowers or music. Neither will you get anywhere by looking at maps without going to sea. Nor will you be very safe if you go to sea without a map. In other words, Theology is practical . . .[2]

THE CRITERIA FOR DISCERNMENT (4:2-6)

John advances his thinking by giving us three standards by which we can differentiate truth from error in the spiritual realm. The first question we must ask is, *"What do they confess about the Son of God?"* John writes, "By this you know the Spirit of God: *Every spirit that confesses that Jesus Christ has come in the flesh is of God."* Remember that John was combating the heresy of Gnosticism which was making inroads into the early church. Central to the Gnostics core teaching was the denial of the humanity of Jesus, an aberration known as docetism which comes from the Greek word *dokeo* meaning "to seem or appear." In other words, according to the Gnostics, Jesus only appeared to have a physical body. This means that Jesus' death and resurrection were merely illusions, which if true, would render salvation in Christ meaningless.

---

2. Lewis, *Mere Christianity*, 154-155.

Church history also tells of another infamous Gnostic teacher by the name of Cerinthus. John MacArthur explains his wild theological speculations:

> One example of how Gnostics tried to subvert the doctrine of the incarnation involved one of the very earliest Gnostic sects, led by a false teacher named Cerinthus. He taught that Jesus (the human person) was actually indwelt by a divine spirit-being known as "the Christ." Cerinthus therefore insisted that Jesus' deity was an illusion. According to this flavor of Gnosticism, Jesus' divine nature was something extraneous to Him—an attribute that belonged to His divine spirit who possessed Him—and not anything essential to His true nature. In other words, Jesus and "the Christ" were supposedly two distinct beings who simply shared the same body."[3]

As you can see the false teachers of John's day tried to explain away the incarnation of Christ by approaching it from opposite ends—one group denied His humanity, the other His deity. John is quick to point out that Christ was both fully God and fully man. Jesus was deity in the garb of humanity; God with skin on. Any teaching that subtracts from Jesus' manhood or His godhood is straight from the forked tongue of the Devil.

People today want to treat Jesus like the Queen of England. The Queen of England is really nothing more than a national dignitary with no real governing power. The Brits let her live in Buckingham palace and they roll out the red carpet and give her due respect at public gatherings, but when it comes down to it she really has no authority. She doesn't make any laws or critical decisions regarding national policy. She's a glorified and pampered mascot; a nostalgic symbol to the faded glory of the British monarchy.

People in our day view Jesus the same way. He is a good moral teacher with excellent values. Most will admit that a historical Jesus appeared in the world, just like they will admit that Alexander the Great was a historical figure, but they will not admit to the fact that God took up residence in a human body. Most will even concede that Jesus had some wonderful teachings and that it was a shame He died a humiliating death. Yet, no skeptic or agnostic is willing to give Christ any authority or say-so in their personal life. Jesus is just one spiritual teacher in a long line of well-meaning, but deluded prophets and preachers.

The only problem is that Jesus never claimed to be just a good man but the God-man (John 8:58). As the classic trilemma states, "Jesus is either

---

3. MacArthur, *The Truth War*, 91.

Learn to Discern (1 John 4:1-6)

a lunatic, a liar, or Lord," but he cannot be just a moral man. John's litmus test for true belief is that one must confess Jesus Christ as the only begotten Son of God, the second person of the trinity, who divested Himself of His privileges, assumed a human nature, was born of a virgin, lived the perfect sinless life, worked miracles, died on the cross as an atoning sacrifice for the sins of the world, was resurrected gloriously three days later, and is the only satisfactory way to the Father in heaven.

In his book, *The Case for the Real Jesus*, journalist and former atheist Lee Strobel gives us a perspective summation of why people resist the real Jesus and search desperately for substitutes:

> The one Jesus that skeptics refuse to tolerate is a uniquely divine, miraculous, prophecy-fulfilling, and resurrected Jesus—even if the evidence points persuasively in that direction. After all, that would put them in the place of being beholden to Him. Their personal sovereignty and moral independence would be at risk. The problem is: *that's* the real Jesus. We are not His equals. We don't occupy the same stratum or possess the same status. He is God, and we're not. For many people that's the crux of their predicament: if Jesus is God incarnate, then He could demand too much. And in fact, He does demand everything . . . That kind of surrender sounds scary for most people. But if Jesus really is God—if He really did sacrifice Himself so that we could be forgiven and set free to experience His love forever—then why would we hesitate to give all of ourselves to Him? Who could be more trustworthy than someone who lays down His life so that others might live?[4]

The second question we must ask when we are testing doctrine is, "*Is it confirmed by the Spirit of God?*" John has written in 4:2, "By this you know the *Spirit of God* . . ." Every believer should be specially tuned into the internal voice of the Holy Spirit. The Holy Spirit acts as a safeguard which keeps doctrine within the parameters of truth. Believers who listen to the Spirit and are acquainted with His voice can discern between what is for real and what is phony. When some spiritual teaching is not right the Holy Spirit will sound off the internal "bologna meter" in your soul.

Jesus refers to the Holy Spirit in John 16:13-14, "When *the Spirit of truth* comes, He will guide you into all the truth, for He will not speak on His own authority, but whatever He hears He will speak, and He will declare to you the things that are to come. He will glorify me . . ." It's the special task of the Holy Spirit to reveal and guide us to the truth. Because

---

4. Strobel, *The Case for the Real Jesus*, 268-269.

the Holy Spirit seeks to glorify Christ then no spirit that is of the Devil will seek to tell the truth about Jesus. The Holy Spirit seeks to put the spotlight on Jesus and any teaching that does not make Jesus the center of attention is not of God.

In contrast to the Holy Spirit, John warns about demonic deception in the form of "the spirit of the antichrist." In its broadest sense "the spirit of the antichrist" is a satanically inspired and energized expression of lawlessness and rebellion against God, the things of God, and the people of God. It's the anti-Christian spirit that works feverishly to oppose, undermine, deny, twist, distort, and reject the truth about Christ.[5]

Have you ever been listening to a preacher and he said something that just didn't sound quite right? After thinking about it you might even begin to feel a little bit uneasy inside. Bells and whistles are going off. Red flags are flying up. That's most likely the Holy Spirit alerting you to the fact that what you just heard is not of God. Even though you may not be alert enough to pick up dangerous spiritual teachings, the Spirit of God is. It's impossible to know everything about every cult and deviant teaching, but if you know right doctrine and are attuned to the Holy Spirit then you will be well equipped for detecting error.

The third question we must ask about our spiritual teacher is *"How do they compare with the Word of God?"* The measuring stick for all true doctrine is not Calvin, Luther, Tozer, MacArthur, Spurgeon, or even Derrick McCarson. It is always the Word of God. As Paul wrote to his young protégé in ministry, "All Scripture is breathed out by God and profitable for teaching, for reproof, for correction, and for training in righteousness" (2 Tim. 3:16).

In order to unpack all that John is saying in this section you'll need to notice the three specific groups of people he addresses—"You" (v.4), "They" (v.5), and "We" (v.6)—that is, believers, the false teachers, and the apostles respectively. In 4:5-6 John contrasts the counterfeit teaching of the false prophets with the authoritative teaching of the apostles.

The false prophets have a message that conforms to the standards of the world. They preach a message that the culture agrees with and that ultimately has its source in Satan (2 Tim. 4:3-4). False prophets always preach an easy message that is agreeable with man's sinful nature. There is no mention of depravity, or the bloody death of Christ, or the need for redemption since this would be offensive to man's pride. With pop-psychology and

---

5. Hitchcock, *Who Is the Antichrist?*, 50.

Learn to Discern (1 John 4:1-6)

self-help sermons, false teachers tickle the ears of their listeners and tell people what they want to hear.

However, God's true prophets preach an undiluted Gospel and are not in the ministry for selfish gain or to win a popularity contest. That is why 4:6 says, "We are from God. Whoever knows God listens to us." In essence, John is saying this: "We, the apostles, were with Jesus for three years—so when we teach you, we are giving you what Jesus gave us—so by way of association when you listen to us, you are listening to God." Ephesians 2:20 reinforces this highlighting that the Church was "built on the foundation of the apostles and prophets, Christ Jesus himself being the cornerstone." Of course we do not have the physical presence of apostles with us today, but we do have them in spirit through their writings. The written Word of God came through the apostles—James, John, Peter, Jude, and Paul—who were guided by the Holy Spirit.

Notice how this process works in harmony with the Spirit of God. The Spirit of God is the internal subjective testimony of truth, while the Word of God is the external objective testimony of truth. The same Holy Spirit who inspired the apostles to pen the Scriptures is the same Holy Spirit who presently illuminates our minds to the truth of God's Word. That is why John writes in 4:4, "You are of God, little children, and have overcome them, *because He who is in you is greater than he who is in the world.*" The one who is "in" us is the Holy Spirit (3:24, 4:2). The Christian does not gain victory over the world by his superior intelligence or because he has done his homework understanding the myriad of cults and false religions (although this might be beneficial). He gains that victory through the Holy Spirit. He puts confidence in the Spirit of God using the Word of God to give understanding of the truth.

Interestingly, one of the Greek names for the Holy Spirit is *paraclete*, which is often translated "Comforter" or "Helper" (John 14:16, 14:26, 15:26, 16:7). The word literally means "one called to the side of another." To have the Holy Spirit as our "Paraclete" is to have God indwelling us as believers encouraging, guiding, teaching, enlightening, and empowering us. The Holy Spirit, because He is God, is greater than Satan who seeks to sabotage our spiritual growth.

This reminds me of a great survivor story. In June of 1992, Jim Davidson and Mike Price climbed Washington's Mt. Ranier. On the way down from the summit, the two climbers fell 80 feet through a snow bridge into a glacial crevasse—a pitch-black, ice-walled crack in the massive glaciers that cover Mt. Ranier. Tragically, Mike Price died.

In his book, *The Ledge*, Jim Davidson tells the story of his miraculous survival and courageous climb out of the crevasse. Throughout the book, Jim reflects back to his childhood and young adult years, describing his relationship with his father.

As early as Jim can remember, his father had shown what some considered an almost reckless confidence in his son. Jim worked for his father painting high, steep-pitched roofs and electrical towers as early as age twelve. The work terrified his mother, but Jim's father kept communicating his belief that Jim could accomplish great things if he pressed through adversity and kept going.

As Jim stood, bloodied and bruised, on the two-foot wide snow ledge next to the body of his climbing partner, he heard the voice of his father. The years of inspiration that Jim's father had invested in him flooded back into his mind and washed over him with encouragement.

With minimal gear and no experience in ice climbing at that level, Jim spent the next five hours climbing out, battling fatigue and the crumbling ice and snow that threatened to bury him. Throughout his ordeal, Jim kept recalling the words of his father. Five grueling hours later, thanks to his father's words, Jim climbed out of the crevasse to safety.[6]

In a similar way, God speaks to us through the Holy Spirit. When we feel like quitting or giving in, The Paraclete revives our beleaguered souls and pushes from the inside when the pressure from the outside seems too great for us to bear. Thank you, Father, for such a wonderful gift!

---

6. Davidson & Vaughan, *The Ledge: An Adventure Story of Survival and Friendship on Mount Rainer*.

14

The Supreme Ethic
(1 John 4:7–21)

IN 1868 A VERY young D.L. Moody let an unknown preacher from England named Henry Moorhouse fill the pulpit of the Chicago church he pastored. Years before while on a crusade in England, Moody and Moorhouse (who was actually an ex-prizefighter) providentially crossed paths. Moorhouse asked Mr. Moody if he would let him preach in his church if he ever came to Chicago. Mr. Moody agreed, thinking he would never have to make good on that pledge, but in time Moorhouse arrived on Moody's doorstep to redeem the pledge. A reluctant Moody surrendered his pulpit, assuring his colleagues that the young man could not do much harm in one night.

As Henry Moorhouse ascended to the pulpit, he announced the sermon text from John 3:16. He preached on the love of God with such passion and power that many hard hearts responded to the message. Every night for the remainder of the week Moorhouse spoke on the topic of God's love.

When Moody returned from his trip he asked his wife how Moorhouse did. She said, "I liked him very much, but he preaches a little differently than you do." "How is that?" asked Moody. "Well," his wife said, "he tells the worst sinners that God loves them." Moody replied, "Well, then, he is wrong." The following Sunday, Moody let Moorhouse preach again so he could hear for himself. Afterward, here is what Moody said of the sermon:

> Moorhouse turned to John 3:16 and preached the most extraordinary sermon from the verse. He went through the whole Bible from Genesis to Revelation, proving that in all ages, God loved the world... Up until that time I never knew that God loves us so

much. That old heart of mine began to thaw out; I could not keep back the tears. He beat the truth down into my heart and I have never doubted it since . . . I used to preach that God was behind the sinner with a double-edged sword, ready to hack him down. But now I realize that God is behind the sinner with his eternal love and that man is running away from the love of God.[1]

The truth of God's love so impacted Moody that he changed his approach to preaching. Afterward, Moody even placed a sign behind his pulpit with the simple declaration, "God is love." Moody became a dynamic evangelist when he began to love people the way that God loved him.

The topic of God's love is a very deep well with no way to plumb its depths. The apostle John has had much to say on the subject of God's love already. No doubt he is called the "apostle of love" because in his three short letters he uses the word "love" over 40 times. When the church father Augustine penned his thoughts about the letter of 1 John he said, "The apostle has spoken many words and nearly all are about love."

John has already pointed out in previous chapters that love is the distinguishing feature of the Christian life. He has taught us that love has both vertical and horizontal dimensions. As a result of responding to God's love, believers reciprocate that same love towards others. Wiersbe insightfully comments on the theme of love throughout 1 John:

> First, love for the brethren has been shown as proof of fellowship with God (1 John 2:7–11); then it has been presented as proof of sonship (1 John 3:10–14). In the earlier passage, love for the brethren is a matter of light or darkness; in the second it is a matter of life or death. But in 1 John 4:7–16 we get down to the very foundation of the matter. Here we discover why love is such an important part of the life that is real. Love is a valid test of our fellowship and our sonship because "God is love." Love is part of the very being and nature of God. If we are united to God through faith in Christ, we share His nature. And since His nature is love, love is the test of the reality of our spiritual life.[2]

In the previous chapters John touched on the tip of the iceberg. Now in 4:7–21, we have come to John's magnum opus on the doctrine of Christian love. This passage begins with God, the source of love, and then moves downward to man where the apostle spells out the specifics of God' love.

---

1. Pollock, *D.L. Moody: Moody without Sankey*, 92.
2. Wiersbe, *The Wiersbe Bible Commentary: New Testament*, 993.

The Supreme Ethic (1 John 4:7–21)

THE DEFINITION OF GOD'S LOVE (4:7-8, 16)

John, the theologian, has taught much about the nature and attributes of God. In John 4:24 we read that "God is spirit." God the Father is an immaterial being, not confined to the constraints of a body, time, or space. In 1 John 1:5 we learn that "God is light." This refers to the holiness of God and his moral purity. God does not have the capacity to sin because there is nothing in His holy nature that can be attracted to sin. The two attributes alone teach us that God is wholly other than His creation, thus when John begins to describe the love of God we should understand the qualitative difference between human love and divine love. God is the origin, fountainhead, and standard of love.

John uses the highest concept in the Greek language—*agapao*—to convey this heavenly brand of love. Notice what John doesn't say here. He doesn't say "love is God." You cannot reverse the word order because if you did then God would be reduced to merely one attribute. If God were merely love then He would become a cosmic teddy bear. There are those who like to overemphasize God's love to the detriment of His other attributes, but we must understand God's love in respect to the rest of His character.

God's love is unconditional, uncaused, unlimited, unending, unstoppable, unchanging, and uncomplicated. Thus, the love of God blends into His other attributes of infinity, eternality, immutability, justice, and so on. A.W. Tozer has written:

> From God's other known attributes we may learn much about His love. We can know, for instance, that because God is self-existent, His love had no beginning; because He is eternal, His love can have no end; because He is infinite, it had no limit; because He is holy, it is the quintessence of all spotless purity; because His is immense, His love is an incomprehensibly vast, bottomless, shoreless sea before which we kneel in joyful silence and from which the loftiest eloquence retreats confused and abashed.[3]

Another important facet of God's love is that it is perfectly communicated in the community of the Trinity. If God were not three-personed then there could be no foundation for love. Since before the creation of the universe God has been in a love relationship with Himself—the Father eternally loves the Son, the Son reciprocates the love of the Father, and the

---

3. Tozer, *The Knowledge of the Holy*, 98.

Holy Spirit in turn adores the Son and the Father. In fact the Gospel of John gives us a sneak peek into the secret inner life of the God-head.

> "The Father loves the Son and has given all things into His hand" (John 3:35).

> "For the Father loves the Son and shows Him all that He Himself is doing" (John 5:20).

> "I do as the Father has commanded me, so that the world may know that I love the Father" (John 14:31).

> "I in them and you in me, that they may become perfectly one, so that the world may know that You sent me and loved them even as You loved me. Father, I desire that they also, whom You have given me, may be with me where I am, to see my glory that You have given me because You loved me before the foundation of the world" (John 17:24).

Christian apologist Norman Geisler helps us understand the profundity of God's love within the Trinity. He explains:

> The Trinity helps us understand how love has existed from all eternity. The New Testament says "God is love." But how can love exist in a rigid monotheistic being? There is no one else to love! Triunity in the Godhead solves the problem. After all to have love, there must be a lover (Father), a loved one (the Son) and a Spirit of love. Because of this triune nature, God has existed eternally in a perfect fellowship of love. He is the perfect being who lacks nothing, not even love![4]

This is an important thought because it means that religions and cults which deny the Trinity have no basis for their god(s) to be discussed as an intrinsically loving being.

God's love helps us understand some of the awe-inspiring things He has done. Why did God create? He didn't do it because He was lonely, for God did not need human beings to be fulfilled. God created out of His own will because He wanted to display His love and glory that came with redeeming the lost.

Why did God make us as free moral agents? God could have made mankind like mindless robots which would automatically worship and serve God, but He didn't. God made man with a free will and the power of choice to love or reject Him. God wanted our love for Him to be a response

---

4. Geisler & Turek, *I Don't Have Enough Faith to Be an Atheist*, 353.

The Supreme Ethic (1 John 4:7–21)

to His love for us, not an arm-twisting coercion. Since forced love is a contradiction, God wanted humans to reciprocate love out of a willing heart.

Why did God send His Son into the world? "For God so loved the world that He gave His only begotten Son . . ." John 3:16 says. God could not love humanity silently from heaven, so He sent His Son in the guise of humanity. God loves each one of us as if there were only one of us to love. The cross proves the extent to which God was willing to go in order to ransom a dying world.

In the same manner, The Father gave believers the gift of the Holy Spirit because He loves us and does not want us to be spiritual orphans (John 14:16–18). The Bible has been called "God's love letter" to humanity, spelling out in sixty-six books His glorious plan of salvation. Like a loving parent, God has carefully preserved His principles for how to live an abundant life. His Word guides us past the dangers, snags, and pitfalls we encounter along life's journey. Heaven will be a place where God's love is ultimately consummated. When we gaze upon Christ for the first time we will have an inkling of God's infinite affection for us.

Karl Barth was probably one of the most prolific theologians of the early twentieth century. The crowning achievement of Dr. Barth was his *Church Dogmatics*, a multi-volume work totaling more than six million words. It is said that when Barth made his only trip to the United States in 1962, a student asked him to summarize the broad-ranging biblical theology he had written in his vast compendium. His audience awaited his reply, expecting to be amazed by the nuggets of truth that would surely fall from the learned man's lips. After a short pause, he said, "Jesus loves me this I know, for the Bible tells me so." In a dozen simple words, Karl Barth, the man who filled reams of paper with theological wisdom, summarized the essence of Christian theology in a way that a child could grasp as easily as a world-class scholar.[5]

The simple truth is that there is nothing you or I could ever do to make God love us any more or any less than He already does. God has a love without motive.

THE DEMONSTRATION OF GOD'S LOVE TO US (4:9–10)

The highest act of love is the giving of the best gift and, if necessary, at the greatest cost to the least deserving. That's what God did when He sacrificed

---

5. Jeremiah, *God Loves You*, 20.

His only Son on the cross for undeserving sinners. John uses the same Greek word from John 3:16 to describe the uniqueness of Christ—*monogenes*. In the classic King James rendering this appears as "only begotten." Literally, the term means, "one-of-a-kind" or "one and only."

God gave the most expensive, valued, and cherished gift in His possession. Paul marveled over this when he wrote, "He who did not spare His own Son, but delivered Him up for us all, how shall He not with Him also freely give us all things?" (Rom. 8:32). John is clear that God took the initiative in sending Christ, ". . . not that we loved God, but that He loved us . . ." This means that true love is willing to take the risk of unrequited affection. God did not wait to see if humanity would love Him before He sent Jesus to the cross. Instead Christ gave Himself, "while we were yet sinners" (Rom. 5:8).

As the Lamb of God, Christ was the once-and-for-all atoning sacrifice for every sin ever committed past, present, and future. John expresses this by using the term *propitiation* for a second time (2:2). Propitiation is a two-part act that involves appeasing the wrath of an offended person and being reconciled to him by way of a gift offering. Mankind's problem is that his relationship with God is utterly broken because of his many transgressions. Because of God's holy hatred of sin, mankind is destined to be an object of God's wrath. However, Christ stepped into man's position on the cross and offered Himself as the perfect offering to turn away God's punishment from man. Therefore, through His son Jesus, God provided the very sacrifice that He demanded. Not only did Christ's death on the cross avert the anger of God, but it provided the basis for us to be reconciled to God. David Jeremiah illustrates the high cost of God's love when he writes:

> Some years ago, before a communion service, I showed a short film clip to illustrate the love of God. It told the story of a farmer and his ten-year-old son who were deeply devoted to each other. The two of them worked side by side on the farm, laughed and played, and spent almost all their time together. The father also had the responsibility of switching the train that passed nearby. Each day he walked to the tracks and pulled the switch that redirected the approaching locomotive to another track. One evening with their farm chores complete, the father and son were fishing in a stream that ran through the farm. When the father heard the distant whistle of the train, he left his son to take care of the track switch. As he walked toward the track, he did not realize that his son had decided to join him. The boy had taken a shortcut

The Supreme Ethic (1 John 4:7-21)

through the woods and was now walking along the tracks to meet his father. The train approached the switching junction moving at high speed, trusting the farmer to switch it to the track that ran straight ahead. Suddenly the farmer saw his son on that track in a place where he could not possibly get off in time. The father's first impulse was to leave the train on its present track. But that track curved away, and the train was moving too fast to negotiate the turn. The father knew that if he switched the train, his boy would die. If he didn't, the train would derail and many people would die. In that moment, the father experienced the most terrible agony imaginable. He had to weigh the life of his son against a railroad of passengers he didn't even know. We sat on the edges of our seats as the film lingered on the father's hand as it gripped the switch. What would he do? The question was not answered. The film concluded right there. But the message was clear: You and I were on that train, and God the Father was at the switch. We know the decision He made.[6]

Perhaps no theologian or gifted writer can better express the love of God than the hymn writer Frederick M. Lehman:

> The love of God is greater far
> Than tongue of pen can ever tell;
> It goes beyond the highest star
> And reaches to the lowest hell.
> Could we with ink the ocean fill,
> And were the skies of parchment made,
> Were every stalk on earth a quill,
> And every man a scribe by trade,
> To write the love of God above,
> Would drain the ocean dry.
> Nor could the scroll contain the whole,
> Though stretched from sky to sky.[7]

THE DEMAND OF GOD'S LOVE ON US (4:11, 20-21)

John argues once again that God's love demands a response. The extent of God's love for us should move us to love others sacrificially and unconditionally. John's argument goes from the lesser to the greater, "... for he who does not love his brother whom he has seen cannot love God whom he has

---

6. Ibid., 127-128.
7. Lehman, "The Love of God," 1917.

not seen." No one who has seen the love of Christ demonstrated on the cross can ever go back to a life of selfishness and hatred. However, if we love only those who have a trace of lovability in them, then we are no different from the world. Jesus preached about raising the bar to another level when it comes to showing love:

> If you love those who love you, what benefit is that to you? For even sinners love those who love them. And if you do good to those who do good to you, what benefit is that to you? For even sinners do the same. And if you lend to those from whom you expect to receive, what credit is that to you? Even sinners lend to sinners, to get back the same amount. But love your enemies, and do good, and lend, expecting nothing in return, and your reward will be great, and you will be sons of the Most High, for He is kind to the ungrateful and the evil. Be merciful, even as your Father is merciful (Luke 6:32–36).

This kind of radical love is impossible and it requires the supernatural love of God in us. In order to love like this we must have a complete revolution in the human heart. God must do open heart surgery and remove our sinful heart and replace with a heart like His which beats passionately for sinners of all shapes, colors, and backgrounds.

Ernest Gordon tells an amazing story in his work *Miracle On The River Kwai* about a band of Scottish soldiers who were forced by their Japanese captors to labor on the infamous Burma Railway during World War II. Under the strain of captivity these beleaguered men had degenerated to barbarous behavior. The hell of war had robbed them of their humanity and turned them into beasts, until one afternoon something tragic happened to change them.

A Japanese guard shouted that one shovel had gone missing and he demanded to know which of the Scotsman had stolen or hidden it. The irate Japanese officer began to rant and rave, working himself up into a paranoid fury and ordered whoever was guilty to step forward. No one moved, "All die! All die!" he shrieked, cocking and aiming his rifle at the prisoners. At that moment one man stepped forward and admitted his guilt. The guard clubbed him to death with the butt of his rifle while the others stood stoically at attention. When the men returned to camp, they buried the body of their fallen comrade, and then the tools were recounted. It was discovered that no shovels were missing.

The Supreme Ethic (1 John 4:7-21)

The word spread like wildfire through the whole camp. An innocent man had been willing to die to save the others! The incident had a profound effect. The men began to treat each other like brothers. When the victorious Allies swept in, the survivors, which were human skeletons by then, were all lined up in front of their captors. Instead of attacking their captors they insisted: "No more hatred. No more killing. Now what we need is forgiveness."

Sacrificial love has transforming power. But we cannot give what we do not have. We can shout from the rooftops, "Jesus Loves You," and preach of God's love until we are blue in the face, but it will not do any good until our love for others is manifested in visible ways.

THE DEVELOPMENT OF GOD'S LOVE IN US (4:12-19)

Learning how to love like Christ doesn't happen overnight. It is the result of a prolonged process of abiding in the love of God. As believers grow in the love of God John identifies three things that happen.

First, *God's love sanctifies us by the Spirit*. John gives another point of application pertaining to the believers' reliance on the Holy Spirit to transform them from the inside-out. John says in 4:13, "By this we know that we abide in Him and He in us, because He has given us of His Spirit." The Holy Spirit is the source of the believer's love and love is one of the precious fruits of the Spirit that should be manifested in our lives (Gal. 5:22). Paul wrote in Romans 5:5, "Now hope does not disappoint, because the love of God has been poured out in our hearts by the Holy Spirit who was given to us."

As the Spirit abides in our heart, God's love has a transforming effect. John writes in 4:12, ". . . God's love abides in us and His love is perfected in us." This does not refer to Christians arriving at sinlessness or achieving a level of moral perfection. Instead, what John has in mind is growing in maturity as we abide in the Spirit. John's logic goes like this: Since God is love, and since the Spirit of God abides in you, and since you abide in God, then the love which comes from God will also come out in you. In other words, God's love sees us grow up from spiritual children into adults.

Second, *God's love secures us in the truth*. As the Spirit dwells in each believer their love for the truth should also increase. That is why John brings up the solid confession of believers in 4:14-16, "And we have seen and testify that the Father has sent His Son to be the Savior of the world. Whoever confesses that Jesus is the Son of God, God abides in him, and he in God." The Holy Spirit is referred to by Jesus Christ as the Spirit of Truth (John 16:13). Among His many job descriptions the Holy Spirit testifies to the truth and glorifies Christ. It makes logical sense then, if the Holy Spirit indwells us, that we would testify to the truth as well and desire to publically profess the Gospel.

Third, *God's love settles our fears.* "Perfect love casts out fear," the apostle tersely encourages us. As we grow in the knowledge and depth of God's love the fears of life melt away under the unrelenting love of God. If God's love for us is more than we can fathom and even extends into our future then we will not fear danger, defeat, death, or damnation.

Because we know that God is watching over us as a loving Father, we can take assurance that His plans and purposes will not be undermined by the events of life. Paul told Timothy, "God has not given us a spirit of fear, but of power and of love and of a sound mind" (2 Tim. 1:7). There is nothing this world can throw at us that can separate us from the love of God (Rom. 8:35–39). Even death, Satan's mightiest weapon against mortals, is rendered ineffective due to Christ's victory. The writer of Hebrews remarks, "Since therefore the children share in flesh and blood, He himself likewise partook of the same things, that through death He might destroy the one who has the power of death, that is, the devil, *and deliver all those who through fear of death were subject to lifelong slavery.*" It's difficult to fear death when you realize that Christ has removed the stinger (1 Cor. 15:55) and He will be there on the threshold of eternity ready with open arms to welcome us into His kingdom.

In the early days of America, a Puritan missionary named John Eliot (1604–1690) came to the frontiers of the New World to evangelize the Indians. Often he was the only white face to be seen in the backwoods where he ministered. Naturally, the Indians were suspicious of him and his motives, thus the preacher received many threats on his life. But whenever he felt endangered by the natives he would tell them in their native tongue, "I am about the work of the great God and my God is with me so that I fear neither you nor all the chiefs of your country. I will go on in my work and you touch me if you dare!" Providentially, Eliot was never harmed during his entire lifetime of ministering to the Native American tribes. What a picture of the knowledge of God's love casting out all fear![8]

Finally John says that believers can have "confidence for the Day of Judgment," because we know that Christ took our punishment and

---

8. Jeremiah, *Living in the Light: Studies in First John*, 116.

judgment on the cross. Romans 8:1 is a good reminder of this, "There is therefore now no condemnation to those who are in Christ Jesus . . ." Perhaps, John had in mind the Judgment Seat of Christ and not the Great White Throne Judgment. The Great White Throne Judgment is for unbelievers who have rejected Christ (Rev. 20:11–15). There standing before Christ as judge, jury, and executioner, all who refused the love of God will be sentenced to eternal separation in the Lake of Fire. Thank God that the Christian will never go to court to be tried as a candidate for hell. His case was settled out of court. Jesus paid the fine when we were flat broke.

However, the Judgment Seat of Christ is for all believers. At the Bema, all Christians will be evaluated on the effectiveness of their life for the Gospel (Rom. 14:10–12, 1 Cor. 3:12–15; 2 Cor. 5:10). There is no punishment at the Bema, only loss or gain of eternal reward. The believer who has practiced love during his earthly life will be able to approach the Judgment Seat of Christ without any shame. By demonstrating the love of God and abiding in the Spirit, we can have confidence that when we stand before Jesus we can hear the sweet words, "Well done my good and faithful servant."

Brennan Manning tells the story of an Irish priest who, on a walking tour of a rural parish, sees an old peasant kneeling by the side of the road, praying. Impressed he says to the man, "You must be very close to God." The peasant looks up from his prayers, thinks a moment, and then smiles. "Yes, he's very fond of me." Indeed, God is very fond of us for "we love because He first loved us" (4:19).

15

We Shall Overcome
(1 John 5:1–5)

WHEN I THINK OF the word "overcomer" there is one name that comes to mind—Nick Vujicic. Nick was born without any arms or legs to Australian parents who loved and served Christ in full-time ministry. Nick candidly speaks about his struggles as a kid under the unrelenting insults from bullies. He even admits his battles with the demon of suicide. Understandably, Nick doubted God's love for him; that was until he read the story of Jesus healing the man born blind (John 9). When he recognized that God had a design for his disability, Nick surrendered his life to Christ.

Even though every day is fraught with hurdles, Nick doesn't let his disabilities define him. One of his most popular YouTube videos shows footage of him skateboarding, surfing, swimming, playing golf, falling down, getting up, and speaking to audiences around the world about the love of God. While many of us would view a life without limbs as a terrible prison, but Nick describes his life as "ridiculously blessed." He writes in his autobiography:

> I am often asked the question: "Nick, how can you be so happy?" You may be dealing with your own challenges, so I'll give you the quick answer up front: I found happiness when I realized that as imperfect as I might be, I am the perfect Nick Vujicic. I am God's creation, designed according to His plan for me. That's not to say there isn't room for improvement. I'm always trying to do better to serve Him and the world! I'm officially *disabled*, but I'm truly *enabled* because of my lack of limbs. My unique challenges have opened up unique opportunities to reach so many people in need

We Shall Overcome (1 John 5:1–5)

... Too often we tell ourselves we aren't smart enough or talented enough to pursue our dreams. We buy into what others say about us, or worse is that when you consider yourself unworthy, you are putting limits on how God can work through you! When you give up on your dreams, you put God in a box. After all you are His creation. He made you for a purpose. Therefore, your life cannot be limited any more than God's love can be contained ... I'm here to tell you that no matter what your circumstances may be, as long as you are breathing, you have a contribution to make.[1]

Words like that help all us with a sound mind and body put our "bad days" into perspective. Nick is a perfect example of what John writes about in 5:4—how faith enables the child of God to overcome the world. John begins chapter five by helping us understand that although the benefits of the victorious Christian life are available to every believer, many of us choose not to enjoy them. Many Christians are content to float to heaven and live just slightly above the level of mediocrity. Why do we live as spiritual paupers when we could live like princes and princesses? I think John would argue that the reason for our lack of vision is because we fail to recognize our distinct standing as blood-bought treasures of Jesus Christ.

According to John, believers in Christ are overcomers—not in themselves or by their own power, but in Jesus and His power. Even though we may lose some minor battles and skirmishes along the way, our ultimate victory is assured in Christ. Not only are we victors in the by-and-by, but also in the nasty now-and-now. Victory is presently available to us and it can be actualized when we tap into it by faith in Christ. The limitless resources of heaven are there and all we simply have to do is take advantage of them. John explains how we can take hold of what God has already secured for us and move from the dumps of defeat to victory.

WE OVERCOME BY PARTAKING IN THE LIFE OF CHRIST (5:1, 4–5)

John uses an important word multiple times in the text which is either translated, "overcome" or "victory." In the original Greek, the word that is used here is *nikao*. You are familiar with this word because you probably own a pair of athletic shoes that bear the brand name Nike. The word has its origins in the athletic competitions of the ancient world in which boxers,

---

1. Vujicic, *Life without Limits*, 2.

sprinters, and wrestlers competed for the glory of a first-place finish. In fact, the Greeks had a goddess named Nike who supposedly helped them defeat their enemies in battle and win the crown in athletics. John, who was writing to a Greek audience in Ephesus, hijacked this concept of being a winner in a conflict and applied it to the Christian life.

So what is an overcomer? Anyone who has been regenerated by the Spirit of God and openly confesses ". . . that Jesus is the Christ is born of God." The mechanism that secures our victory is the gift of faith which transfers our trust from false religion and self-reliance to the sinless Son of God. When believers partake in the new life secured by Christ, old things pass away (2 Cor. 5:17). Those who are born from above are equipped with a new nature, a new set of desires, a new way of thinking, and a new ability to forsake our old sinful habits. As sons and daughters of God we now have His spiritual DNA implanted in us (2 Peter 1:4).

While the text doesn't specifically use the word, the term that is often used to describe the new birth is "regeneration." This is the act whereby God imparts His life to us through the work of the Holy Spirit. Every time that John mentions being "born of God" he has this theological concept in mind. Regeneration is also described in a couple of places in the Gospel of John:

> But to all who did receive Him, who believed in His name, He gave the right to become children of God, who were born, not of blood nor of the will of the flesh nor of the will of man, but of God (John 1:12–13).

> Jesus answered him, "Truly, truly, I say to you, unless one is born again he cannot see the kingdom of God . . . Jesus answered, "Truly, truly, I say to you, unless one is born of water and the Spirit, he cannot enter the kingdom of God" (John 3:3, 5).

Understanding our status as believers is made even more profound when we parallel John's words in 5:4–5 about being an overcomer with Jesus' words from John 16:33, "In the world you will have tribulation. But take heart; *I have overcome the world.*" Don't miss this because there is an important connection between our victory and Christ's victory. It is through the life, death, and resurrection of Jesus that believers can lay claim to ultimate victory through what Christ has already accomplished. This is why Paul is so ecstatic in Romans 8 when he's trying to plumb the depths of Christ's love for us and His conquest over sin:

We Shall Overcome (1 John 5:1-5)

No, in all these things we are *more than conquerors* through him who loved us. For I am sure that neither death nor life, nor angels nor rulers, nor things present nor things to come, nor powers, nor height nor depth, nor anything else in all creation, will be able to separate us from the love of God in Christ Jesus our Lord (Rom. 8:37-39).

Perhaps a pithy illustration will help. I had the privilege of attending the University of North Carolina from 2002-2006. During the 2005 season coach Roy Williams recruited, trained, and led one of the most talented and dominating basketball teams in the history of the school. After a great regular season the team rolled into the post-season with their eyes on a National Championship. "March Madness" was particularly memorable that year because UNC crushed the completion all the way to the Final Four in St. Louis. When the final buzzer sounded, UNC had defeated the Fighting Illini 75-70 and proceeded to cut down the nets.

Meanwhile, in Chapel Hill, celebrations broke out across campus. A sea of students dawned in powder blue descended upon Franklin Street and everyone reveled in the glory of being number one. The next day classes were all but cancelled. The student store sold thousands of championship T-shirts and everyone bought at least a half dozen for themselves and other fans. I saved the front page of *The Daily Tar Heel* which publicized the team's victory and a special edition of *Sports Illustrated* which chronicled the Tar Heels' road to the top. For weeks everyone was on cloud nine because our basketball team trounced the competition. Most importantly we secured bragging rights over our arch rivals, the Duke Blue Devils, whose lair was just eight miles down the road. The campus was electrified with the sense that we knew we were winners.

I mention that because I was the recipient of a victory that I played no part in achieving. I had done nothing to contribute to my school's victory. I hadn't played one single minute of basketball, yet I got to strut around school with a Final Four championship shirt on my back as if I was a sixth man on the team. Simply by carrying around a UNC student ID card I was associated with a team of champions.

In a sense, this is the message that John is trying to convey to believers with respect to the victory secured by Jesus Christ. We had nothing to do with Christ coming to this world, His vicarious death or triumphant resurrection, yet because He demolished our greatest enemies we have assurance that we are forever winners. By placing our faith and trust in Him, we receive the spoils of Christ's victory having not sacrificed anything ourselves. Just reflect on all that Jesus conquered on our behalf:

- Jesus destroyed *the Devil*, "The reason the Son of God appeared was to destroy the works of the devil" (1 John 3:8).
- Jesus defeated *death*, "'Death is swallowed up in victory. O death, where is your victory? O death, where is your sting?' The sting of death is sin, and the power of sin is the law. But thanks be to God, who gives us the victory through our Lord Jesus Christ" (1 Cor. 15:55-57).
- Jesus dismissed our *debt*, "And you, who were dead in your trespasses and the uncircumcision of your flesh, God made alive together with Him, having forgiven us all our trespasses, by canceling the record of debt that stood against us with its legal demands. This He set aside, nailing it to the cross" (Col. 2:13-14).
- Jesus diverted our *destiny*, "Truly, truly, I say to you, whoever hears my word and believes Him who sent me has eternal life. He does not come into judgment, but has passed from death to life" (John 5:24).

There is no place we can tread on this earth that Christ has not already claimed as His. No obstacle is too tall, no challenge is too great, no foe too daunting, and no fear is too demoralizing that it hasn't been dealt with in some way by the victory of Christ. The final outcome has already been decided and all those on Jesus' team win.

WE OVERCOME BY PERFECTING THE LOVE OF CHRIST (5:1-2)

I once saw a bumper sticker that summed up a good portion of John's message to us. It read: "Know Christ, know love. No Christ, no love." John reminds us again that it is impossible to love the Father and not the child who bears His same spiritual features. He argues that we should naturally love fellow believers because they are our brothers and sisters in the family of faith. Once again, John says "love" and not "like." We are not always going to like everyone, but we can love them. The reason is because loving someone is a decision of the will, whereas liking someone is a matter of preference. Love chooses to put the good of the other ahead of our own desires and needs. John Phillips writes:

We Shall Overcome (1 John 5:1–5)

John's statements are interlocking. More yet, they are like the revolving doors in large buildings. Once you get into one of them, it's sometimes hard to get out, especially if the place is busy and each of the compartments in the contraption is full and everybody is in a hurry, and everyone is pushing on the part of the door in front of him. It's possible to go round and round, locked in by the motion . . . That seems to be John's idea here. He wants us to get locked into the endless round of loving God and loving man, loving man and loving God. Round we go in a cycle, which will continue throughout the endless ages of eternity.[2]

Paul instructed the Romans about the liberating effects of love. When his statement in Romans 13:8–10 is paraphrased it goes like this:

> Don't run up debts, except for the huge debt of love you owe each other. When you love others, you complete what the law has been after all along. The law code—don't sleep with another person's spouse, don't take someone's life, don't take what isn't yours, don't always be wanting what you don't have, and any other "don't" you can think of—finally adds up to this: Love other people as well as you do yourself. You can't go wrong when you love others. When you add up everything in the law code, the sum total is love.[3]

Loving others automatically fulfills the requirements of the Law. In other words, when love is supreme then you don't need a rulebook anymore.

Tony Campolo once told the story of Joe, a drunkard who was miraculously converted at a Bowery mission in New York City. Prior to his conversion, Joe had gained the reputation of being a dirty wino for whom there was no hope—only a miserable existence in the ghetto. But following his conversion to a new life with God, everything changed.

Joe became the most caring person that anyone associated with the mission had ever known, doing whatever needed to be done. There was never anything that he was asked to do that he considered beneath him. Whether it was cleaning up the vomit left by some violently sick alcoholic or scrubbing toilets after careless men left the men's facility filthy, Joe did what was asked with a simple smile on his face and a seeming gratitude for the chance to help. He could be counted on to feed the feeble men who wandered off the street into the mission, and to undress and tuck into bed men who were too out of it to take care of themselves.

---

2. Phillips, *Exploring the Epistles of John*, 158–159.
3. Eugene Peterson, *The Message*, Rom. 13:8–10.

Living in the Light

One evening, when the director of the mission was delivering his evening evangelistic message to the usual crowd of still and sullen men with drooped heads, there was one man who looked up, came down the aisle to the altar, and knelt to pray, crying out for God to help him change. The repentant drunk kept shouting, "Oh God! Make me like Joe! Make me like Joe! Make me like Joe!"

The director of the mission leaned over and said to the man, "Son, I think it would be better if you prayed, 'Make me like Jesus.'" The man looked up at the director with a quizzical expression on his face and asked, "Is He like Joe?"[4]

There is no substitute for the love of God. Not only does it transform us, but it reaches out to those starved for love. It is the greatest magnet to draw in sinners to the Savior.

WE OVERCOME BY PRACTICING THE LAW OF CHRIST (5:2-3)

The three-fold cord of truth, love, and obedience once again emerges. It has been the scarlet thread which weaves its way in and out of the tapestry of 1 John. Truth—"believing that Jesus is the Christ;" love—"loving the children of God;" and obedience—"keeping His commandments," are the tests by which we stay in the fellowship of God both doctrinally and morally.

Finally, John touches again on the necessity of obedience. John says that the inward sign of our love for God is shown by the outward obedience to His commandments. There is nothing new here. John has already talked about this in 2:4 and 3:22. John is once again restating Jesus' command in John 14:15, "If you love me, you will keep my commands."

However, this time there is a little nuance at the end of 5:3, ". . . His commands are not burdensome." That word "burdensome" carries the thought of heavy, weighed down, grievous, oppressive, troublesome, or stern. Perhaps, John had in mind the suffocating demands of legalism which epitomized the duty-bound Pharisees. As the custodians of the Law, the Pharisees invented 613 laws in an attempt to not break any of God's original commandments. The result was the tedious, hair-splitting religion of memorizing man-made rules and dragging around the ball-and-chain of traditions. For example, if the Pharisees were alive today, they would probably prohibit the opening of the refrigerator door on the Sabbath. Why?

---

4. Gray, *More Stories for the Heart*, 29.

We Shall Overcome (1 John 5:1–5)

Because by opening the door, that would inadvertently trigger the light inside, thus "kindling a fire" which would constitute an act of work. That's burdensome!

However, the law of Christ is not merely tethered to duty, but it flows out of a relationship of love. For the believer, it's not so much that obeying Christ is a "have to" but a "want to." There is an added incentive for you and me when we are obedient to the Word of God. The commandments of Christ are there to protect us from danger and maximize joy in our lives. Think about it—God is the author of life and because God loves us He is not going to give us commands that rob us of life, but He gives us commands to enhance the quality of life. God has our best interest in mind. In this way, His commands are not burdensome, but a blessing.

Remember the scene when Jesus performed His first miracle at the wedding festival in Cana (John 2:1–11)? If you will recall, when Jesus agreed to deal with the embarrassing shortage of wine, Mary gave a simple command to the servants, "Do whatever He tells you." The servants then followed what must have been a strange request by Jesus, "Take six water pots and fill them with water." In unquestioned obedience the servants filled the jars to the brim. Jesus miraculously sped up the fermentation process from six months to six seconds. The servants didn't fully understand, but their simple obedience was rewarded with hundreds of gallons of the sweetest wine any of them had ever tasted. This lesson is simply this: a brimful of obedience equals a brimful of blessings.

I am reminded of the old story told about the American Civil War veteran who used to wander from place to place begging for a bed for the night and a bite to eat. No matter where his travels took him, he always talked about his friend, Mr. Lincoln. Because of his serious injuries, he was unable to hold a steady job, but as long as he could keep going he would chat about his beloved president. "You say you knew Mr. Lincoln," a skeptical bystander retorted one day. "I'm not so sure you did. Prove it!" the cynic badgered.

Well, the old soldier had his wits about him and replied, "Why sure I can prove it. In fact, I have a piece of paper here that Mr. Lincoln himself signed and gave to me." From his old tattered wallet, the beggar took out a much-folded piece of paper and showed it to the inquisitive man. "I never learned how to read," the old man apologized, "but I know that's Mr. Lincoln's signature."

"Man, you don't have a clue what you have here, do you?" the other man said. "Huh? What do you mean?" the old soldier grunted. "You have a generous federal pension authorized by President Lincoln. You don't have to walk around like a poor tramp living on scraps in the garbage cans. Mr. Lincoln has made you rich and you didn't even know it!"

Because of Jesus Christ, we Christians don't have to walk around defeated. Our Lord has made us victors in every area. He has felled every enemy and equipped us with the tools needed to live like an overcomer.

16

How to Be Absolutely Sure
(1 John 5:6–13)

IN 1853 A MODERN marvel of human ingenuity was unveiled to the world. E. G. Otis invented the first passenger elevator safe enough for widespread public use. However, Otis had a peculiar problem. The visionary innovator could not find any buildings that were willing to buy his elevator design because the public perception was that elevators were unsafe and liable to come crashing down.

Unable to sell his elevators, Otis decided to demonstrate to the world how safe they were. In 1854 he took his invention to the Crystal Palace Exhibition in New York City. There, he set up an exhibit of his elevators in which the shaft was open and it would allow people to view the mechanics of the elevator.

Crowds watched as Otis rode his elevator up and down. When the elevator was up several flights, he had an assistant cut the cable that was holding the elevator up. Onlookers gasped, and waited for the inventor to end up buried under a twisted heap of metal on the exhibition floor. Instead, there was Mr. Otis still high in the air, bowing and waving to his stunned audience.

The secret to his success was a simple spring mechanism that when released would propel metal bars into the sides of the elevator shaft, thus bringing it to a safe halt. While, Otis did not actually invent the first elevator, his patented brake system was enough to convince the general public that taking the "lift" was better than huffing and panting up flights of stairs. Now that the public perception of elevators had changed, Otis' little company couldn't make elevators fast enough. Perhaps more than any other man, E. G. Otis made the modern skyscraper possible.

That story highlights a basic need in the human psyche—assurance. Man has a deeply rooted requirement for security and certainty. How many of us would board an airplane if we thought there might be a ten-percent chance it would crash? Why do our children demand that we leave a nightlight in the hallway on for them when we tuck them into bed? Why is it that I nervously grab hold of my wallet when I'm walking down a crowded street? Doubt, suspicion, and uncertainty are paralyzing feelings that can rob us from enjoying something of great benefit.

If there is one thing that can erode away a believer's confidence faster than anything else it's a lack of assurance. There are many Christians who are stymied in their spiritual walk because they are constantly tortured by nagging questions. Questions like: "How do I know that I am saved?" or "How can I be sure that I won't lose my salvation?" or "I think I prayed and accepted Jesus when I was a kid, but now I'm not sure?" This is why you can have people walking down the aisle multiple times professing salvation in Jesus.

D.L. Moody once said, "I've never met anybody who was any good to the service of Christ who first of all did not have the assurance of his or her salvation." Adrian Rogers, talking about salvation added, "If you could have it and not know it, then you could lose it and not miss it. But the truth of the matter is, if you do have it, you will know it. And if you have it and know it, you can never lose it." I have heard that when it comes to salvation and assurance, there are three groups of people: those who are secure but not sure, those who are sure but not secure, and those who are secure and sure.

The apostle John is concerned about of our level of certainty with regards to salvation. If the Gospel of John was written to tell us how to be saved (John 20:30–31), then the epistle of 1 John was written to tell us how to know that we are saved (1 John 5:13). In the passage before us, John is going to help us know that our faith is built on facts and that we can know beyond a shadow of a doubt that we are saved.

CERTAINTY BY THE ATONING WORK OF THE SON (5:6)

There is perhaps no other figure in all of history who is as scrutinized, maligned, or beloved as much as Jesus Christ. Hate Him or love Him, you cannot ignore Him. No one really knows quite what to do with Jesus. He defies

How to Be Absolutely Sure (1 John 5:6–13)

all of our neat conventions and cannot be neatly placed into a polished box. Philip Yancey reflects on the various interpretations of Jesus when he writes:

> If you peruse the academic books available at a seminary bookstore you may encounter Jesus as a political revolutionary, as a magician who married Mary Magdalene, as a Galilean charismatic, a rabbi, a peasant Jewish cynic, a Pharisee, an anti-Pharisee Essene, an eschatological prophet, a hippie in a world of Augustan yuppies, and as the hallucinogenic leader of a sacred mushroom cult.[1]

These same wild and fluctuating opinions about the true identity of Jesus were floating around in the first century as well. John steps in as the voice of reason to try and quell the spurious claims of heretical groups trying to project their ideas on Christ. In the previous verses (5:1–5), the emphasis of John's argument is placed on being "born of God" by trusting in Jesus as God's Son. His train of thought continues and now he deals with a follow-up question, "How do we know that Jesus is God's Son?" John brings to the witness stand several testimonies which he believes will vouch for the authenticity of Christ. The apostle doesn't want believers to doubt their salvation because they have trusted in some phony-bologna Jesus.

John begins by using a peculiar phrase, "blood and water." Then again in verses 5:7–8 he adds that "there are three that testify the Spirit and water and blood and they agree as one." We can see that John is reverting back to the Old Testament tradition by introducing these witnesses. Since the days of Moses it was God's established rule was that if an event was going to be credible then it would need the backing of two or three witnesses who could testify to the truth (Deut. 19:15).

While there is much speculation on their meaning, I believe the "blood and water" refers to two distinct moments in the ministry of Jesus—the beginning and the end. The water refers to Jesus' baptism and the blood refers to Jesus' crucifixion. So what do these events have to do with giving us assurance of salvation? In both cases, Jesus was validated by the testimony of God and other reliable witnesses to be the unique Son of God.

First, let's consider *the water of His baptism*. It was at Jesus' baptism that He was publically identified to the nation of Israel as God's beloved Son. When John the Baptist saw Him coming from afar he said, "Behold the Lamb of God who takes away the sin of the world" (John 1:29). The baptism can be thought of as Jesus' "coming out" event as He made a splash

---

1. Yancey, *The Jesus I Never Knew*, 19.

Living in the Light

on the public scene. When John dunked Jesus under the water, Matthew tells us that the heavens opened up and the audible voice of the Father was heard, "This is my beloved Son in whom I am well pleased" (Matt. 3:13–17). In that glorious moment, Jesus was anointed by the Holy Spirit, who descended upon Him in the form of a dove. All members of the Trinity were acting in concert. John 1:32–34 describes the scene like this:

> And John bore witness: "I saw the Spirit descend from heaven like a dove, and it remained on Him. I myself did not know Him, but He who sent me to baptize with water said to me, 'He on whom you see the Spirit descend and remain, this is He who baptizes with the Holy Spirit.' And I have seen and have borne witness that this is the Son of God."

In that scene we have a human witness in John, the audible voice of the Father and the Holy Spirit—three credible witnesses all saying the same thing, "Jesus is the unique Son of God." Since Jesus was perfectly approved by the other members of the Godhead then He was qualified to be an all sufficient sacrifice when it came time for Him to carry the cross up to Golgotha.

Second, let's ponder *the blood of His cross*. If we go back to John 19:33–34 we see the specific event which triggered John's memory as he penned this thought in the epistle. "But when they came to Jesus and saw that He was already dead, they did not break His legs. But one of the soldiers pierced His side with a spear, and at once there came out blood and water."

John makes the point that Jesus came "by water and blood, not by water only." Why is this important? Remember that at this time John is combating the Gnostics who were teaching false doctrines about Christ. One heresy among the Gnostics was the idea that a special, divine anointing came upon Jesus at His baptism but left Him before He died. John is putting an end to all of that nonsense by saying, "No, the entire ministry of Jesus was perfectly planned and authorized by God, including His death."

Just as in the baptism of Christ, the death of Christ was also authenticated by supernatural acts. Matthew 27 records that while Jesus was on the cross a trio of unexplained events converged which pointed to the fact that the man dying between the two thieves was no common rabble-rouser. There was darkness in the middle of the day from 12:00 to 3:00 PM (Matt. 27:45). Then the veil in the temple was rent in two from top to bottom (Matt. 27:51). This showed that the temple sacrificial system was no longer needed because the ultimate sacrifice was given and man could now have

How to Be Absolutely Sure (1 John 5:6–13)

direct access to God. To add to the eeriness, there was an earthquake which caused the tombs around Jerusalem to split open (Matt. 27:51–53). As Jesus took His final breaths, the Roman Centurion at the foot of the cross said, "Truly, this is the Son of God" (Matt. 27:54). It is fascinating that at both ends of Jesus' ministry you have human witnesses attesting to His deity (John the Baptist and the Roman centurion)—one Jewish and the other Gentile.

Now let's bring this back to our assurance of salvation. What John is getting at here is the credibility of Jesus Christ. We can know that we are saved because of Jesus in whom we have believed. If Jesus would not have been the all-sufficient Savior then we could have no hope of salvation. His death would have been in vain. However, Jesus lived the perfect life of obedience to the Father which was evidenced at His baptism. Then His death on the cross was also divinely affirmed by signs and wonders. Therefore, Jesus' perfect life and His sacrificial death satisfied the demands of God in every way. Our salvation is complete because the Father and the Spirit put their stamps of approval on the Son's ministry.

I once read a story about Michelangelo, the great renaissance artist. Michelangelo was known to never sign any of his great works of art. In his pride he thought that his genius was so recognizable that anyone could look at one of his sculptures and know immediately that he had done it. However, after he finished a sculpture of Mary and Jesus called *the Pieta*, Michelangelo was walking by it and he overheard a peasant attributing his work to another artist. He became so enraged that his work was confused with an inferior artist that he snuck into the cathedral under the cover of darkness and etched his name on the sculpture so there would be no doubt whose work it was.

God the Father has uniquely put his signature on His Son so that there would be no confusion that He was indeed the Savior of the world.

THE ABIDING WITNESS OF THE SPIRIT (5:7–8)

Another character witness that John calls to testify is the Holy Spirit. If Jesus Christ is the superstar then the Holy Spirit is His promoter. Not only does the Spirit make Christ known, but the Spirit also makes it known to us that we belong to Christ (Rom. 8:16). Wiersbe has written, "We were not present at the baptism of Christ or at His death, but the Holy Spirit was present. The Holy Spirit is the only person active on earth today who was present when Christ was ministering here. The witness of the Father is past history, but the witness of the Spirit is present experience. The first is external, the second is internal—and both agree."[2]

Before we are saved the job of the Holy Spirit is to act as the prosecuting attorney which presents the evidence of our guilt and then points us in the direction of Jesus Christ. Jesus said, "But when the Helper comes, whom I will send to you from the Father, the Spirit of truth, who proceeds from the Father, He will bear witness about me" (John 15:26). In John 16:8–9 Jesus added, "And when He comes, He will convict the world concerning sin and righteousness and judgment: concerning sin, because they do not believe in me . . ."

Before we are saved we must first be convinced that we are lost. The Holy Spirit's ministry of conviction is underrated and oft-resisted. His gentle pricks slowly crack and fracture the tough veneer of sin that has encased our hearts.

When I was a kid I remember getting pink dye tablets from the dentist. After we brushed our teeth we would chew up those tablets and the pink dye would stick to the plaque and other places that were still dirty. The pink dye showed how much we missed trying to clean our teeth by our own effort. The Holy Spirit is our pink dye. He gets deep in your life and points out all the places where there is sin and dirt so that you will be convinced to turn to the blood of Jesus which cleanses us from all sin. Consequently, one way we know that we are saved is if we have become sensitive to the promptings of the Spirit over sin issues. I like the way John Phillips summarizes John's three-fold witness:

> Many a time I have stood at Niagara Falls and watched the endless flow of water pouring over the precipice and down into the yawning gulf below. Every minute, thirty-five million gallons of water fall with a thunderous roar 180 feet into the gorge, sending up voluminous clouds of spray. On the Canadian side of the falls, it's possible to descend a shaft and then proceed along a tunnel to a ledge behind the falls. All around the water thunders down, so it is no place to make a speech or conduct a conversation. The Indians who inhabited Niagara long before the advent of the white man actually called it the Place of Thundering Waters. Niagara, then can be likened to God's answer to all our foes—let them try to make themselves heard in the face of the united thundering voices of the Father, Son, and Holy Spirit.[3]

2. Wiersbe, *The Wiersbe Bible Commentary: New Testament*, 1003.
3. John Phillips, *Exploring the Epistles of John*, 165.

THE AUTHORITATIVE WORD OF THE SCRIPTURES (5:9–12)

The final affirmation of salvation comes from the witness of the Word. The believer has two ways to verify his salvation. Not only the internal subjective witness of the Spirit but the external objective Word of God. John says that the ultimate and final authority in bringing assurance to the heart and mind of the believer comes from the written testimony that God has given. Follow his logic as it moves from the lesser to the greater. If you trust the testimony of a mortal, finite man, then surely you will trust the testimony of immortal, infinite God. In other words, if you read a science book and believe in the existence of invisible subatomic particles, then you should have no problem accepting what God has said because His testimony is perfect and inerrant. God's revelation to man is contained in the Bible. So in effect, when we trust the Bible, which God wrote through the pen of the apostles and prophets, then we accept the testimony of God.

Skeptics say, "Yeah, but God used men to write the Bible so it cannot be trusted." To that I say, "If every year the Yellow Book can produce an accurate record of everyone's phone numbers, then why can't God accurately record history?" Just because God used fallible men to record His Word, it doesn't follow that the product is also fallible. God can write straight with a crooked stick. Moreover, the Bible is attested to be the most trustworthy and accurate source from antiquity with more archaeological support and more manuscript evidence than any other ancient text. The veracity of the Bible is proven when skeptics like Frank Morrison, Josh McDowell, and Lee Strobel come along and try to disprove the resurrection of Christ only to be converted under the weight of evidence in favor of the empty tomb.

John ends by reinforcing the exclusivity of the Gospel in 5:12, "He who has the Son has life, whoever does not have the Son of God does not have life." Jesus is the litmus test for true spirituality. In our pluralistic culture, Christians are often reviled in the public square for being narrow-minded and arrogant because we confess unapologetically that Christ is the only way to heaven (John 14:6). However, truth is not determined by feelings, sincerity, majority vote, or public opinion. The religions of the world all hold mutually exclusive beliefs at their core. Just look at the three major worldviews: atheism says "No God at all," pantheism says "God is all," and theism says, "God made all." Likewise, they all say different things about Jesus. There is no way all these contradictory claims can be right.

Living in the Light

What makes Jesus unique? First, Jesus lived a perfect, sinless life (Heb. 4:15). Examine the founders of world religions and you will not find anyone who can stand in the same league with Jesus in terms of moral purity. Joseph Smith was a polygamist who died in a gunfight trying to break out of prison. Muhammad, also a polygamist, waged several bloody wars and beheaded many Jews and Christians on his way to building a "religion of peace." Jesus challenged His greatest critics to accuse Him of one sin, but all turned away in disgust (John 8:46). Instead of taking life, Jesus gave His life out of love (John 3:16).

Second, Jesus proved His audacious claims to be God by performing many signs and wonders (John 20:30–31). By healing the sick, raising the dead, and restoring sight to the blind, Jesus gave us a model of compassion and love that had never been seen before or since. His mighty miracles are unparalleled by other religious gurus. Neither Buddha nor Muhammad ever claimed to be God or forgave sins. Likewise, their claims to be religious authorities were never substantiated by reaching out to a leper and causing his spots to leave instantly.

Third, Jesus fulfilled prophecies. Only Jesus met the messianic profile described by the Old Testament prophets. During His life, Jesus fulfilled hundreds of prophecies spoken about Him hundreds of years in advance. The prophets foretold His lineage from Abraham and the house of David (Gen. 12:3, 7, 49:10, Jer. 23:5–6, 2 Sam. 7:16), the sight of His birthplace in Bethlehem (Micah 5:2), His virgin birth (Is. 7:14), the year of His death in 30 AD (Dan. 9:26), His brutal crucifixion (Ps. 22, Is. 53), and His resurrection (Ps. 16:10). There is no way anyone could engineer their life in such a way to meet these strict predictions unless, of course, they were the eternal God invading our time and space.

Finally, Jesus alone conquered death. The risen Jesus appeared to over 500 eyewitnesses, on twelve separate occasions, over a period of forty days (1 Cor. 15:3–8). His resurrection led to the conversion of hardened skeptics like Thomas, Paul, and James and gave the scared disciples the courage they needed to preach the Gospel without fear. If the resurrection were a grand hoax then the Church would not have ever made it out of the first century. Yet, every Easter the skeptics are still rolling out new speculations trying to explain away the empty tomb. Meanwhile, every other religious founder is cold in the ground and faithful pilgrims journey to pay their respects to their tombs. However, Jesus' tomb is vacant. Indeed, he who has the Son has life!

How to Be Absolutely Sure (1 John 5:6–13)

    As we close this chapter I am reminded of the believer's untouchable security in Christ. Some Christians believe that it is possible to lose their salvation due to sin or apostasy. However, think about it like this—since there is nothing you can do to gain your salvation then there is nothing that you can do to lose your salvation. Eternal life is a free gift with no strings attached. Our salvation is dependent upon Christ keeping hold of us, not on us keeping hold of Him. Jesus promised, "I give them eternal life, and they will never perish, and no one will snatch them out of my hand. My Father, who has given them to me, is greater than all, and no one is able to snatch them out of the Father's hand" (John 10:28–29).

    There is a great scene from one of the old Superman movies which illustrates this. Superman rescues a man from a burning building by picking him up off the top of a roof. As they are flying through the air to safety, the man looks at Superman and then looks down to the ground. He says, "I'm scared Superman! Look how far down it is!" Superman gives him the greatest answer: "Now if I delivered you from the burning fire, what makes you think I'm going to drop you while carrying you to safety?" The same is true of Christ. We are secure in Him.

17

Living Above the Level of Mediocrity (1 John 5:13-21)

SEVERAL YEARS AGO A man was browsing around a flea market in Adamstown, Pennsylvania. Walking through the tables and booths, he was suddenly attracted to a painting of a pastoral landscape in an ornate, gilded frame. After negotiating the price down with the seller, the man walked out of the flea market with a four dollar picture frame. Back at his home the man took the frame and set it in his garage. There it stayed for several months collecting dust and all but being forgotten.

One day the man was doing some spring cleaning and found the four dollar picture frame that he bought years ago at the flea market. As he began to clean the frame he removed the old torn painting in the frame and found a folded document between the canvas and the wood backing. He took the folded parchment out and could hardly believe his eyes. What he found inside the frame turned out to be a 1776 copy of the Declaration of Independence—one of 24 known to remain. On June 13, 1991, it was sold at an auction for $2.4 million.[1]

Unbelievable! The man was an accidental millionaire and didn't know it! By his own dumb luck he stumbled onto a priceless piece of history disguised as a dusty family heirloom. That story reminds me that there are many Christians who are living the same way. They possess something of eternal value, yet they are largely ignorant of its true worth. I find that many

---

1. Reif, "Declaration of Independence Found in $4 Picture Frame, Online: <http://www.nytimes.com/1991/04/03/arts/declaration-of-independence-found-in-a-4-picture-frame.html>.

Living Above the Level of Mediocrity (1 John 5:13-21)

believers are living just above the level of mediocrity when they could have abundant life now. Most are content to simply float through a hum-drum life until they get to heaven. The Church has simply become eternity's waiting room. All the joy and zeal of the Christian life was sapped out of them long ago; now all that remains is empty routine and spiritual slumber.

Call me gullible or a holy-roller, but it seems to me that it's impossible to have Jesus Christ and live like Eeyore. Read through the Gospels and you'll notice that life with Jesus was anything but ordinary. Walking in fellowship with Christ promises adventure, hair-pin turns, brushes with danger, and deep personal transformation.

For five chapters John has been writing about how believers can maximize their intimacy with God. The apostle has given us several tests to tell us how well we are doing. Do we love one another? Are we abiding in the truth? Are we living in obedience to the commands of Christ? John's three-fold test for fellowship has centered on right belief and right behavior.

In the last section of his epistle, John has been focused on living the victorious Christian life, namely by overcoming the world (5:1–5) and having assurance of eternal life (5:6–12). The apostle doesn't want us to be content with our four dollar experience with God when lying just below the surface is a wealth of spiritual treasure. John wants us to have the full-orbed experience of the Christian life that comes through intimacy with Christ.

In the final passage of 1 John, the apostle concludes by giving us four certainties that every believer can build their life upon. These guarantees are intended to help believers live as victorious overcomers.

CERTAINTY OF ETERNAL LIFE (5:13)

In December of 2011 the world saw the death of Christopher Hitchens, a prominent writer, speaker, and outspoken atheist. Hitchens was not just an atheist; more like an anti-theist, as well as anti-religion. He argued in his book, *God Is Not Great*, that religion is tantamount to brainwashing and it poisons everything in human society. Even as he neared death, he did not change his mind about God or the possibility of life after death. In one of his last debates Hitchens spoke of death when he said, "It will happen to all of us that at some point, you get tapped on the shoulder and told not just that the party's over, but slightly worse: The party's going on, but you have to leave."

Living in the Light

Believers in Jesus Christ have a different point of view. However much we may enjoy this life, we believe that when we leave this earth we are actually going to the party that will never end. How do we know? Because we have unchanging promises from Christ Himself:

> "For God so loved the world, that He gave His only Son, that whoever believes in Him *should not perish but have eternal life*" (John 3:16).

> "Truly, truly, I say to you, whoever hears my word and believes Him who sent me *has eternal life*. He does not come into judgment, but has passed from death to life" (John 5:24).

> "For this is the will of my Father, that *everyone who looks on the Son and believes in Him should have eternal life*, and I will raise Him up on the last day" (John 6:40).

> "I am the resurrection and the life. Whoever believes in me, though he die, yet shall he live, and *everyone who lives and believes in me shall never die*" (John 11:25–26).

The statement in 5:13 is one of the four purpose statements in this letter (1:4, 2:2, 2:26). John wants us to have complete assurance that we are eternally secure in Jesus. According to John we can have assurance of our salvation when we maintain close fellowship with Christ by resting in the knowledge of God's word (5:6–9), listening to the internal witness of the Holy Spirit (3:24), keeping the commandments of Christ (2:5–6), not conforming to the world (2:15), loving the brethren (4:7), and believing the truth (4:1).

Faith is merely taking God at His word and trusting the truth claims of God, especially when it comes to what He says about eternal life. This is where Christianity takes a radically different departure from the cults and religions of the world. Christianity is not a "hope so" religion where we hitch our never-dying soul to the cart of good works and are expected to pull our own weight to earn our salvation. Christianity is built on the solid, immovable promises of God which are sturdier than the bedrock under our feet.

Ergun Caner was a devout, practicing Muslim until a concerned friend began relentlessly witnessing to him about Jesus Christ. Finally, young Ergun attended a church service with his Christian friend. After hearing the simple Gospel message and seeing the love of believers for him, Ergun gave his life to Jesus Christ. In his book, *Unveiling Islam,* Caner talks about the oppressive demands that Islam forces on its followers:

> The ultimate question in any religion addresses an eternal life after death: "What must I do to go to heaven?" In Islam, the answer to this question remains as mysterious and complex as was the founder of its religion, Muhammad . . . the Qur'an hints that the believer in Allah can be confident of his or her eternal destiny, but there is no guarantee, even for the most righteous. So Muslims strive mightily to get to paradise, but they continually fear that Allah will judge their arrogance and send them to hell . . . Muslims believe that each person must be 51 percent good. Therefore, those who know they have lived a life of misery and shame have no hope of heaven if they are nearing death. Accordingly, they live in despair and destruction, for they can only expect hell. The divine balance scale is the ultimate demonstration of precise mathematical judgment. Each person is literally accountable for each act performed. Consequently, the scales become more important as one approaches the end of life, especially for those on the edge. They have to work harder, live better, and give more. Then, they can hope, the scales will tip in their favor . . . In Islam, you place your hope in good works, trying to please Allah more than you offend him . . . In Islam sin is not paid for, it is weighted on a balance scale.[2]

Imagine going through your whole life trying to please God never knowing when enough was enough and ultimately not knowing where you would go when you die! Yet, this is the plight of millions of sincere Muslims, Hindus, Mormons, Buddhists, and "spiritual people." Ultimately, this leads to a life of insurmountable fear and nagging uncertainty. However, God's perfect love casts out all fear (1 John 4:18). We can be assured that our salvation in Christ is signed, sealed, and delivered.

F.B. Meyer once wrote about two Germans who wanted to climb the Matterhorn. They hired three guides and began their ascent at the steepest and most slippery part. The men roped themselves together in this order: guide, traveler, guide, traveler, guide. They had gone only a little way up the side when the last man lost his footing. He was held up temporarily by the other four, because each had a toehold in the niches they had cut in the ice. But then the next man slipped, and he pulled down the two above him. The only one to stand firm was the first guide, who had driven a spike deep

---

2. Caner & Caner, *Unveiling Islam*, 142–151.

into the ice. Because he held his ground, all the men beneath him regained their footing. F.B. Meyer concluded his story by drawing a spiritual application. He said, "I am like one of those men who slipped, but thank God, I am bound in a living partnership to Christ. And because He stands, I will never perish."

CONFIDENCE IN PRAYER (5:14-17)

If you are like me, you've used the excuse more than once, "I don't have the time to pray." However, if I go for too long without spending time in prayer I begin to notice a real disconnect in my spiritual life. Suddenly, I find myself getting impatient, my words can be sharp and critical and the cares of everyday life consume my joy. The truth is I can't afford not to pray, because when I'm alone with God my soul is refreshed, my sins are confessed, and my perspective gets corrected. Oswald Chambers added his insight:

> Remember no one has time to pray; we have to take time from other things that are valuable in order to understand how necessary prayer is. The things that act like thorns and stings in our personal lives will go away instantly when we pray; we won't feel the smart anymore, because we have God's point of view about them. Prayer means that we get into union with God's view of other people.[3]

John reminds us that believers who stay intimate with Jesus can go into the prayer room with boldness and confidence, knowing that when we ask of God we will get an answer. The writer in Hebrews said, "Let us then with confidence draw near to the throne of grace, that we may receive mercy and find grace to help in time of need" (Heb. 4:16). However, it is critical to take note of the condition that John places on prayer, "... *if we ask according to His will* He hears us." In other words, there are many prayers that don't get any higher than the ceiling because they fall outside of God's will.

Over the years I have saved the artwork that my niece, Grace, has done for me. I have a drawer at home that is filled with pages that she colored from a coloring book and gave to me. Some of the pages that she did as a small girl are quite humorous. Two things give me a chuckle when I look at her earliest colorings: First, many of the colors that she chose were inappropriate. It's common to see pink hair and purple elephants and blue grass

---

3. Chambers, *Prayer*, 97.

Living Above the Level of Mediocrity (1 John 5:13-21)

in those early works. Second, like all kids learning how to color, often her crayons got outside the lines. However, as she matured her coloring progressed. Now every time I see some of her work hanging on the refrigerator I think to myself, "Wow, I don't even think I could color that well."

As I look at those pages, I thought that often our prayer lives resemble a kid's coloring book. At first, we don't know what to pray for, nor do our prayers stay within the guidelines of God's will. However, as we mature in the faith and continue praying, our praying gets better with practice.

Praying in God's will means that you are asking for the right things, in the right way, for the right reasons. It's not praying out of our greed but out of our need. We can know the will of God in prayer by knowing His word. If we ask for something that is in violation of His word then we can expect for our request to be rejected.

John also addresses an oft-neglected aspect of prayer—intercession. In 5:16-17 John is dealing with a special case in which believers can pray for a backslidden brother or sister. He refers to this situation as "the sin that does not lead to death." If a Christian sees a brother or sister caught in sin, he should pray for them, imploring that they would turn from their wayward path, repent, and confess their sins to God. This happened in the case of Peter. On the night of His arrest, Jesus turned to prideful Peter and said, "Simon, Simon, behold, Satan demanded to have you, that he might sift you like wheat, but I have prayed for you that your faith may not fail. And when you have turned again, strengthen your brothers" (Luke 22:31-32). While Peter stumbled, denying the Lord three times, he eventually was restored and God used him greatly.

Paul also referred to the ministry of restoration in Gal. 6:1, "Brothers, if anyone is caught in any transgression, you who are spiritual should restore him in a spirit of gentleness." James 5:14-20 is another parallel to what John is talking about. James described a believer who had fallen ill because of his sin. As a result of his straying, God sent divine correction in the form of sickness. When the sickly saint confessed his sins and the prayer of faith was offered by elders in the church, his health was restored.

In these instances of intervention we learn that Christians should be like the U.S. Marines. We leave no fallen comrades behind. This intercession is effective only in the case of sin not leading to death—that is, the person has not reached the end limits of God's patience and grace.

However, John also issued a strong warning about calloused believers whose sinning put them on a collision course with premature death. John

Living in the Light

writes at the end of 5:16 about the mysterious "sin that leads to death." Apparently, John's audience knew what he meant by this, because he doesn't take the time to explain it. How should we understand this cryptic but deadly transgression?

Let's begin by identifying what it is not. We shouldn't confuse "the sin that leads to death" with "the unpardonable sin." The unpardonable sin refers to an unbelievers' ultimate and final rejection of Christ (Matt. 12:31–32). Otherwise known as "blasphemy of the Holy Spirit," the unpardonable sin cannot be forgiven because the infidel has gone past the point of no return and is not responsive to the conviction of the Holy Spirit. Moreover, the unpardonable sin applies strictly to unbelievers.

Instead, "the sin that leads to death" refers to a Christian's sin that is so serious that God sends discipline to them in the form of premature death. The Scriptures are filled with examples of people who died because of their grievous actions. Nadab and Abihu, the two sons of Aaron, were charbroiled by God because they fooled around with the sacrificial system (Lev. 10:1–7). Korah and his band of insurrectionists tried to usurp authority from Moses and as a result God swallowed them up in a bottomless pit (Num. 16). Achan and his entire family were stoned to death when he openly defied God's command and hid Jericho's treasures under his tent (Josh. 6–7). When Ananias and Sapphira lied to God and the Jerusalem church about their offering, they dropped dead on the spot (Acts 5:1–11). Paul wrote to the Corinthians that "the reason many among you are weak and sick, and a number sleep [have died]" was because they were abusing the Lord's Table (1 Cor. 11:30).

Cerinthus was a first century Gnostic who opposed much of John's teaching. There is a legendary story told by Polycarp (John's disciple), which was passed on to Irenaeus, about an instance in which John exited the public baths of Ephesus in great haste when he heard that Cerinthus had entered. John reportedly said, "Let us flee, lest the baths fall in while Cerinthus the enemy of truth is within."[4] If the ancient story is true, apparently John feared that his Gnostic opponent was under the condemnation of the "sin that leads to death."

God, in His grace, allows believers to sin without immediately punishing them. However, there comes a point when God will no longer allow a believer to continue in unrepentant sin. When this point is reached, God sometimes decides to punish a Christian, even to the point of taking his or

---

4. Bruce, *The Epistles of John*, 23.

her life. John's advice in such an extreme situation is found in 5:16, "I do not say that one should pray for that," meaning that there are some people whose sinning is so deep that no amount of prayer will help their incorrigible heart. Frankly, we do not know another's heart condition before the Lord and we are not encouraged to speculate about the cause of any believer's untimely death. In our prayer life, we can continue to intercede for a wayward brother or sister, but there are some cases where no amount of intercessory prayer will alter God's judgment.

CONQUEST OVER SIN AND SATAN (5:18-19)

Billy Graham once said, "Conversion is a revolution in the life of the individual." What he meant was that those who come to Christ do a complete 180 degree turn away from sin and self and go the opposite direction towards holiness and righteousness. New life in Christ results in a new set of desires to please God and shun evil. This is what John had in mind when he said, "We know everyone born of God does not keep on sinning . . ." a topic which he has already explored in 3:9. He is not talking about reaching a point of sinless perfection. John is merely conveying the idea that Christ gives each believer the ability to resist a lifestyle of sin.

As a result of Christ's stronghold "the evil one" or Satan can never repossess us. Satan can tempt and harass the saints, but he can never lay his chains over them and drag them back into eternal damnation. Even though the whole world system belongs to Satan, the inner witness of Christ reassures us that we belong to God. Erwin Lutzer gives the following illustration of the believer's security:

> A butterfly was observed inside a windowpane, fluttering in great flight. It was pursued by a sparrow which kept pecking at the butterfly eager to devour it. What the butterfly could not see was the pane of glass that separated the two of them. The butterfly did not realize that he was as safe next to the sparrow as he would have been had he flown to the South Pole. Just so, the invisible Christ comes to shield us from Satan's power. The Serpent can hiss and taunt, but he cannot devour. We have a different King; we serve in a different kingdom.[5]

---

5. Lutzer, *The Serpent of Paradise*, 96.

CONSISTENCY BY KNOWING THE TRUTH (5:20-21)

Truth is the most powerful ally in the cosmic battle which we find ourselves embroiled. As Jesus stood before Pilate he said, "For this purpose I was born and for this purpose I have come into the world—to bear witness to the truth. Everyone who is of the truth listens to my voice" (John 18:37). God's word is truth (John 17:17). The truth liberates us from the world's lies (John 8:32) and Jesus is the fountainhead of all truth (John 14:6).

John's final words remind us that those who stay close to God have a keen sense of spiritual discernment. Lovers of the truth gain knowledge and understanding about spiritual matters that casual Christians are not sensitive to or unbelievers are blind to (2 Cor. 4:4). Truth corrects the skewed lenses of a fragmented worldview and allows us to perceive reality the way God does. By internalizing the truth we get God's perspective on every aspect of life from money, sex, relationships, politics, ethics, philosophy, and parenting.

The command at the end of this epistle may seem like an afterthought, "Little children, keep yourself from idols." However, it fits nicely with the theme of abiding in the truth. When believers are familiar with the truth they will not be fooled into accepting a counterfeit. Idols are simply that, false gods that obscure the true and living God.

John's original audience in Ephesus would have immediately picked up on this warning against idolatry. Ephesus was home to one of the wonders of the ancient world—the Temple of Diana (Artemis). This pagan shrine created an entire industry of manufacturing and selling of silver Diana statues (Acts 19:21-41). The first recipients of John's letters were under tremendous pressure to conform to this pagan worship.

We may not bow down to blocks of stone or totem poles today, but we are tempted to worship our jobs, bank accounts, possessions, or personal pleasures as if they were real gods. Anything that takes the rightful place of God becomes an idol to us (Ex. 20:3). In his book, *Surrounded by the Sacred*, evangelist Clayton King writes about how God gave him an unforgettable lesson on idolatry from the most unlikely of sources:

> I admit that I love rock-and-roll. Not all of it, and certainly not the offensive crude messages portrayed by many of the bands that fill the genre. But there is something raw and real about rock-and-roll that I have always appreciated. And God showed me some very interesting and important things one day while watching one of the biggest rock concerts in history on TV. I was at a friend's

Living Above the Level of Mediocrity (1 John 5:13–21)

house during summer break, and it was too hot to go outside. The TV was on and tuned to MTV. Immediately I realized who was playing, and I was drawn to the set and the man all the cameras were focused on. His name was Axl Rose, the lead singer for Guns-N-Roses. They were performing at an event in honor of the late Freddie Mercury, former lead singer of the rock group Queen, who had just passed away as a result of the AIDS virus. It looked like Axl had a picture of a man on his shirt, and I was curious. He was moving so much that I couldn't really make it out. When he finally faced the crowd, I saw the words "Kill Your Idols." Underneath the words was a picture of Jesus Christ.[6]

The irony of that story is difficult to miss. A rock star who was an idol of a godless lifestyle to so many wearing a shirt with a message that he neither lived nor understood. Such is the deceptive quality of idolatry.

At its heart, idolatry is nothing more than making a god to suit our own sins. John's final admonition encourages believers to see through the smoke-screen of the world and take hold of the truth. It is the truth which keeps us from error and makes us invincible to the lies of the enemy. It is by knowing the truth that we kill our idols, claim victory, and live consistently.

---

6. King, *Surrounded by the Sacred*, 84.

18

The Message of 2 John
(2 John 1-3)

SECOND AND THIRD JOHN have the distinction of being the shortest letters in the New Testament. Coming in at just under 300 words each in the original Greek language, these two letters could fit on a single page of papyrus. You might think of these brief letters as postcards from the ancient world. Their similarity in length, structure, style, and content justifies the description of them as "twin sisters."

While these epistles may be short in length, they are long in practical application. Taken together, both epistles focus on the importance of Christian hospitality as well as balancing the virtues of truth and love. As you study 2 John you will notice the overlap from 1 John. In fact, of the thirteen verses in 2 John at least eight of them are found directly or indirectly in 1 John. Thus, much of what the apostle John wrote the first time around is revisited in some form or fashion. With this letter's thematic similarity to 1 John, it is best to suggest that John wrote from Patmos in about AD 90.

AUTHOR: WHO WROTE 2 JOHN?

John did not identify himself by name in this letter, but he did adopt the term "elder" for himself (2 John 1). The term "elder" is derived from the Greek word *presbuteros* and it carries the general meaning of an "old man." However, it is most likely that John is not referring to his old age but to his office in the church. Like Peter, he saw himself as an overseer of the church (1 Peter 5:1).

The Message of 2 John (2 John 1-3)

AUDIENCE: TO WHOM WAS 2 JOHN WRITTEN?

The apostle clearly identifies his audience as "the elect lady and her children." This is a mysterious phrase and scholars have been divided over its interpretation. It either refers to an actual woman or serves as a metaphor for the church abroad. Those who lean more towards an individual have ventured some fantastic guesses as to the identity of his recipient. Without a shred of evidence, some have fancied that Mary, the mother of Jesus, is the "elect lady."

On the other hand, if this happens to be a title given to the personified church, then the reference to the "chosen sister" in verse 13 is another figure of speech intended to apply to a sister church in the same geographical area. In either case, whether to a smaller family group related by blood or to a larger one joined by confession, the application of the letter should remain unchanged.

AIM: WHY WAS 2 JOHN WRITTEN?

We can understand the theme of 2 John by underlining the five times he uses the word "truth" in the first four verses. The gist of John's message is this: "Make sure your practice of love is kept within the parameters of truth." Thus, 2 John makes clear what our position should be regarding enemies of the truth. In 1 John 2:18-19 the apostle warned against the dangers of false teachers which he called "antichrists." Second John focuses on protecting our fellowship from those antichrists (2 John 7). The apostle went so far as to warn his readers against inviting false teachers into their congregation or even offering them a greeting (2 John 10).

The problem of false doctrine in John's day was exacerbated because the early church did not have the full canon of Scripture. At best they only had access to the Old Testament and a few epistles or perhaps the Gospels from the New Testament. It was customary for circuit-riding evangelists and self-proclaimed prophets to make their way from church to church spreading their heresy as they went. In those days the itinerant preachers would not stay in the local Motel 6 since they were just a notch above a roach-infested brothel. Many times this meant that believers in the local assembly would open up their homes to these traveling teachers. John R.W. Stott summarizes the thorny situation when he adds:

Living in the Light

> But where should travelling Christians stay when they came to some city on a business journey, or more important still, on a missionary journey? The comforts of the modern hotel, or even of the village inn, were then unknown. Besides, according to W.M. Ramsey "the ancient inns . . . were little removed from houses of ill-fame . . . the profession of inn-keeper was dishonorable, and their infamous character is often noted in Roman laws." Inns were notoriously dirty and flea infested, while innkeepers were notoriously rapacious. As a result, it was natural that Christian people on their travels should be given hospitality by members of local churches. There are many traces in the New Testament of this custom . . . (Acts 16:15, 17:7, 21:8, 16; Rom. 16:23). Such hospitality was open to easy abuse, however. There was the false teacher, on the one hand, who yet posed as a Christian: should hospitality be extended to him? And there was the more obvious mountebank, the false prophet with false credentials, who was motivated less by creed than by greed, namely the material profit and free board and lodging he hoped to receive. It is against this background that we must read the second and third letters of John, for in them "the elder" issues instructions concerning whom to welcome and whom to refuse and why.[1]

Thus, John's second and third epistles were inspired by his pastoral concern for the general health of the church and a staunch opposition against the antichrists.

ARRANGEMENT: HOW IS 2 JOHN STRUCTURED?

I. **Greeting (1–3)**

II. **Balancing the Truth with Love (4–11)**

    A. Practicing the Truth (4–6)

    B. Protecting the Truth (7–11)

III. **Conclusion (12–13)**

---

1. Stott, *The Letters of John*, 201–202.

19

Balancing the Truth with Love (2 John 4–13)

BALANCING TRUTH AND LOVE can be a tall order. However, this was exactly what Jesus was known for, "And the Word became flesh and dwelt among us, and we have seen His glory, glory as of the only Son from the Father, *full of grace and truth*" (John 1:14). Like the double helix of a DNA strand, we must have a tight grasp on the twin virtues of truth and love. I like the way Randy Alcorn challenges us:

> The apparent conflict that exists between grace and truth isn't because they are incompatible, but because we lack perspective to solve their paradox . . . It reminds me of Moses our Dalmatian. When one tennis ball is in his mouth, the other's on the floor. When he goes for the second ball, he drops the first. Large dogs can get two balls in their mouths. Not Moses. He manages to get two in his mouth only momentarily. To his distress, one ball or the other spurts out onto the floor. Similarly, our minds don't seem big enough to hold on to grace and truth at the same time. We go after the grace ball—only to drop the truth ball to make room for it. We need to stretch our undersized minds to hold them both at once.[1]

Second John is a reminder that as believers we must maintain a careful balance between truth and love. Many of us know that some churches can major on truth and minor on love, while others are exactly the opposite. In an attempt to not offend anyone, some churches focus on love to the detriment of the truth. Both extremes are unhealthy and deadly. If we possess

---

1. Alcorn, *The Grace and Truth Paradox*, 16–17.

the truth without a heaping handful of love then we become religious terrorists. On the other hand, if we embrace everyone in the name of love and cast away the truth then we don't help them either; we just bear-hug them into hell. Like two wings on a plane, we need both the truth and love to maintain a balanced approach. Thus, 2 John serves as a fulcrum to keep the two playmates of truth and love in a happy balance so that neither gets hurt.

PRACTICING THE TRUTH (4-6)

In the first section of this short letter John is repeating old material that he tried to hammer home in his previous epistle. Three times he uses the term "walk" to describe the Christian life (v.4, 6). When the Bible refers to our walk, it generally speaks of our daily pattern of behavior. Walking in the light (1 John 1:5) is synonymous with walking in the truth (2 John 4). Notice that the three-fold chord of abiding in the truth (v.4), loving one another (v.5), and obedience to the commands of Christ (v.6) resurfaces again. Truth keeps us in check doctrinally, love keeps us in check socially, and obedience keeps us in check morally. Taken together these three virtues keep us walking straight on the balance beam of the Christian life. If we get one of these attributes out of equilibrium then our spiritual life is compromised and we are susceptible to falling away in apostasy or falling down into sin.

    I once had a vehicle that was constantly on the brink of mechanical failure. When I fired it up on a cold morning the engine would spit and sputter, knock and kick. On multiple occasions I would pull up to a traffic light and I would watch the RPMs decrease, knowing that as the engine cycle dropped the vehicle would inevitably lose power and shut down. The check engine light would come on and I would take it to the auto shop to have the diagnostic tool run on it. Invariably, there would be an assortment of sensor and part failures pop up. Then I would dump hundreds of dollars into various parts trying to cause the light to go away and get the vehicle to run properly. Nothing worked and I was getting tired of the guessing game.

    Finally I broke down and took it to a seasoned mechanic. Within a day he identified the problem and had it fixed. "The problem," he said, "was a simple gasket leak." This leak threw the entire engine into a frenzy and as a result the computer indicated every warning code in the book. When the leak was stopped and the simple repair was made, the vehicle ran better than the day I bought it.

Balancing the Truth with Love (2 John 4-13)

The Christian life, according to John, is a delicate balance of truth, love, and obedience. When one of these things is malfunctioning then our entire Christian life is thrown off kilter and we become as dysfunctional as that malfunctioning auto. A leak in one of these areas—truth, love, or obedience—can cause all kinds of other problems in our Christian walk. The reason John has harped on these topics so much is because they are so simple, yet so essential for genuine spirituality. Notice the overlap from the first epistle to the second.

1 John	2 John
Walk in the light (1:5)	Walk in the truth (v.4)
Love one another (4:7)	Love one another (v.5)
Keep His commandments (5:2-3)	Keep His commandments (v.6)
Beware of antichrists (2:19, 4:1)	Beware of antichrists (v.7-8)
Christ has come in the flesh (4:2)	Christ has come in the flesh (v.7)

PROTECTING THE TRUTH (7-11)

In discussing the exclusive nature of truth, G.K. Chesterton wrote, "There are an infinity of angles at which one falls and only one at which one stands." When you examine all the truth claims put forth by the multiplicity of religions and cults it becomes clear that they cannot all be true at the same time. This applies especially when we come to the subject of Jesus. Jesus cannot be a good moral teacher, a revered prophet, an enlightened guru, and the Son of God all at the same time. These contradictions are enough to cause intellectual constipation. The question of Christ's true identity as either a bad man, a mad man, or the God-man is the most divisive topic of all-time.

That is why John pulled no punches when he warned the readers of this epistle that there were wolves in sheep's clothing who were denying the humanity of Christ (v.7). No doubt, John had in mind the Gnostic opponents who had concocted all sorts of theological forgeries. Two thousand years later, enemies of the truth are doing the very same thing in their caricatures

Living in the Light

of Jesus. I think Erwin Lutzer sums up this epidemic of Jesus-bashing and historical revisionism when he writes:

> Whenever I see a picture of Jesus on the cover of *Time* magazine or *Newsweek*, I pick up the magazine with misgivings. I know that Jesus will be dissected, analyzed, and stripped of His deity. The man from Nazareth will be putty in the hands of scholars who are bent on fashioning Him according to their preference and liking. He will be a no-frills Jesus—a remarkable man to be sure, but just a man nevertheless. He will be an object of fascination, not adoration. And in the end, they'll come up with a Jesus who is not qualified to be our Savior, much less one worthy of worship.[2]

Like a mighty river that overflows its banks and causes damage, so too biblical love must be kept within the banks of truth or else people will get hurt. The apostle was reminding these first century readers not to swallow every spiritual teaching hook, line, and sinker without first checking to see if it cleared the test of truth.

In 2012 the unthinkable happened in the sports world when Lance Armstrong, the renowned cyclist, cancer survivor, and poster-child for the "Live Strong" campaign, was stripped of his seven Tour de France titles. His fall from grace reverberated among athletes and fans universally. He even lost his multi-million dollar endorsement deal with Nike. After a detailed investigation it was discovered that Armstrong engaged in serial cheating through the use, administration, and trafficking of performance enhancing drugs. This "doping scandal" tarnished the hero status of Armstrong among many fans that bought his iconic yellow armbands.

Similarly, John identified that falling victim to false doctrine could result in the loss of eternal reward (v.8). The New Testament reminds us that all believers must one day stand before the Bema Seat of Christ to receive rebukes and rewards (Rom. 14:10, 1 Cor. 3:11–15, 2 Cor. 5:10). It is here that we will be given our final job performance assessment. How tragic to watch a crown slip through our fingers because of a lack of discernment or because our walk faltered (Rev. 3:11). In much the same way that Armstrong watched his medals and trophies disappear, the careless believer can watch his earthly work go up in smoke when Christ judges it. Thus, guarding against error is serious because it has eternal consequences.

Eugene Peterson paraphrases verse 9 like this, "Anyone who gets so progressive in his thinking that he walks out on the teaching of Christ,

---

2. Lutzer, *Slandering Jesus*, 77.

Balancing the Truth with Love (2 John 4-13)

walks out on God."[3] The peril John is warning of here is going beyond the limits of the Word of God and either adding to or subtracting from it. Consequently, this sounds a lot like the thinking of cult leaders who see themselves with infallibility when it comes to their new spiritual insights. The original "Bible Answer Man," Walter Martin, defined a cult this way:

> By "cult" we mean a group, religious in nature, which surrounds a leader or group of teachings which either denies or misinterprets essential biblical doctrine. Most cults have a single leader, or a succession of leaders, who claim to represent God's voice on earth and who claim authority greater than that of the Bible. The cultic teaching claims to be in harmony with the Bible but denies one or more of the cardinal doctrines presented therein.[4]

Cultic leaders say they have a direct pipeline to God and they place greater emphasis on their new revelations which supersede old ones.

I'm thinking of one particularly charismatic televangelist who is known for slapping people on the head and rendering them "slain in the Spirit" during his healing sessions. I remember hearing him claim that God gave him new revelation concerning the nature of the Trinity. In front of a packed auditorium and TV cameras he announced that there were nine parts to the Trinity. According to him, each member of the trinity was a separate tri-unity of body, soul, and spirit. I almost got a headache. I thought, "Let me get this straight, the Spirit has a spirit?" Another infamous Scripture-twister who has a prime slot on TBN revealed that God the Father actually has a spirit-body. According to this guy, "God stands about six feet, two inches tall, has a hand-span of about nine inches and lives on his own planet in a galaxy far, far, away." Sometimes I don't know whether to laugh or cry when I hear things like that.

John's point is clear. Unless we keep doctrine in the boundaries of truth it is liable to overflow in all directions. Every teaching should be measured by the plumb line of Scripture. In his first letter, John reminded his readers that they had been anointed by the Holy Spirit and possessed all knowledge (1 John 2:20-21). They knew the truth and did need any new-fangled teaching or doctrine. Thus, there is simply no need for any "extra-biblical revelation."

It's shocking to see the stern words which come off the pen of "the apostle of love" in verses 10 and 11. We forget that the man who could be

---

3. Peterson, *The Message*, 2 John 9.
4. Martin, *The New Cults*, 16.

found leaning on the bosom of our Lord, was also the man who wanted to call down fire from heaven on the Samaritans who insulted Jesus (Luke 9:51–56). In the face of potential danger, John protected his "little children" against the enemies of truth the way a mama bear goes after predators threatening her cubs.

In essence, John tells his first century audience to be very careful who they show hospitality to and invite into their church fellowship. John is not advocating that we go on a witch hunt but that great discernment must be exercised when it comes to who we allow to sit at our dinner tables and preach from our pulpits. Shepherds would be blind or just plain stupid to allow wolves into the sheepfold. In much the same way, John is instructing his church people to tell the traveling heretics coming to prey on the congregation to "Get lost!" when they come knocking on the front door. Sam Gordon has written, "Love is the hinge on which hospitality turns to open its door. But just as the door has hinges, it also has a lock. And love never opens a locked door to a wolf—even if it is dressed in sheep's clothing."[5]

Do these verses prohibit you from inviting Mormons and Jehovah's Witnesses into your home? At first look, it would seem so. However, we must understand that John's command was given to the first-century believers who were being hoodwinked by false teachers. Today, the warning still applies and we should be careful who we allow to stand behind the podium and speak on behalf of God. At the same time, we should take great care in witnessing to cultists and we should know our Bible backwards and forwards, as well as their doctrines before matching wits with them. F.F. Bruce adds:

> The injunction not to receive any one who does not bring "the teaching of Christ" means that no such person must be accepted as a Christian teacher or as one entitled to the fellowship of the church. It does not mean that (say) one of Jehovah's Witnesses should not be invited into the house for a cup of tea in order to be shown the way of God more perfectly in the sitting-room than would be convenient on the doorstep.[6]

I agree wholeheartedly. We must be winsome to win some. Yet, we must also not compromise the truth.

---

5. Gordon, *Living in the Light*, 253.
6. Bruce, *The Epistles of John*, 142.

20

The Message of 3 John
(3 John 1–4)

TROUBLE WAS NOT IN short supply during the days of the early church. The first believers were under a constant barrage of attacks from both inside and outside the church. If the iron boot of Rome didn't squash the early church with its relentless persecution, then false doctrine or infighting would promise to kill her from within. The early church was fractured and scattered among the vast empire of the Caesars. Various counterfeit pockets like the Gnostics had sprung up and taken root. In the beginning, the beleaguered band of believers scraped by, surviving as tiny assemblies tucked away in home churches. The times were urgent and uncertain for those who first called themselves Christians.

For the third time, John picked up his pen to write another memo to a beloved brother in desperate need of encouragement and direction. Like his second letter, this epistle was written to address a specific problem in a particular congregation. Once again the issue was showing Christian hospitality and balancing the virtues of truth and love. Third John has the honored distinction of being the shortest letter in the New Testament. It is just one line shorter than the second epistle of John—that is, in the original Greek language.

AUTHOR: WHO WROTE 3 JOHN?

The apostle John identified himself in his third letter as "the elder" (3 John 1:1), the same as he did in 2 John. At the writing of this, his final epistle,

John was nearing the end of his life, a life that had changed dramatically decades before when Jesus called John and his brother James out from their fishing boat (Matt. 4:21–22). While the other disciples had been killed as martyrs—James was beheaded by Herod (Acts 12:2), Peter was crucified upside down, Paul was also beheaded in around 68 AD—John was allowed to live out his final years in Asia Minor. His years of experience and wisdom guided the church out of the tail end of the first century.

AUDIENCE: TO WHOM WAS 3 JOHN WRITTEN?

John wrote his letter to Gaius, a leader of one or more churches in Asia Minor. The New Testament mentions several men by the name of Gaius. In fact, historians have informed us that Gaius was probably the most popular name in the whole of the Roman Empire. In Acts 19 we read of Gaius of Macedonia who, together with Aristarchus, was seized by the rioting mob at Ephesus. Then there was another Gaius who accompanied Paul the apostle on his last trip to Jerusalem. In Acts 20, he formed part of the group of delegates that presented the offering from the Gentile churches to the church in Judaea. Then there is Gaius of Corinth, in whose house, scholars believe Paul lived while he was dictating the epistle to the Romans (Rom. 16:23). The real question is, "Who is this Gaius?" The simple answer is—we really don't know. Almost nothing is known of John's dear friend except what this letter reveals.

AIM: WHY WAS 3 JOHN WRITTEN?

Specifically, 3 John was written because one of the church leaders, a man named Diotrephes, had asserted control over the congregation and was refusing to show hospitality towards faithful ministers of the Gospel. Apparently, the church had seen some leadership quality in Mr. Diotrephes and had placed him in charge, but now in the top spot the power had gone to his head. Upon receiving an earlier correction from John, Diotrephes refused to listen (3 John 9). In many ways, John was addressing in his third epistle the converse of the problem he was addressing in his second epistle. Examine the chart below to see the differences.

The Message of 3 John (3 John 1-4)

2 John	3 John
Written to a lady and her children	Written to a man and his acquaintances
The main problem was giving hospitality to the wrong people	The main problem was not giving hospitality to the right people
Truth was needed to bring love back in balance	Love was needed to bring truth back in balance
Hospitality was misplaced	Hospitality was missing

Taken together, these two epistles give us the mirror reflections of truth and love. In 2 John we have the toughness of love; a love that does not open its doors to everything and every thought. Yet in 3 John we have the tenderness of love, a love that extends charity to those who are truly in Christ and serving God faithfully.

ARRANGEMENT: HOW IS 3 JOHN STRUCTURED?

John writes about three different men serving in this particular church. These men and their character form the skeleton on which the apostle arranges his content.

I. Gaius: A Commendable Christian (1–8)
- John's Focus—Commendation

II. Diotrephes: A Conceited Christian (9–10)
- John's Focus—Confrontation

III. Demetrius: A Consistent Christian (11–12)
- John's Focus—Challenge

IV. Conclusion (13–14)

21

Three Men and a Church
(3 John 5–14)

"Icy-cold" is how I would describe the atmosphere of the church I entered to preach one Wednesday evening. As a guest speaker, I expected at least one person there who would greet me and direct me around the campus, but no one was found. Meandering around the dark hallways of the church I finally found my way down to the fellowship hall. "Who are you?" a little lady asked me all bedecked in an apron and plastic gloves. "I'm Derrick McCarson. I was invited to come and speak at the evening service," I said. The lady looked puzzled, "Well, you're early, so come on in and have a hot dog before we get started."

I went through the line and fixed my plate, telling everyone the same story I had just relayed to the lunch-lady that ushered me in. As I sat down at one of the plastic fold-out tables, I could almost feel their eyes gawking at me like I was some kind of freakish science experiment gone wrong. I sat there in the cramped fellowship hall eating my hot dog all alone. No one introduced himself. No one came over to sit to with me; instead they just stared in my direction like a calf bewildered at a new gate. Apparently social interaction was something not afforded to "outsiders."

After I hurriedly choked down one of the worst hot dogs ever, I made my way back up to the sanctuary and prepared for my message. Since Easter was right around the corner, I spoke to a group of about fifteen or twenty teenagers on the resurrection of Christ and presented evidence arguing for the historical fact of the empty tomb. It was difficult to tell if anyone was listening or if they were remotely interested.

Three Men and a Church (3 John 5-14)

Things got worse about halfway through my presentation when a man came from a side-door, walked up on stage while I was preaching, pulled me aside and said, "Listen, we need you to wrap up in about five minutes; we are planning on having an important business meeting in here after you're done." It's hard to describe the surge of emotions I had in that moment. I recall a strange mixture of anger, humiliation, and disappointment. I didn't even try to finish. I just looked into the faces of my apathetic audience and said, "Let's close with a word of prayer."

As I walked to the parking lot I was totally defeated. This was one of my first experiences in the ministry. I could count on my hand the number of times I had been invited to speak publically. I wanted to quit already. I can honestly say the only meaningful interaction I had in that church was with the sound guy who handed me my flash drive on the way out.

Eventually my ego recovered and as I was invited to other churches I saw a completely different side of hospitality. Other congregations were the total opposite of that church which shall remain nameless. The people in other assemblies were warm, friendly, helpful, and expressed gratitude after we had spent time in the Word. I am thankful for those early experiences in the ministry because the Lord gave me a glimpse of the good, the bad, and the ugly.

Third John is a short epistle that deals with just that—the good, the bad, and the ugly sides of church ministry. Much like my experience of being jilted by that inhospitable church, John was dealing with a similar problem in this epistle. While there were good people in the leadership of the church John was addressing, there was one rotten apple who was giving the church a bad name. Rather than building a warm and hospitable congregation, this church was gaining the reputation of being unfriendly.

Third John is yet another example of the statement found in the *Westminster Confession of Faith* that "the purest churches under heaven are subject both to mixture and error" (25.5). John is writing not only to praise and encourage the believers who were laboring graciously for Christ but also to correct those who were abusing their office and disfiguring the church's witness.

GAIUS: A COMMENDABLE CHRISTIAN (1-8)

I once heard the story of a poor vagabond traveling a country road in England. Tired and hungry, he came to a roadside inn with a sign reading: "George and the Dragon." He knocked gently on the door. The innkeeper's wife stuck her head out a window. "Could ye spare some victuals?" he asked politely. The woman glanced at his shabby clothes and obviously poor condition. "No!" she said rather sternly. "Could I just have a pint of ale?" "No!" she said again. "Could I at least sleep in your stable?" "No!" by this time she was shouting. The vagabond said, "Might I please . . ." "What now?" the woman interrupted impatiently. "D'ye suppose," he asked, "I might have a word with George?" Apparently "The Dragon" believed in the old saying which goes, "After three days, both fish and guests begin to smell."

John uses most of his ink praising the character and dependability of Gaius. If his name lined up with his character then we could surmise that he was a down-to-earth kind of guy for Gaius means "of the Earth." It seems certain that Gaius was a convert of John. The apostle expressed to Gaius that nothing brought more joy to him than to hear that his children walked in the truth (v.4). Thus, it seems that John counted Gaius as one of his children in the faith.

Apparently Gaius was known for his heart of gold. He supported itinerant preachers and even strangers with food, housing, and money (v.5). Anyone who came into town to minister found a place to stay at Gaius' house. We can imagine that Gaius kept a spare bedroom at his house for just such an occasion. Perhaps boisterous laughter could be heard around his dinner table as he entertained his guests for an evening. As they left Gaius' home, I imagine that he handed them a care package for the road and there was a coin or two hidden in his handshake.

In opening up his heart, his home, and his pocketbook Gaius was fulfilling the words of Paul, "Therefore, as we have opportunity, let us do good to all, especially to those who are of the household of faith" (Gal. 6:10). Gaius put his love for the Lord into practice. The weary travelers that had spent a night at Gaius' house heralded his name around the Christian community (v.6). When word got back to John his heart was delighted and he encouraged his dear friend to continue his ministry of hospitality (v.7–8). John Stott comments on this passage:

> An important principle lies buried here, namely that we Christians should finance Christian enterprises which the world will not, or should not be expected to support. Indeed we have an obligation to do so. There are many good causes we may support, but we must support our brothers and sisters whom the world does not support.[1]

---

1. Stott, *The Letters of John*, 227.

Three Men and a Church (3 John 5–14)

Many of us may not be called to be preachers, teachers, or missionaries, but we still have our part to play in spreading the Gospel. If God has given you a heart for hospitality like Mr. Gaius, don't underestimate its value to the kingdom. You don't have to have eloquent words or a degree in theology to share Christ, just a loving heart and willing hands.

I can think of several "Gaius'" that God put in my path. God's people have helped me in innumerable ways. Through the years those with the heart for giving have lent me their vehicles, took me out to lunch, bought me clothes, helped me move, sent over a warm meal, donated thousands of dollars to the ministry, and prayed with me. These selfless acts came from people who loved Jesus and wanted to see the ministry flourish. When Christian love is unleashed there is no need that can stand in the way of the advancement of God's kingdom.

For many years Dr. Frances Schaeffer and his wife Edith ran a house of Christian hospitality and study in Switzerland called L'Abri. They opened their hearts and homes to hundreds of people seeking biblical answers to life's challenges. Schaeffer's profound theological works line the libraries of scholars and pastors around the world. Yet, for all those volumes, Schaeffer's wife, Edith, is remembered for this timeless truth, "Every Christian home is meant to have a door that swings open." Gaius would give a hearty, "Amen!" to that.

DIOTREPHES: A CONCEITED CHRISTIAN (9-10)

The name "Diotrephes" will always be remembered in the annals of Christendom as a title synonymous with "a pastor's headache." His was a case of lay-leadership gone wild. In these two verses, there is much we can deduce about his pompous character. Diotrephes was the opposite of Gaius. Gaius was the quiet, dependable servant content to do his ministry off the radar. Diotrephes, on the other hand, was a control freak with a type-A personality that loved to dominate the reins of power. Thus, he monopolized the pulpit and pounded on it like an overbearing dictator. Diotrephes fancied himself to be the alpha male around this church and no one dared usurp his authority.

Apparently, John had previously written this particular church, but the letter was either lost or destroyed by Diotrephes (v.9). When the correspondence slid across his desk and his eyes scanned its contents, the insidious Diotrephes promptly shredded the apostolic letter and tossed it in the garbage. Somewhere in the molecules of the universe lies a lost letter of John that never saw the light of day. Imagine all that Diotrephes and the church at large could have gleaned from John. This was a bold move of defiance that John intended to address personally when he arrived (v.10).

C.S. Lewis once wrote of pride as "the essential vice, the utmost evil . . . unchastity, anger, greed, drunkenness, and all that are mere fleabites in comparison: it was through pride that the Devil became the devil: pride leads to every other vice: it is the complete anti-God state of mind."[2] John identifies the sin of pride which had taken over Diotrephes when he said of him, "Diotrephes, who likes to put himself first . . ." The church under Diotrephes was a dictatorship and it was either his way or the highway. John's denunciation of Diotrephes reminded me of James' words to the worldly bunch of Christians he was addressing, "For where envy and self-seeking exist, confusion and every evil thing are there" (James 3:16).

It's fairly easy to spot a Diotrephes when you see one. I recall several years ago attending a small church and on this particular day the pastor was out of town, so a retired minister was brought into to do the preaching. I can't say that I remember any of his message. He yelled and screamed around the platform as if he had a chip on his shoulder. It was obvious that his message had no real content and most of what he did was in the flesh.

I do remember one moment in his tirade where he slammed the pulpit and said, "Everyone is supposed to be looking up here at me!" I doubt if anyone in the congregation gave him the courtesy of making eye contact with him. I noticed that many in the crowd concentrated on the floor. It was a painful and traumatic experience for one lady who was called down because she got up for taking her crying infant to the bathroom. There was a collective sigh when the red-faced Napoleon ran out of gas and finally ended his "message," if that's what you want to call it. Later on I learned that the reason that the man was retired was because he had pastored several churches and each one he was in nearly imploded under his heavy-handed approach.

John also informs us that Diotrephes did his dirty work with an assault of malicious words (v.10). Working in the shadows, Diotrephes started a gossip mill that sought to defame the character of the aged apostle and his friends. The tongue may only be three inches long, but it can slay a man six feet tall. Diotrephes unleashed a hailstorm of slanderous arrows

---

2. Lewis, *Mere Christianity*, 122.

Three Men and a Church (3 John 5-14)

against John and Gaius in an attempt to divide the congregation and garner support for himself. Worse yet, Diotrephes closed the doors of the church to traveling preachers and missionaries and threw out a large mat on the front step which read, "GO AWAY!" Sam Gordon appraises the situation accurately:

> As time passed a fissure ran through the church, forming a hairline crack between the leadership of the local congregation and the itinerant ministers. Eventually the division became so great that a fault line formed. Tremors of resentment and refused hostility radiated from the local church's leadership, at the epicenter was a man named Diotrephes. In a quake of rejection, he shook off John's teaching and tried to bury the apostle in a rock slide of sharp-edged words. As an aftershock, Diotrephes' refusal of hospitality extended to such that he not only forbade his members to receive these visitors, but expelled them from the church if they did so.[3]

There was only one solution to the impasse created by this opposition—Diotrephes had to go. When John arrived he would put down the insurrection with grace and truth. Power-hungry preachers and mossy-back deacons with an inflated sense of importance are a cancer on the local church. When a dictator takes over a church, the Spirit leaves, attendance drops, and eventually financial support dries up. If new leadership is not brought in, the church will wither up and die under the suffocating presence of a Diotrephes.

In his classic work, *Word Pictures in the New Testament*, A.T. Robertson recalls, "Some forty years ago I wrote an article on Diotrephes for a denominational paper. The editor told me that twenty-five deacons stopped the paper to show their resentment against being personally attacked in the paper."[4] Sadly, this problem still plagues the church today. Let us take a heaping helping of humble pie and remember that the church belongs to Christ and not us.

DEMETRIUS: A CONSISTENT CHRISTIAN (11-14)

Very little can be known of Demetrius save for what John tells us. Many believe that he was John's postman assigned to deliver this epistle by hand to Gaius thus ensuring that Diotrephes would not intercept it. Demetrius was

---

3. Gordon, *Living in the Light*, 276-277.
4. Robertson, *Word Pictures in the New Testament*, 3 John 1:9.

a common name in the first century which means "belonging to Demeter" (the Greek goddess of agriculture). It is likely that Demetrius probably had a pagan background. However, this is probably not the Demetrius of Acts 19:24, who was a silversmith in the city of Ephesus.

The best thing about this man was that he had John's stamp of approval. Like Gaius, Demetrius had proved his integrity, fidelity, and commitment to the truth. Demetrius met one of the qualifications of an overseer, "Moreover he must have a good report of them which are without; lest he fall into reproach and the snare of the devil" (1 Tim. 3:7). Everywhere Demetrius went he testified to the truth through his words and deeds. John admonishes Gaius to choose who he imitates very carefully (v.11). The options laid before him were the example of Diotrephes or the example of John and Demetrius.

I am reminded of a story that Ravi Zacharias retells which illustrates the power of our testimony:

> There is a magnificent story in Marie Chapian's book *Of Whom the World Was Not Worthy*. The book told of the sufferings of the true church in Yugoslavia where so much wrong has been perpetrated by the politicized ecclesiastical hierarchy. That which has gone on in the name of Christ for the enriching and empowering of corrupt church officials has been a terrible affront to decency. One day an evangelist by the name of Jakov arrived in a certain village. He commiserated with an elderly man named Cimmerman on the tragedies he had experienced and talked to him of the love of Christ. Cimmerman abruptly interrupted Jakov and told him that he wished to have nothing to do with Christianity. He reminded Jakov of the dreadful history of the church in his town, a history replete with plundering, exploiting, and indeed with killing innocent people. "My own nephew was killed by them," he said and angrily rebuffed any effort on Jakov's part to talk about Christ. "They wear those elaborate coats and caps and crosses," he said, "signifying a heavenly commission, but their evil designs and lives I cannot ignore." Jakov, looking for an occasion to get Cimmerman to change his line of thinking, said, "Cimmerman, can I ask you a question? Suppose I were to steal your coat, put it on, and break into a bank. Suppose further that the police sighted me running in the distance but could not catch up with me. One clue, however, put them onto your track; they recognized your coat. What would you say to them if they came to your house and accused you of breaking into the bank?" "I would deny it," said Cimmerman. "Ah, but we saw your coat, they would say," retorted Jakov. This anal-

Three Men and a Church (3 John 5-14)

ogy quite annoyed Cimmerman, who ordered Jakov to leave his home. Jakov continued to return to the village periodically just to befriend Cimmerman, encourage him, and share the love of Christ with him. Finally one day Cimmerman asked, "How does one become a Christian?" and Jakov taught him the simple steps of repentance for sin and of trust in the work of Jesus Christ and gently pointed him to the Shepherd of his soul. Cimmerman bent his knee on the soil with his head bowed and surrendered his life to Christ. As he rose to his feet, wiping his tears, he embraced Jakov and said, "Thank you for being in my life." And then he pointed to the heavens and whispered, "You wear His coat very well."[5]

I have always heard that there are five Gospels—Matthew, Mark, Luke, John, and You. While most unbelievers may never read the first four, they will read your life. Their conclusions about Jesus will be made by how well you wear His coat.

As we close this study on the letters of John we are reminded that our example is all that we will leave behind. We are either imitating good or imitating evil. The legacies of these three men were summed up in just a few short verses. If your life were to be summed up in just a few sentences, what would they say? Just so, we write our legacy by the daily choices we make to either walk in the light or the darkness.

---

5. Zacharias, *Can Man Live Without God?*, 101-102.

Bibliography

Alcorn, Randy. *The Grace and Truth Paradox*. Colorado Springs, CO: Multnomah, 2004.
Augustine. *The Confessions of St. Augustine*. Translated by John K. Ryan. Garden City, NJ: Doubleday, 1960.
Bonhoeffer, Dietrich. *The Cost of Discipleship*. New York, NY: Touchstone, 1995.
Bethge, Eberhard. *Dietrich Bonhoeffer: A Biography*. Minneapolis, MN: Fortress Press, 2000.
Bruce, F.F. *The Epistles of John*. Grand Rapids, MI: Eerdmans, 1970.
Caner, Ergun Mehmet and Caner, Emir Fethi. *Unveiling Islam*. Grand Rapids, MI: Kregel, 2002.
Chesterton, G.K. *Orthodoxy*. Mineola, NY: Dover Publications, 2004).
Chambers, Oswald. *Prayer: A Holy Occupation*. Grand Rapids, MI: Discovery House, 1992.
Dalia Lama. "The Karma of the Gospel." *Newsweek*, March 27, 2000.
Davidson, Jim and Vaughan, Kevin. *The Ledge: An Adventure Story of Survival and Friendship on Mount Rainer*. New York, NY: Ballantine Books, 2011.
Eusebius, *Ecclesiastical History*.
Evans, Tony. *Tony Evans Book of Illustrations*. Chicago, IL: Moody Press, 2009.
Evans, Tony. *Totally Saved*. Chicago: Moody Press, 2002.
Geisler, Norman and Turek, Frank. *I Don't Have Enough Faith to Be an Atheist*. Wheaton, IL: Crossway, 2004.
Gordon, Sam. *Living in the Light: 1, 2, 3, John*. Greenville, SC: Ambassador, 2001.
Graham, Billy. *Just As I Am*. New York, NY: Harper Collins, 1997.
Gray, Alice, *More Stories for the Heart*. Eugene, OR: Multnomah, 1997.
Gray, Alice. *Stories for the Heart: The Original Collection*. Sisters, OR: Multnomah, 2001.
Hamilton, Ian. *Let's Study the Letters of John*. Carlisle, PA: Banner of Truth, 2008.
Hiebert, Edmond D. *The Epistles of John: An Expositional Commentary*. Greenville, SC: Bob Jones University Press, 1991.
Hitchcock, Mark. *Who Is the Antichrist?* Eugene, OR: Harvest House, 2011.
Hybels, Bill. *Too Busy Not to Pray*. Downers Grove, IL: InterVarsity Press, 2008.
Jeremiah, David. *God Loves You: He Always Has, He Always Will*. Nashville, TN: Faith Words, 2012.
Jeremiah, David. *Living in the Light: Studies in First John*. San Diego, CA: Turning Point, 2009.
Kennedy, D. James and Newcombe, Jerry. *What if Jesus Had Never Been Born?* Nashville, TN: Thomas Nelson, 1994.

Bibliography

King, Clayton. *Surrounded by the Sacred*. Fort Washington, PA: CLC Publications, 2009.
Lehman, Frederick M. "The Love of God," 1917.
Lewis, C.S. Online: <http://bible.org/illustration/become-dog> accessed 26 October 2012.
Lewis, C.S. *Mere Christianity*. San Francisco, CA: Harper Collins, 2001.
Lewis, C.S. *Surprised by Joy: The Shape of My Early Life*. New York, NY: Harcourt, Brace, Jovanovich, 1994.
Lewis, C.S. *The Four Loves*. Orlando, FL: Harcourt, Brace and Company, 1988.
Lewis, C.S. *The Screwtape Letters*. San Francisco, CA: Harper Collins, 1942.
Lutzer, Erwin. *Oprah, Miracles and the New Earth*. Chicago, IL: Moody Press, 2009.
Lutzer, Erwin. *Slandering Jesus*. Carol Stream, IL: Tyndale House, 2007.
Lutzer, Erwin. *The Serpent of Paradise*. Chicago, IL: Moody Press, 1996.
MacArthur, John. 12 *Ordinary Men*. Nashville, TN: Thomas Nelson, 2002.
MacArthur, John. *The MacArthur New Testament Commentary:1-3 John*. Chicago, IL: Moody, 2007.
MacArthur, John. *The Truth War*. Nashville, TN: Thomas Nelson, 2007.
Martin, Walter. *The New Cults*. Ventura, CA: Regal Books, 1980.
McCasland, David C. "Contact," *Our Daily Bread*, 24 August 1996, accessed 20 October 2012, Online: http://odb.org/1996/08/24/contact/.
Peterson, Eugene. *The Message: The Bible in Contemporary Language*. Colorado Springs, CO: Nav Press, 1993.
Phillips, John. *Exploring the Epistles of John*. Grand Rapids, MI: Kregel, 2003.
Pollock, John. *D.L. Moody: Moody without Sankey*. Fearn, Scotland, UK: Christian Focus, 1995.
Rader, Dotson. "Elton John: There's a Lot of Hate in the World," Parade, 17 February 2010 <http://www.parade.com/celebrity/celebrity-parade/2010/elton-john-web-exclusive.html>, accessed 31 August 2012.
Reif, Rita. "Declaration of Independence Found in $4 Picture Frame." *The New York Times*, 3 April 1991. Online <http://www.nytimes.com/1991/04/03/arts/declaration-of-independence-found-in-a-4-picture-frame.html> accessed 25 October 2012.
Rhodes, Ron. 1001 *Unforgettable Quotes about God, Faith and the Bible*. Eugene, OR: Harvest House, 2011.
Rhodes, Ron. *Find It Quick: Handbook on Cults and New Religions*. Eugene, OR: Harvest House, 2005.
Rhodes, Ron. . Grand Rapids, MI: Zondervan, 2001.
Riddle, Regan. Mountain Heritage Music, 2007.
Robertson, A.T. . Nashville, TN: B & H Publishing, 2000.
Schaffer, Francis. . Downers Grove, IL: InterVarsity Press, 1970.
Stark, Rodney. *The Rise of Christianity: A Sociologist Reconsiders History*. Princeton, NJ: Princeton University Press, 1996.
Stott, John R.W. *The Cross of Christ*. Downers Grove, IL: InterVarsity Press, 2006.
Stott, John R.W. *The Letters of John*. Downers Grove, IL: InterVarsity Press, 1988.
Stowell, Joe. *Fan The Flame*. Chicago, IL: Moody Press, 1986.
Strobel, Lee. *The Case for the Real Jesus*. Grand Rapids, MI: Zondervan, 2007.
Swindoll, Charles R. *Day by Day with Charles Swindoll*. Nashville, TN: Thomas Nelson, 2000.
Swindoll, Chrales R. *Swindoll's Ultimate Book of Illustrations and Quotes*. Nashville, TN: Thomas Nelson, 1998.
Tertullian, *The Apology*.

Bibliography

Tozer, A.W. *The Knowledge of the Holy*. San Francisco, CA: HarperCollins, 1961.
Vujicic, Nick. *Life without Limits: Inspiration for a Ridiculously Good Life*. New York, NY: Double Day, 2010.
Wiersbe, Warren. *The Wiersbe Bible Commentary: New Testament*. Colorado Springs, CO: David C. Cook, 2007.
Wright, N.T. *Judas and the Gospel of Jesus*. Grand Rapids, MI: Baker, 2006.
Wurmbrand, Richard. *Tortured for Christ*. Bartlesville, OK: Living Sacrifice Book, 1990.
Yancey, Philip. *The Jesus I Never Knew*. Grand Rapids, MI: Zondervan, 1995.
Zacharias, Ravi. *Can Man Live Without God?* Dallas, TX: Word, 1994.
Zacharias, Ravi. *Deliver Us From Evil*. Nashville, TN: Thomas Nelson, 1998.
Zarrella, John and Oppmann, Patrick. "Pastor With 666 Claims to Be Divine." Online: <http://articles.cnn.com/2007-02-16/us/miami.preacher_1_cult-leader-followers-tattoo?_s=PM:US> accessed 31 August 2012.
Zuck, Roy B. *The Speaker's Quote Book*. Grand Rapids, MI: Kregel, 2009.

www.ingramcontent.com/pod-product-compliance
Lightning Source LLC
Chambersburg PA
CBHW071444150426
43191CB00008B/1233